Algernon Charles Swinburne, E. B. Lanin

Russian Traits and Terrors

A faithful Picture of the Russia of to-day

Algernon Charles Swinburne, E. B. Lanin

Russian Traits and Terrors

A faithful Picture of the Russia of to-day

ISBN/EAN: 9783337172589

Printed in Europe, USA, Canada, Australia, Japan

Cover: Foto ©ninafisch / pixelio.de

More available books at **www.hansebooks.com**

RUSSIAN TRAITS AND TERRORS

A FAITHFUL PICTURE OF

THE RUSSIA OF TO-DAY

BY

E. B. LANIN

THE COLLECTIVE SIGNATURE OF SEVERAL WRITERS IN THE
"FORTNIGHTLY REVIEW"

WITH AN ODE BY

ALGERNON CHARLES SWINBURNE

BOSTON, MASS.
BENJ. R. TUCKER, PUBLISHER
1891

CONTENTS.

CHAPTER		PAGE
I.	LYING	1
II.	FATALISM	28
III.	SLOTH	47
IV.	DISHONESTY	66
V.	RUSSIAN PRISONS: THE SIMPLE TRUTH	107
	RUSSIA: AN ODE	137
VI.	SEXUAL MORALITY IN RUSSIA	141
VII.	THE JEWS IN RUSSIA	172
VIII.	RUSSIAN FINANCE: THE RACKING OF THE PEASANTRY	208
IX.	THE RUSSIAN CENSURE	256

RUSSIAN TRAITS AND TERRORS.

CHAPTER I.

LYING.

THE history of Russian civilization will, when written, furnish the most striking and convincing proof of the theory advanced by certain modern thinkers, that the loftiness or baseness of the ethical code of a people bears a strict relation to the degree of their intellectual enlightenment; morality being the ethical equivalent of a nation's mental attainments. For the theory of right conduct universally accepted and acted upon in Russia may be truly affirmed to be on a level with the egotistic principles or instincts which determine the unheroic actions of the average man and woman — which is another way of declaring it devoid of ideals. And that this low level of morality is in perfect keeping with the crass ignorance and brutalizing superstition in which the masses are still hopelessly plunged, is abundantly evident to all who possess even a superficial knowledge of the country and the people. Moreover, the efforts that have occasionally succeeded to an appreciable extent in raising the standard of morality in certain circumscribed districts of the empire, owe whatever success they have had to the spread of knowledge among the population; the fluctuations of the intellectual level having always made themselves immediately felt in the moral sphere. In this Russians admirably exemplify the actions of that interdependence which is no less a law of our intellectual and moral faculties than of our physical senses; and it is not more natural that the color which produces the deepest impression on the sight should at the same time heighten the intensity and increase the delicacy of our hearing, touch, and taste, than that the ignorance, superstition, and apathy which cloud the intellect, should keep down the standard of right living to their own low level. What is more surprising, however, and not explicable by the operation of any known law, is the circumstance that the lower classes of Russians are mostly found to be bereft of those ethical qualities which, although of the essence of all true morality, yet have no traceable connection with pure intellect; such, for instance, as sensibility to the appeal of moral obligation, or that fervid enthusiasm which is the chief ingredient of heroism.

I may state here, what should be obvious enough without any express declaration, that neither these general assertions nor the facts that I shall presently bring forward to illustrate and support them, imply anything in the nature of censure or reproach. To blame a people for habits which are the outcome of conditions over which they had practically no control, would argue ignorance of their history and of the nature of morality itself. It would be just as reasonable to condemn the moth for eating woollen stuffs, or to wax indignant at the depravity of those female spiders of certain species of Epeirides, who coolly devour the males as soon as the latter have discharged their natural functions, as to allot praise or blame for conduct and principles which are practically as independent of the will of the nation as its physical type. One should bring to the study of the ways and habits of men, no less than of animals, if the results are to be worth having, a spirit of intelligent curiosity equally free from prejudice and passion. When, therefore, I affirm that a careful survey of the facts of Russian social life warrants — nay, imperatively calls for — the employment of a standard of judgment widely different from that which we are wont to apply to other European people — the Russians being, as Burke would say, still in the gristle, not yet hardened in the bone of manhood — I merely state a fact which can at worst discredit their spiritual or political guides, if proved to be the result of their negligence or malice. And even a slight acquaintance with the facts of the case is sufficient to show that an abyss divides Russian civilization from that of Western Europe on the one hand, and that this is, to a very considerable extent, the result of what may be termed artificially arrested development on the other.

By nature the Russians are richly endowed : a keen, subtle understanding ; remarkable quickness of apprehension ; a sweet, forgiving temper; an inexhaustible flow of animal spirits; a rude, persuasive eloquence,[1] to which may be added an imitative faculty positively simian in range and intensity, constitute no mean outfit even for a people with the highest destinies in store. But these gifts, destined to bring forth abundant fruit under favorable circumstances, are turned into curses by political, social, and religious conditions which make their free exercise and development impossible, and render their possessors as impersonal as the Egyptians that raised Cheops, or the coral-reef builders of the Pacific. In result we have a good-natured, lying, thievish, shiftless, ignorant mass whom one is at times tempted to connect in the same isocultural line with the Weddas of India or the Bangala of the Upper Congo, and who differ from West European nations much as Sir Thomas Browne's vegetating "creatures of mere existence" differ from "things of life." For most of them, indeed, life, dwarfed to its narrowest conceivable limits, is void of meaning. Hopes, fears, love, sorrows (wholesome hatred has no place in their composition), all are compressed into the narrow compass of their relations to the various manifestations of a tyrannical will; and it is no wonder that the most healthy moral instincts, those that are usually marked by enduring vitality, are utterly crushed out in the process. The following incident, illustrative of a whole category of such, will give some idea of the extent to which not only moral instincts but plain common sense are absorbed by that brutalizing awe of the authorities which is ever uppermost in the minds of the people, hypnotizing and deadening them to every human instinct, and which the Russian Government is assiduously striving to perpetuate and develop. In the village of Stepantsy (district of Kanevsky) a peasant hanged himself in April, 1889 — a merciful death in comparison with that which would have otherwise ended his sufferings. At the inquiry made into the circumstances of his death, it was elicited that hunger and want were, as usual, the motives. The evidence given by some friends of the suicide who discovered him a second or two after he had tied the fatal knot.is instructive because emi-

---

[1] The celebrated Danish *littérateur* Georg Brandes has a very poor opinion of Russian eloquence at its best — when inspired by genuine enthusiasm. This, however, is not a question of personal appreciation; it is a matter of fact, to the perception of which a thorough knowledge of the Russian tongue is indispensable, and every one possessed of this qualification knows that the Russians are naturally eloquent.

nently characteristic. I translate a portion of it literally from the Russian. " Now he's stark and cold," one witness remarked, " but when we first came up and saw him hanging, he was warm enough; and he dangled his legs about a good deal. There was plenty of life in him then, and for a good while after too. It's gone now." *Q.* " Why did you not cut him down at once?" *A.* " Cut him down, is it? Well, at first we were going to do it. But then we said, ' Best let him take the road he chose for himself; for if we cut him down and save him, *we shall have to* answer to the authorities.' So we let him hang there. And he's as cold as a stone now."[1] There are numbers of Russians whom, in similar circumstances, fear of being answerable to the authorities would keep from saving their own fathers. That same awe of the authorities is firmly implanted in the breasts of most of the members of the educated classes, for whom no infamy is too enormous, if commanded or desired by the Government; and it is developed in them, and as fruitful of results, as that fear of God and awe of their own consciences which was the guiding principle of English Puritans. " What is your view of the immortality of the soul, gentlemen?" the Russian satirist, Schtschedrin, makes a police official inquire of two highly educated Russian Liberals who are disciplining themselves and qualifying for the degree of " loyal " men. " In order to solve this problem in a perfectly adequate manner," is the orthodox reply, " it is absolutely necessary first of all to consult the sources. That is, to discover whether we can lay our finger upon any paragraph of the law, or even upon any command issued by the authorities, in virtue of which we are authorized to hold the soul immortal; if so, then there is no manner of doubt, we are bound to act in strict accordance therewith; but if the laws and precepts contain no such paragraph, then it is incumbent upon us to await further orders thereunto appertaining."[2] This is as true and accurate an account of the manner in which the minds of the Russian people are hypnotized by the central power, as if it had appeared in a sober history instead of a biting satire.

Veracity, which has been justly called the vital force of human progress — the one thing needful in the journey onwards and upwards *ad majora* — is precisely that quality

---

[1] Cf. Russian newspapers of 5th April, 1889.
[2] Cf. *A Modern Idyll*, p. 34.

in which Russians are most hopelessly deficient. Indeed, in that respect they may without exaggeration be said to outdo the ancient Cretans and put the modern Persians to shame. They seem constitutionally incapable of grasping the relation of words to things, between which, to their seeming, the boundary is shadowy or wholly imaginary; and they lack in consequence that reverence for facts which lies at the root of the Anglo-Saxon character. A Russian can no more bow to a fact, acknowledging it as final and decisive, than he can to a personal appreciation or a mere opinion founded upon insufficient or no grounds; he is ever ready to act in open defiance of it; and the most serious statesman, the most sober thinker, will eagerly start a discussion on such topics as the geographical position of Java, Borneo, or Madagascar, with the same trustful, childlike expectation of seeing entirely new light thrown upon it, as if it were of the Thirty-nine Articles or Kant's theory of time and space. A lengthy and lively conversation was lately begun between two Russian statesmen by the question put by one of them, a man who had governed his country for half a generation: "Why do you suppose that the Caroline Islands are not in the Indian Ocean?" and the discussion continued quite as long, and was to the full as lively, as if it were upon some obscure question of metaphysics; nor did it once occur to either of the disputants to consult a trustworthy map. This same airy independence of facts is visible like a white thread on a black ground in all departments of Russian life, public and private. Ask a peasant how many miles you have to walk to the next village, and if you look footsore and weary he will tell you three or four. Let your friend, looking blithe and gay, put the same question to him five minutes later, and he will answer fifteen. Facts to him are purely subjective, and he arranges them to his taste, which is often capricious, and according to circumstances which are ever varying. "You lie," is a most common expression in the mouth of one gentleman to another whom he suspects of dealing arbitrarily with the facts, whether deliberately or inadvertently; and the answer of the corrected party is not infrequently, "Yes, I do lie; it is as you say." Instead of correcting himself by saying, "I am mistaken," a Russian, who is relating an incident and has inadvertently misstated some trivial fact, will gravely say, "I am lying to you; it was not so, it was otherwise."

It is quite natural under such circumstances that comparatively little attention should be paid to words as exponents of facts, that solemn assurances should be disbelieved, promises distrusted, and calumnies be almost powerless for evil; nor can one feel astonished at that strongly marked tendency to exaggeration which disgusts the newly arrived Englishman in Russia. Russians lack the delicacy of perception requisite to discriminate the degrees that separate extremes, and the consequences of this defect stand out in bold relief in everything they put their hands to: three-fourths of the address on an envelope are underlined; half a book is printed in italics; in conversation statements about the veriest trifles are emphasized by tone, pitch, gesture. People passionately appeal to their Creator in corroboration of the assertion that there were more gnats last year than this, or that the hat you wore on your birthday fifteen years ago was trimmed not with blue ribbon but black. Your ears constantly tingle with the stereotyped oath, "*Yay-ee-bó-goo*" uttered by the costermonger, the goods-clerk, the tradesman, solemnly taking Almighty God to witness that the ribbon for which you offer him sixpence cost him tenpence half-penny; and if you are a new-comer in the country you are considerably startled to find half a minute later, as you are leaving the shop, that he lets you have it at your own valuation, and if you indignantly refuse, even for less.

A celebrated Russian General, almost as well known in this country, where he has some enthusiastic admirers, as in his own, whose name has gradually grown synonymous with that of liar *par excellence*, is erroneously looked upon as a contemporary Münchausen, the embodiment of a grotesque exaggeration of the least veracious of his countrymen, whereas in sober reality he is merely the sublimated expression of all that is characteristic of the average Russian. His verified sayings would, perhaps, if collected and published, successfully compete with the most popular book of Mark Twain or the "Danbury Newsman," and deservedly take a high place in that equivocal class of literature, notwithstanding the circumstance that the statements of the American humorists were made to amuse, while those of the Russian statesman were intended to mislead. "Why do you abstain from wine, General?" asked the host one day at dinner, seeing this Russian diplomatist persist in filling his glass with water. "Because," interposed one of the guests, in a somewhat loud aside, "*in vino veritas.*" There is a respectable, but what our Transatlantic cousins would term "shoddy" family in St. Petersburg, consisting of two elderly ladies and a brother [the Netschaïeff-Maltseffs], who, having spent the best portion of their lives in the country, suddenly inherited an immense fortune and straightway abandoned tranquillity and the province for fashionable life in the capital, where their simple, artless ways and their profound veneration for the aristocracy are unfailing sources of delight to the *blasé* princes and princesses who enjoy their hospitality and their *naïveté* with equal gusto. The General, questioned one day why he never appeared at their dinners and balls, replied in a tone of engaging confidence that the fortune they had lately inherited belonged of right — moral and legal — to him, and that they knew it. He scorned, however, to take legal proceedings to recover it, and his kindliness and gentlemanly feeling forbade him to awake in them or intensify by his presence those qualms of conscience which must, he knew, be destructive of all peace of mind. Hence he systematically kept out of their way. And he tells this story with such bland, childlike simplicity and candor, that some persons are to my knowledge still persuaded of its truth. It is perhaps superfluous to remark that as a matter of fact the General has as much right — moral or legal — to the property in question as the Tichborne claimant or Buffalo Bill, and that, not being of insane mind, he knows.

Some people maintain that faces never lie. The clearness or muddiness of the eye, the tell-tale shade of expression, the unmistakable accents of sincerity or prevarication combine, they say, to stamp every statement with its true moral value. To this one can only reply that the physiognomists who think thus would do well to come to Russia to study faces. There the most damnable lie, the lie that blasts and kills, is sometimes uttered with apparent reluctance, with visible pity clothed in a voice trembling with compassion — a voice that seems to come from the heart and to go straight to the heart, pleading, as it were, for the wretched creature it dooms to ruin. The features of the speaker are open, manly, noble; his expression angelic; Carlo Dolci would have been proud to transfer his face to canvas; and yet his soul Dante would have had a grim satisfaction in burying in the nethermost pit of hell. I once had dealings with a favorable specimen of the Russian peasant — at least he was recommended to me as such — a class of men whom until a few months ago Panslavists and Liberals vied with each other in idealizing, and who are still regarded by most educated Russians as inarticulate Homers, potential Napoleons, undeveloped Charlemagnes, obscure Bayards — a view which I cannot term utterly groundless. He was a giant in size and an angel in look, and his features seemed of pellucid crystal through which his soul shone visible and pure. The late Edward Fitz-Gerald would have called him "a grand, tender soul lodged in a suitable carcass." He was a member of an *artel* — a sort of Russian trades union — to which I had entrusted the removal of some personal property to a distant city. After a few conversations he charmed me. So much practical wisdom, such perfect tact and nobility of soul in one so untutored, seemed like the realization of a miracle. I could not look upon him without comparing him with a huge uncut diamond of untold price. I soon learned to trust him as a brother, and when he presented his bill for payment, though I winced on seeing so many extras, I paid the money unhesitatingly and without remark. Emboldened by this he went on to mention in a very casual manner an item of £30 insurance money which he had forgotten, he said, to include in the estimate or mention in the contract. Here, however, I drew the line and flatly refused to pay, my belief in his honesty becoming mere notional assent. He looked at me for a long time in silent sadness, then tried to speak, but his voice faltered and he burst into tears, and Goliath that he was wept like a helpless child for nearly half a day, bitterly bewailing his impending ruin and that of his large family in the picturesque and forcible language of a child of nature. The servants involuntarily wept with him; perfect strangers espoused his cause and joined in. I thought myself that I felt something like a film gathering over my own eyes at last. I had already paid more than I was bound to pay by the terms of the contract, and £30 more seemed a large sum to throw away, as it were. Yet I would not willingly contribute to ruin an unoffending man with a large family, merely because he had been guilty of an oversight in my favor and to his own prejudice. So I finally handed him the money in return for a receipt. A week later I learned that not an article had been insured by him; two months afterwards I discovered that this angel in human form had fleeced quite a flock of easy-going persons who believed in undeveloped Charlemagnes and peasant Bayards; that he was a regular embezzler, an inimitable comedian, who could draw tears from a stone and money from a miser.

Apart from cases of this kind, which in commercial dealings are extremely frequent, a Russian, it should be remembered in mitigation, is not conscious of guilt when telling a deliberate untruth. It is very doubtful whether, even in such aggravated instances as the above, he is really conscious that he is violating any law human or divine. For it should not be forgotten that he is suffering from complete anæsthesia of that moral faculty which in more or less-developed peoples is so prompt to condemn lying. To a Russian words are his own, and he simply does what he likes with them, thus exercising an indefeasible right which he freely concedes to others. Being superstitious and impressionable, he attaches great weight to religious and other ceremonies; and the complicated formalities with which an oath is sometimes administered — formalities occasionally as solemn as those that accompanied Harold's oath to William of Normandy — will at times determine a man to change a specious and elaborate lie into a simple statement of facts. Notwithstanding this, however, perjury is extremely rife in Russia; indeed, I fear that the facts which will be set forth in another paper will show it to be an acknowledged and indispensable institution in the social life of the country as now constituted, regularly and more or less satisfactorily discharging certain functions for which no other machinery at present exists. "You can get as many witnesses as you like," we are gravely informed by the most accredited organs of the Russian press, "for a measure of *vodka;* witnesses who will go anywhere and testify to anything you tell them."[1] " In Lodz an admirably organized band exists for the purpose of bearing false witness," says the journal *Svett.* "The affairs of this gang are in a prosperous condition; for those classes of the population which have need of their services remunerate the members of this curious institution on a liberal scale. The chief of the gang has drawn up a tariff: for evidence in a case of slander three roubles (about six shillings);[2] in cases of violence to the person from five to fifty roubles, and so

---

[1] Cf. *Grauschdanin*, April 15th, 1889.
[2] Labor is comparatively cheap in Russia.

on."[1] "If I wanted three or four perjurers," said a friend of mine once to me when speaking on this question, "I am acquainted with two lawyers of whom I might bespeak them, without euphemistic paraphrase or apprehension of failure." The journal *Svett*, which has devoted so much of its space from time to time to show up this strange state of things, for which the Government is mainly responsible, is yet highly indignant whenever criminal judges of the Lutheran persuasion, accustomed to a high standard of truth, express doubts of the veracity of witnesses belonging to the orthodox Church. Whether in the following case the hesitation of the judges or the wrath which it roused in the *Svett* is more intelligible may safely be left to the judgment of the reader. A person occupying a responsible position in the capital of one of the Baltic provinces prosecuted a servant for theft and incivility, and produced two witnesses — members of the orthodox Church — to prove the charges. Having heard the case for the prosecution, the judge declared that he felt unable to act upon the testimony of the two Russian witnesses, and dismissed the case; nor did he reopen it until a fresh witness — a Lutheran — was produced,[2] when the prisoner was condemned and punished. For Lutheran judges — Finnish and German — have been taught by long experience that average Russians, like the prophet Jeremiah's beloved people, "bend their tongues like their bow for lies," and are "not valiant for the truth upon earth."

Whatever blame may appear to attach to this wholesale demoralization of a people capable of quite other things should fall almost entirely upon the Government, which, as will be shown later on, directly and deliberately encourages and fosters this unveracity and makes itself answerable for the result. Unfortunately the very Bayards and Washingtons of Russia, those guiding spirits who serve as a pillar of cloud by day and a pillar of fire by night to the people wandering wearily through the wilderness of despotism and ignorance, even they are deeply marked with this national trait. Born into the world tainted with this original sin, it never wholly leaves them, but breaks out at unexpected

---

[1] *Svett*, 5th February, 1880. It should not be forgotten that the journal is describing not something that has been and is now no more, but a phenomenon that still exists and is developing, and is one of the complex forces of modern social life in Russia.
[2] *Svett*, 20th June, 1889.

seasons and in unforeseen ways to the amazement of Europeans, who are at a loss to account for the mystery. What, for instance, would be said and thought in England of a gentleman of culture, a scholar, a university professor, a modern Samuel chosen from among millions to instil principles of truth and honesty into the tender mind of his future emperor, who systematically lied in the most solemn manner imaginable; who in a text-book on civil law written for his students, deliberately ignored the vast judicial reforms which constitute one of the most durable and solid services that the late Emperor rendered his subjects; and this simply because he disapproved them? Suppose a work were written in this country in the year 1884 on the machinery of English law courts, to serve as a text-book for students, in which the author purposely omitted to treat the Judicature Acts, passed during the Chancellorship of Lord Selborne, as accomplished facts, out of prejudice against the party to which Lord Selborne belonged; spoke of the old system of pleading, procedure, and appeal as still in existence; cited earlier and now obsolete statutes as still in force, and allowed his book to *go through three editions* in the space of several years without changing an iota, knowing that it was being made practically obligatory for all students in the Empire; what, I ask, would be said and thought of such a man in England? In Russia he was first made tutor to the Prince Imperial, now the Czar Alexander III., and then appointed virtual head of the orthodox Church, Ober-Procuror of the Most Holy Synod, for the gentleman in question is M. Pobedonostseff.[1] To give some idea of the extent to which this scholar carries his dislike of the reforms of the late Emperor, and his forgetfulness of the requirements of truth, I may mention that he gravely declares that according to the laws in force in the year 1883, a man or woman may be still disposed of by testament or by deed of sale.[2]

---

[1] " According to the laws now in force every actual possession of real estate, even though illegal, is deemed undisputed, and is protected by the law against violence, until a claim is preferred or a suit begun, and the estate adjudged to belong to another." [Here follow citations from old obsolete statutes.] — *Course of Civil Law*, by K. Pobedonostseff, 3d edition, 1883, p. 168, etc. This is but one of innumerable instances.

[2] In the following passage, for instance: "Things capable of being possessed are: 1st. Documents testifying to the entry into possession, if the thing is of such a nature that it cannot be delivered up otherwise than by document, even though it be *personal estate*, as a ship, a sea-faring vessel, *serfs who have no land.*" — *Course of Civil Law*, 3d edition, 1883, 1st Part, p. 44.

Examples of this systematic unveracity are as numerous as the sands of the sea; there is an *embarras de richesse*. They may be conveniently summed up in the saying of the Russian poet Testscheff: "The thought expressed is already a lie." Turghenieff was in most respects one of the most typical of educated Russians, gifted in an eminent degree with the good qualities, and not lacking those of the bad which distinguish his countrymen, and which a life-long sojourn among cultured foreigners did not suffice to rub off. One or two instances, therefore, of the value which he was wont to set upon his pledged word, his solemn promise, will do more to give English readers an insight into the Russian theory and practice on this subject than whole pages of careful psychological analysis. The great Russian novelist was a regular contributor to the *Contemporary* — a Russian monthly magazine — and once, when it was on the eve of bankruptcy, the novelist, being in pressing need of money, asked the editor for an advance of 2,000 roubles. The editor hesitated, was about to refuse, but the contributor clenched the matter by saying: "I am in sore need of this sum; if you do not let me have it, I shall be compelled, to my great regret, to go and *sell myself* to the *Memoirs of the Fatherland* (a rival review), and you will not soon get any of my productions again." This threat worked. The editor obtained the money, we are told by the eye-witness who tells this story, "through my intervention and under my guarantee." Soon afterwards Turghenieff, who had solemnly promised to send a story for the forthcoming issue of the review, failed to keep his word, and had not come to the office for a whole week previous to the latest day fixed for sending it, though he was wont to come every day and dine or take tea at the office. The editor grew nervous; drove over twice to see him, but not finding him at home, forwarded him a note, imploring him to send the manuscript without delay. Turghenieff came, and walking into the office said: "Abuse me, gentlemen, as badly as you like; I know that I have treated you very scurvily, but what could I do? An unpleasant thing has happened to me . . . and I cannot give you the story that I promised. I'll write another for the following number." This statement took away the breath of the two editors Nekrasoff and Punaïeff. At first they were silent — lost in amazement — then they bombarded him with questions: "I was ashamed to show myself," he explained, "but I deem it puerile to deceive you any longer, and thus delay the printing of the review. I have come to ask you to insert something else. I give you my word of honor that I will write something for the following number." "Why? why?" asked the editor. "Will you first promise not to reproach me if I tell you?" "Yes, yes; we promise; say on." "Well, I loathe myself for what I have done. I have sold the story that I promised you to the *Memoirs of the Fatherland*. Now execute me. I was in sore need of 500 roubles. It would have been *impolite* to come to ask you for the money, as I have done too little for the 2,000 roubles you lately gave me." "Is your manuscript already in the hands of the editor of the *Memoirs of the Fatherland?*" was Nekrasoff's next question. "Not yet," was Turghenieff's reply. Nekrasoff's countenance suddenly beamed, and opening his desk, he took 500 roubles from one of the drawers and handed them to Turghenieff, saying, "Here, take this, and write him a letter of apology." The novelist hesitated, but at last said: " Gentlemen, you are placing me in a stupid position. . . . I am a miserable man. . . . I deserve a flogging for my weak character. Let Nekrasoff write a letter of apology. . . . I will copy it and send it with the money." Then to Nekrasoff: "Smear Kraieffsky's (the editor of the rival review) lips with the honey of promises. Tell him I shall soon write another story for him. I can well picture to myself his black disappointed face when reading my letter."[1]

Another habit of Turghenieff's was to invite friends to dinner and be absent when they came, not deliberately of set purpose, but because of the little value he set on his pledged word, and the very faint impression it used to make upon his mind. He once invited the famous critic Belinsky and five others to dine with him at his house in the country, where he had a *chef de cuisine* whom he looked upon as a genius. "I will organize a banquet for you, the like of which you never dreamt of." He fixed the day, and *made each person give his word of honor* that he would come. "Don't fear for us," remarked Belinsky. "We shall be there without fail; but you must not repeat the trick that you played upon us last winter, when you asked us to dine and were not at home when we came; but lest you should forget your invitation, I shall write to you on the eve of the

---

[1] Cf. *Historical Messenger* (a monthly review), May, 1889.

day of our arrival." "It was a sultry day when the whole six of us set out for Pargolovo in an open calèche at eleven o'clock in the morning," says one of the persons invited. "We were thoroughly fatigued by the heat and dust of the road. Arrived at Turghenieff's country house we alighted with joy in our countenances, but we were all struck with the circumstance that Turghenieff did not come out to meet us. We knocked at the door of the glass terrace. The silence of death reigned in the house. All our faces grew visibly longer. 'Can Turghenieff have played the same trick as last winter?' exclaimed Belinsky. But we all calmed him, saying that we probably arrived earlier than we were expected. 'But I wrote to him that we should be here at one o'clock,' objected Belinsky, 'what can it mean? If they would only admit us into the room we could wait, but here we are scorched.' At length a boy came out of the door and we all plied him with questions. His master had gone off, he said, and the *chef de cuisine* was in some public-house. We gave the urchin money, sent him to fetch the *chef* who should let us in, and meanwhile we sat down on the steps of the terrace. We waited long in vain. Belinsky wanted us to return, but our hired coachman refused to take us back until the horses had had a long rest. So we sat on, hungry and hot. Panaieff went to the public-house to see if anything eatable could be procured, but there was nothing to be had. . . . At last the *chef* made his appearance. 'Where is your master?' cried Belinsky. He did not know. 'Did not your master order a dinner for us to-day?' insisted the critic. 'He did nothing of the kind,' was the reply. Amazement and terror were depicted on all faces. Belinsky flamed up, and looking at us in his significant way, exclaimed, 'Turghenieff has indeed given us a banquet!'"[1]

These things — which are but samples and not by any means the worst — need no comment. Taken absolutely they indicate the width of the gulf that divides the views on veracity in particular and morality in general which are current in this country from those prevalent in Russia, and considered as the genuine characteristics of a man of Turghenieff's truly excellent disposition and noble aspirations, they amply confirm Pascal's thesis that morality — and the great novelist was from a Russian point of view a

---

[1] Cf. *Historical Messenger*, February, 1889, and *Novoye Vremya*, 12th March, 1889.

highly moral man — changes its aspects with the climates in which it is cultivated. This fact has never been acknowledged fully and frankly enough by those who sit in judgment on foreign men of note, and are wont to look upon Mrs. Grundy's maxims as the only standpoint whence everything and everyone should be judged without appeal. Does the weeping willow violate a law of nature in growing downwards or Australian cherries in wearing their stones on the outside? Was Epictetus depraved because he made no attempt to realize certain of the ideals put forward in the Sermon on the Mount, or Julian the Philosopher immoral because in the absence of the sun and moon he shaped his course by the light of the stars?

Whatever the causes of this unveracity — and they are numerous and complicated — it has struck deep roots in the Russian character, and it would need the Herculean labors of many generations of earnest men to eradicate it. If a prophet, as in olden times, were to rise up among the people, and show them whither this was leading them; were he furthermore fortunate enough to inspire them with a sincere desire of mending their ways, they are and would necessarily remain powerless to carry out their wish as long as those who govern them pursue a policy which is avowedly dependent for success on the crassest ignorance of the masses and the absence, in their intellectual outfit, of a rudimentary sense of duty. As the Russian satirist Schtschedrin said: "It has been ordained on high, by the powers that be, that if a man is uneducated he is bound to work with his hands; and if a man is educated, his duty is to take pleasant walks and to eat. Otherwise there would be a revolution."[1] No man, whatever his calling, whatever his religious, political, or social convictions, can at present live and prosper in Russia without constantly paying a heavy tribute to the father of falsehood, the patron of the Empire. Take a journalist, for instance. He lives, moves, and has his being in an atmosphere of hypocrisy and deceit which would prove quickly fatal to the toughest moral nature of the west. Ibsen's Hovstad and Billing of the *People's Messenger* are models of fidelity to principles, positive angels of integrity, in comparison with the average editor of a Russian journal, and this, though the latter does not cease to retain and develop those other moral qualities

---

[1] *A Modern Idyll*, p. 28.

which favorably distinguish him from the majority of his countrymen. Suppose this Russian journalist publishes an article with the Censor's *imprimatur*. If it possesses any real merit, it is almost certain to be denounced by a zealous official, a mischievous busybody, or an envious rival, who writes to some one in authority, attributing a hidden meaning to it. The Minister at once calls the Censor-General to account, who in his turn summons and censures his subordinates. The official who signed the *imprimatur* is dismissed or severely reprimanded, and the writer of the obnoxious article is sent for and treated more like a dog than a human being. He gladly draws up a document, solemnly assuring the authorities that not one of the obvious meanings of the passages objected to was his, and that nothing was further from his intention than to insinuate that anything in the administration needed improvement. The next day he publishes an article embodying his recantation and branding the principles laid down in the obnoxious paper as infamous. And a month afterwards he returns to his old sins of suggestion, insinuation, and writing between the lines, which may possibly again pass unnoticed for an indefinite period. The unfortunate journalist is compelled daily, nay hourly, to sell his soul that his body may not perish — if, indeed, that be the summing up of his life's purpose — or that he may do some little good to his fellow-men, if, as one may charitably hope, that is his object in doing and suffering. Under such circumstances political and religious apostasy is of every-day occurrence; nor does it take moral rank among crimes or sins; it is a result of the law of political gravitation, to which all Russians are subject alike, everything drawing the journalist to the side of power; life, on the other side being only for the extinct race of heroes and martyrs, or for those vain creatures who deem the doubtful good which their words can effect cheap at the price of daily hypocrisy. One is naturally astonished at the Escobar-like immorality of Diderot, who, with perfect coolness and composure, swore that he had no hand in the composition of the *Letters to the Blind*, of which he was the sole author. This, however, was an exceptional occurrence in that philosopher's life, and an oath, it should be remembered, was no more to him than a simple affirmation. But in Russia there are journalists who insert theological sermons unabridged in their newspapers, and profess firm belief in the truths they contain, and yet regard such hateful prevarications and never-ending tissues of lies as part of their daily work which they ask God to bless and their fellow-citizens to admire.

Journalists, however, are not alone. There is scarcely a human being in all Russia who has it in his power to consistently shape his living and working in accordance with the elementary principles of morality. A hero, no doubt, could accomplish it; a John the Baptist, a Fabricius, a Regulus; but heroes are uncommonly scarce in the empire of the Czars, where autocracy, like a scythe, has been for ages occupied in cutting down every head that presumed to raise itself above the low level of the common herd. The average man makes no effort to be consistent. The conception of the unity of human life is unknown there, existence being but an amalgam of fragments, heterogeneous, accidental, mutually inimical, the ever-varying combination of which determines the man's character at a given moment. Thus there are nominal members of the Orthodox Russian Church who have no more faith in the truth of its doctrines or the efficacy of its sacraments than in the stoicism of Epictetus or the teaching of Laou-tsze : some, because they have lost faith in the supernatural ; others, because they are at heart Jews, Catholics, Lutherans, Dissenters. Yet they are one and all compelled to stretch their consciences on the Procrustean bed of orthodoxy, and, what is stranger still, most of them comply with but the ghost of a struggle. Many of them receive the sacraments of confession and communion from the Orthodox popes, thus committing an act of sacrilege — one of the most heinous sins in the long catalogue of religious crimes, which it is their constant endeavor to avoid. Jews, for instance, are positively driven in thousands "into the true fold" by measures which Julian would have scorned to employ, and which even the popes who maintained most zealously Holy Cross Day in Rome would have been ashamed to countenance. They have to blacken their souls with falsehood, bowing down and worshipping strange gods in whom they believe not. I am personally acquainted with several young men, once honest Jews and now spurious Christians, whose sentiments towards their adopted Church resemble those which a young healthy man might be supposed to entertain towards the corpse strapped on his back for the remainder of his life. Even Rabbi Ben Ezra's "Song of Death" is too feeble to adequately express the boundless hate and unutterable loathing which they feel for their new spiritual and old political guides. It is thus no uncommon thing for a man's life to be turned into one continued abominable lie; it is, on the other hand, extremely uncommon for any one to think a bit the worse of him on that account; whether the proximate cause of this profanation be dire necessity or mere avarice. When a forest is being hewn down, says a Russian proverb, the chips fly about in abundance; nor does any one stop to inquire from which of the trees they are falling.

Since M. Pobedonostseff has taken up the reins of Church government in Russia, unrecognized talents, slighted merits, deserved misfortune, all are wont to seek, and generally to find, in religion, not a spiritual consolation for the rebuffs of mankind, but a vulgar stepping-stone to advancement. I have known the editor of a newspaper, which was about to disappear for want of subscribers, to fall back upon religion as a last resource. Nor was his faith belied by the results. He had tried that other salable commodity, loyalty; but there was quite enough of it to be had for the asking, and when he requested a subsidy from the Minister on the ground that he was zealous and indefatigable in defending the good and bad measures of the Government, the late Count Tolstoy significantly dared him to do otherwise. He then returned unabashed to his native city, took to attending divine service every morning, taking up an ostentatious position before two rich and bigoted merchants, beating the ground with his forehead, injuring his knees with genuflexions, watering his handkerchief with tears, and in various other ways behaving like a penitent of the early churches. He published, *verbatim*, the sermons of all Church dignitaries in the diocese; bared his head before the ecclesiastical buildings; and was before long caressed by the bishops, and received large subsidies from the merchants who had witnessed his devotions. His paper is now flourishing and his financial condition highly satisfactory.[1]

---

[1] This paper was already finished when another striking instance of the practical uses of "religion" in Russia under the present emperor was announced in the Russian *Government Messenger* — the appointment of M. Tertius Philippoff to the high post of Controller-general, in spite of the strenuous opposition of M. Pobedonostseff, the other great light of the Russian Church. For M. Philippoff is known chiefly as a theologian, an indomitable champion of Russian Orthodoxy, and as such was appointed to the honorary post of Guardian of the Holy Sepulchre in Jerusalem. Molière might have profitably cultivated the acquaintance of this gentleman before he wrote *Tartuffe*, and Dickens would have been delighted to know him when drawing the portrait of the "sleek, smiling surveyor of Salisbury."

Another gentleman, with whom I am also personally acquainted, who is well known to certain special circles outside Russia, had to abandon his religion in order to qualify for a position which his education and peculiar studies admirably fitted him to fill. He joined the Lutheran Church and received the post. Soon afterwards he became a Roman Catholic in order to qualify for another situation, which he also obtained, holding it simultaneously with the first and unhesitatingly avowing his sordid motives. He had not yet, however, discovered the *truth;* he was only drawing near to it by easy stages. He at last embraced the doctrines of the Orthodoxy to qualify for another position; and here his religious Odyssey came to an end; for out of the Orthodox Russian Church as out of the Orthodox Hell there is no redemption. No man or woman who has once belonged to it can ever again leave it. This gentleman, known by name probably to many readers of this book, boasts an excellent education and considerable special acquirements, which it is perhaps superfluous to say lie outside the sphere of ethics; and, what will seem strangest of all to an Englishman, he is highly respected. It would be interesting to learn such a man's view of truth; but whether he deems it absolute or relative, he would no doubt heartily agree with Lessing that it is far more profitable to pass one's life in seeking for it and groping after it than to discover it off-hand.

Thus religious belief, which might become in the Empire of the North what it has occasionally been in other countries — a germ of true progress, an unfailing source of inspiration, a temporary substitute for that positive knowledge which is the basis of all true morality — is deliberately transformed in Russia into an efficient instrument of demoralization. Genuine faith, as distinguished from blind superstition, is rare; yet, whenever and wherever manifested, it is ruthlessly crushed unless it assumes the form of belief in the talismanic power of hollow forms and unintelligible ceremonies. The dragonnades in which Louis XIV. gave vent to his Christian zeal are occasionally rehearsed in Russia with variations suited to the country and the time, as M. Makoff, the late Minister of the Interior, could testify. But they are enacted in silence and in grim earnest. The outer world, like the spectators in a theatre, rarely learns anything but the final results, set forth in short, dry paragraphs, or in flowery official reports suggestive of Bertrand Barère's masterpieces of state rhetoric. " So and so many Catholics of the United Russian Church have humbly petitioned the Most Holy Synod to receive them into the true fold of the Orthodox Communion, and their prayers have been most graciously accorded "; such is the pithy account that usually finds its way into the newspapers; but thereby always hangs a tale, and invariably a woeful one, strongly suggestive of that appalling story of unparalleled barbarity which was euphemistically wrapped up in the decent historical formula, "Order is restored in Warsaw." I have had occasion to observe somewhat closely the machinery employed in bringing about these conversions, and I can truly say that the details are sickening. If conversion to the Russian Church meant the beginning of a veritable millennium, even for such a boon the price exacted would seem exorbitant. A whole parish or an entire village retires to rest Catholic, and awakes at cock-crow to learn that it has denied its religious faith, and is severely punished for taking the well-beaten road to the Catholic church instead of the unfrequented path to the Orthodox chapel. Agents had persuaded the peasants to sign a paper described as an address of congratulation to his Majesty or some member of the Imperial family, but which was really a petition asking for admittance into the "true fold." At other times a Roman priest secretly secedes to the Orthodox Communion, and transfers the allegiance of his flock, who have not the faintest inkling of his intentions, a procedure the more feasible that the ceremonies and liturgy of the United Catholic Church are identical with those of the Orthodox Church of Russia. When the trick is discovered there is no remedy. Many of the peasants prove refractory and are deported to Siberia or to the coast of the White Sea. The remainder are awed but not convinced, and gradually take to a life of hypocrisy, openly worship in the Orthodox Church, privately receive the Sacrament in Roman Catholic places of worship, or in holes and corners visited by priests of that communion; marry secretly according to their old customs, and consent to have their wives publicly treated as concubines and their children handicapped as bastards.[1]

---

[1] Such marriages are perfectly valid in Russian law, though of course unlawful. The punishment decreed against those who contract them is sufficiently severe to outweigh all ordinary considerations, and it is at least intelligible that simple peasants should expose their offspring to the painful treatment which the Russian law reserves for illegitimate children rather than be separated from them for ever and sent into life-long exile.

In no other country of the world — except perhaps in the Paraguay of Dr. Francia — are the functions of the legislator so entirely merged in those of the moralist. Nowhere else could the standard of right living be so rapidly and so considerably raised, or the whole social state so readily remoulded by the law-maker as in Russia; and yet in no other country is he so reluctant to make any better use of the sublime office which he exercises than that of prostituting it to the most ignoble ends. The result of this gross neglect of duty upon the masses is not a mere matter of opinion; it is writ large and legible in the history of the country, in the character of the people, whose thoughtless, shiftless, trusting nature has been rendered utterly unfit for an encounter with a strong blast of bitter experience; their *morale* being as morbid and unequipped for the trials, temptations, and ordinary duties of every-day life as their over-sensitive bodies — made delicate and effeminate by the artificial heat of rooms — are for the fresh breezes of spring. A Russian has no latent power of reaction stored up within him to enable him to recover from the moral shocks and blows which await him at every step in life; and so crude and undeveloped is his sense of the relation of things to one another that it seems to have been given him for some other world than ours. His lying and all the other immoral habits of which it is the taproot, are unaccompanied by even the most rudimentary consciousness of guilt; for he suffers from complete anæsthesia of that moral faculty by which in other people these habits are prevented or condemned. The following incident may help to illustrate my meaning and to throw a side-light on the peasant's views on the relations of things to each other, and his idea of veracity. In the Government of Kieff some time ago the inhabitants of thirty-six villages, after due deliberation, decided that no public-houses for the sale of alcoholic drinks should be opened in any of the villages whose representatives took part in the deliberation. All peasants who were of age voted for the measure, and each village feed a public writer, to draw up a petition to the Government asking that the decision be registered and sanctioned. Thirty-five petitions were rejected by the Ministry, and the *kabaks* duly opened in the villages, the thirty-sixth was favorably received, and the publicans excluded. The reason assigned for the success of the thirty-sixth petition was the eloquence and force with which the public writer put the case; and on learning this, the inhabitants of the fortunate village, disappointed that their *kabaks* were closed, though *at their own request*, condemned the writer of the petition for excess of zeal and superfluous eloquence to be flogged. And he was duly flogged.[1]

It is only fair to say that the acts of the authorities have not at all times that tendency to demoralize which is their usual characteristic; they are occasionally even salutary, and one would be glad to give the government credit for those motives which are at once the most obvious and most honorable, were it not that the real reasons, which no effort is made to conceal, are wholly foreign to considerations of morality. Russian newspapers, with a few exceptions, seem to make a specialty of lying, and apparently thrive upon it. Of course the inventive or mythopæic faculty of the pressmen is almost exclusively employed upon the affairs of foreign countries: for, like Hovstad, of the *People's Messenger*, they "have learned from experience and thoughtful men that in purely local matters a paper must observe a certain amount of caution." An unsuspecting foreigner is thus sometimes puzzled to discover how a provincial newspaper with fifteen hundred or only a thousand readers can keep special correspondents in all the large cities of the world, and pay for whole columns of costly telegrams. The secret was officially disclosed a few weeks since, when the Government ordered all the editors of the city of Odessa to cease publishing foreign telegrams "from our own correspondents," without first proving to the satisfaction of the local censors that they were *bonâ fide* telegrams and not paragraphs fabricated at the office. The result was immediate and striking: silence fell upon the special correspondents — as deathlike and prolonged as that with which the Delphic oracle was struck after the birth of Christ. One's satisfaction at this laudable intervention of the government is considerably diminished by the circumstance that it was determined upon on purely political grounds, several forged "foreign" telegrams being gross calumnies upon foreign governments, whose representatives were instructed to protest.

Wholesale lying of this kind would presumably cause a bloody revolution in this enlightened country, judging by the terrible shock which public opinion sustained here some time

---

[1] *Kievsloic Slovo*, July 16, 1887, and *Odessa Messenger*, July 18, 1887.

ago on learning that Mr. Parnell endeavored by an exaggeration in terms to deliberately mislead the House of Commons. What would be said, or rather done, by such virtuous public opinion, were the elaborate defence of lying lately published in all seriousness by the editor of an official journal, to have appeared in London instead of St. Petersburg? In a leading article upon the death of the late Crown Prince of Austria, written before the melancholy circumstances of his death were fully known, the *Graschdanin* bitterly lamented the decay of lying in a strain worthy of a Jeremiah bewailing his country's fate. "If he really put an end to his life," says this moralist, whom the Government subsidizes to spread the light, "is it possible that there was not a single individual sufficiently alive to the interests of the family, the dynasty, and the throne, to insist upon the concealment of the fact of suicide, and to hush up the details of it, leaving no trace discoverable? What would be easier than to conceal the suicide, if it really took place? 'He was toying with a revolver,' one might say, 'when it caught the button of his uniform,' or a number of other very natural and likely statements might have been put forward, and there is no doubt that people would have believed them much more readily than the story of suicide."[1] On the other hand, that same journal and others of its way of thinking, or rather writing, are at a loss for words emphatic enough to adequately express their indignation whenever this convenient principle is acted upon by others in a manner injurious or displeasing to themselves. Thus in the *Novoye Vremya*, the Russian telegraphic agency is plumply accused of systematically communicating to the inhabitants of Omsk false statements concerning the prices of the shares of various banks, now immoderately exaggerating, now lowering their real value on the exchange. Thus, on the 18th of September last year, the shares of the Volga-Kam Bank were quoted by that news agency at 500 roubles, whereas in reality they stood at 645 roubles, a difference of about £15 sterling per share; the shares of the Siberian Bank were given at 645 roubles, whereas they were only 460 roubles, that is, about £19 difference on each share. "Such garbled figures," exclaims the writer, "are *systematically repeated every day*. Fancy the predicament of those who purchase shares of the above-named companies on the basis of the telegrams of this

---

[1] *Graschdanin*, February, 1889. Cf. also *Novosti*, 19th February, 1889.

agency!"[1] These things, it should be borne in mind, are confined to no one portion of Russia, to no particular class or classes of the population; they are universal, pan-Russian, inborn in every individual like a species of original sin inherited from forgotten ancestors and deliberately perpetuated by present sponsors. If moral blame attaches to any one, it can only be to the Government and the Church in the past and to the press of very recent years. The masses are wholly blameless. To them lying has ever been as natural as singing. It is as old and as respectable as the universe. "Lying began with the world," says one of their proverbs, "and with the world it will die." What force of expression, lucidity, eloquence, is to our speech, lying is to theirs. "Rye beautifies the field," says another Russian proverb, "and a lie beautifies speech." And again, "A palatable lie is better than a bitter truth." But even had mendacity been foreign to their nature, the practical experience of a generation or two of veracious men acquired under the Government and in the Church of any of the past nine centuries of Russian history would have amply sufficed to teach this docile people that unblushing falsehood is the only coin that passes current in their native country. The accuracy of this statement is vouched for by history; it is confirmed by the evidence of the people themselves embodied in their countless proverbs, which constitute nearly three-fourths of the spoken language of the uneducated. "Do not mourn for truth: make terms with falsehood." Or, "It is by falsehood that men live: it is not meet that we should die." Not only have they everything to gain by deceiving and cheating their fellow-men and those unprincipled slavemasters whom they looked upon as maleficent deities, but they have no penalty to undergo in the shape of remorse here or hell fire hereafter. If detection is not followed by physical punishment, there is no cause for apprehension. "Lying," according to another proverb, "is not like chewing dough: it won't choke you." It is not that they do not honor and revere truth for itself, whenever they hear of it; but they look upon it as a sort of Noumenon far

---

[1] *Novoye Vremya*, 6th November, 1888. This is one of numerous such accusations against the same agency. It is not my wish or purpose to discuss the truth or falsehood of these accusations of deliberate lying. They may be cases of inadvertent errors. A Russian proverb truly says, "We cannot creep into another's soul" to learn his intentions. Cf., however, *Graschdanin*, 8th August, 1889, and *Novoye Vremya*, 3d August, 1889.

too precious for this sinful phenomenal world of ours — a holiday garment for the soul to be worn in the Elysian fields prepared for them by an indulgent Creator after they have thoroughly cleansed themselves in the bath of death. "Truth is sacred," says a Russian proverb, "but we mortals are sinful." Or in a variant which is also explanatory, "Sacred truth is good, but not for mortals." What it is good for is made clear in another proverb, "Truth is not good for being put in action: it should be put in an *icon*-glass case and prayed to."

One of the disadvantages inseparable from an attempt to prove a comprehensive thesis by a series of particular instances is the danger of the conclusion being held to be a wholly unwarranted or a greatly exaggerated generalization. As a matter of fact, it has been my earnest endeavor to state the case as moderately as is compatible with a due regard for incontrovertible facts; and English travellers in Russia who may still feel inclined to make exceptions from the general rule in favor of such apparently trustworthy sources of information as government institutions, ministries, statistical bureaus, and the like, would do well to act only on good cause shown, taking with them the prudence of the serpent and leaving at the frontier the simplicity of doves. A few months ago a case illustrative of the necessity for this precaution was published in the Russian newspapers, not as a matter of wonder, but merely as an ordinary stop-gap to fill in the fragment of a column. The occasion was the reading before the Governor of Baku of the official report of the Statistical Department of Baku on crime in that district during the year 1888. It was then solemnly affirmed, with all the *aplomb* which objective science and professional assiduity can inspire, that there were but three cases of highway robbery and two murders during twelve months — a remarkably clean bill of moral health for such a district. Now the subject of the report was very simple, one would imagine. Apparently no one would ever dream of deliberate lying in the presence of the governor of the very district of which it was question, surrounded as he was by officials provided with excellent means of testing every statement. And least of all would one suspect a statistical department of being foolish enough to attempt such a thing, seeing that its only *raison d'être* is the issue of trustworthy reports calculated to inspire confidence. What actually happened is this: the governmental attorney (procurer), who was attentively listening to the report, quietly remarked that to his personal knowledge, which may have been incomplete, there had been not tens but hundreds of murders and robberies committed in that district during the year 1888.[1] The statistics of education are rich in equally eloquent illustrations of the same inborn aversion of the Russian, even though educated and trained to better things, to

> "let truth's lump rot stagnant for the lack
> Of a timely helpful lie to leaven it."

Thus, among the schools which figured in the official list of educational establishments of the government of Kherson during the past twelve years, it has now been disclosed that *two hundred and seventeen* (217) are mere figments of the brain of some unduly zealous official, they never having had an objective existence.[2] How many such paper schools there are in other governments of Russia, no man knows.[3]

Certain persons with broad views on the doctrine of compromise and accommodating readiness to subordinate ethics to the practical exigencies of daily life may perhaps be tempted to explain all these symptoms as merely the result of a passing moral aberration such as we observe in one form or another in most nations and epochs, rather than as indications of a specific difference of moral code. To these large-minded moralists a convincing reply within the limits of a review article would be impossible. I would ask them, however, to give careful attention to the following fact and to draw a mental picture of the state of society in which alone such a state of things is possible. A well-known journalist of Odessa (Dulsky by name), who himself some time since occupied an editor's arm-chair in the office of the *Odessky Listok*, published a very curious letter some months ago in which he laughs to scorn the editor of another journal (*The New Russian Telegraph*) whom he had been deliberately and systematically deceiving for several years. "As I had complete control of the depot for intelligence of all kinds," this high priest of modern journalism frankly writes, "in the

---

[1] *Graschdanin*, April 16, 1889.
[2] *Novoye Vremya*, August 31, 1888.
[3] These and a hundred similar instances should be carefully borne in mind by travellers like Mr. Landsdell and others whose faith in Russian official statements is Tertullian-like in its ravenous appetite for the wildest and most indigestible assertions.

government of Bessarabia, most of the items of news published in the *New Telegraph were forged in my lodgings and at my dictation.*" Yet this gentleman is still an active member of the staff of the most widely circulated daily newspaper in all South Russia, and is highly respected — as respect goes in those parts — in the social circles in which he moves. Nor is this indulgent treatment the result of repentance and a firm resolve to amend in future; for not only does this prophet and guide publicly avow acts which in western climes would be branded as infamous by the least pharisaical of journalists, but he positively glories in them as if he could possess no better titles to public esteem. Nay, he does not hesitate to humbly implore the assistance of God to enable him to lie and mislead with as much success in the future as in the past. "So matters have gone on," he writes, "for the space of four or five years, and I shall not hide from you that with God's help I shall continue this harmless occupation until I grow tired of it."[1]

---

[1] Cf. *Northern Messenger* (monthly review), February, 1889, pp. 67, 68.

CHAPTER II.

FATALISM.

WHERE the great guiding principles of social conduct universally accepted by civilized peoples are not yet assimilated by a nation, it would be puerile to expect the observance of those minor practical rules which are usually included under the name of propriety. This may be an enviable blessing or the opposite, according to the point of view from which we consider it, but in either case it is an incontrovertible fact. In no other civilized people is the sense of the fitness of things and the perception of the incongruous so undeveloped and rudimentary as in the Russians. This defect can be satisfactorily accounted for in many ways; for instance, by the listless, unreal, dreamy life led by the people, who are ever glad to flee from the dread realities around them, to sleep, drunkenness, phantasy, for transient relief; by their childish view of the relation of cause and effect, which to their thinking is as necessary or as accidental as the falling of rain in answer to the prayers of the priest for moisture for the crops. Thus a most trivial act — such as spitting over one's shoulder, for instance — performed by a nobody will work revolutions in the heavenly spheres, producing effects that are nothing if not infinite. The stroke of a pen of a country boor, who is a copyist in some government office, will thwart the will of the Tsar and baffle the efforts of the entire Government;[1] a few genuflexions in church and the burning of a penny wax taper before an *icon* will straightway restore to pristine innocence the abandoned wretch whose soul is black with the guilt of inexpiable crimes, to which Tannhäuser's were mere peccadilloes. To the average Russian mind every

---

[1] This is literally true. I could bring forward several curious cases in proof of this statement, which is well known to business men in the country — natives and foreigners, who have always to begin the distribution of the indispensable bribes with the lowest officials, ascending gradually upwards. The omission of a single intermediate link would be as fatal to final success as the passing over of a proposition in Euclid to the boy who learns geometry for the first time.

cause is a talisman between which and the effect to be produced there need be no proportion whatever. The scholastic law — *Nemo dat quod non habet* — would be rank heresy to the mind of the Russian, who has no eye for the perception of the grotesqueness that so often results from the logical application of his own view of causality. The talisman once put in requisition, the necessary effect must follow; if it does not, the reason thereof surpasses the understanding of the poor helpless mortal who had best leave things to right themselves. At the root of this slipshod way of conducting the most serious business of life is the absence of reflection, which during ages of demoralization, when all the expanding intellectual energies of the people were systematically driven into the narrow channel of emotion, was paralyzed for want of exercise, like the ventral fins of the mudfish (*Siluridæ*, etc.), or the eyes of the sightless *amblyopsis* of the Mammoth Cave of Kentucky. A man is appointed to a post which requires constant hard work, he shirks the hard work and accepts the emoluments in conformity with a confused half-conscious feeling that the nomination and his occupying the post constitute as it were the talismanic formula; the results intended should somehow come of themselves, or at any rate with very little co-operation from him. A typical instance of this view of one's life-work occurred in the beginning of the present year. The secretary of the Town Council of the city of Taraschtscha (Government of Kieff) for a long time discharged his professional duties in accordance with this curious conception of his obligations, until at last it occurred to certain town councillors that they might get on fairly well without him. They drew up a report to this effect, which had first to be privately read and signed by him, and then publicly read by him to the Town Council. He actually signed the report, having shirked his duty of first perusing it, and afterwards publicly read about half of it to the Town Council before he became aware of its drift.[1] This same conception of duty was manifested some time ago in a somewhat emphatic manner by a favorite pianist whose concerts are eagerly visited by friends of music in Russia. This gentleman sometimes deems that he has satisfactorily performed his duty if he merely shows himself to the public assembled to hear him playing. In the spring

---

[1] *Novoye Vremya*, 18th February, 1889.

of 1888, he was advertised to give a concert in the University of Dorpat. The seats were filled by an appreciative audience, which grew impatient when the artist failed to put in an appearance at the hour fixed. At last he arrived, staggered along the platform, turning his dull unmeaning eyes upon the audience, and fell heavily into the seat beside the piano. Then he laid his bushy head upon the candle-stand, and let his hands drop motionless to his side. The public grew nervous; several ladies cried out that he had a stroke of apoplexy, and were imploring medical assistance for him when he fell heavily to the ground. "He is dead," they cried despairingly, and the confusion became indescribable, until a friend of the artist came forward and said: "It is nothing dangerous; our dear artist is only dead drunk."[1] And the "dear artist" is as great a favorite as ever. Improprieties of this kind are constantly passing without notice in Russia, where the manners of the rudest elements of society — the not yet amalgamated Armenians, Georgians, Mingrelians, etc. — have an irresistible tendency to keep the general standard rather low. Turghenieff was one day complaining to his friend Panaïeff of the queer (to an Englishman's way of thinking outrageous) manner in which the well-known *littérateur*, Pissemsky, had conducted himself the evening before, when reading a new novel he had written to a circle of well-born ladies and gentlemen in a salon of St. Petersburg. "I shall take care never to be present again when Pissemsky is reading, unless it be in our own circle," exclaimed Turghenieff. "Just fancy, gentlemen,. he undertook to read his novel though suffering from a disorder of the bowels. As usual, he incessantly belched, constantly jumped up and went out of the room, and returning adjusted his dress before the ladies. *Lastly, and to crown all*,[2] he called for a glass of *vodka*."[3]

Is there any country but Russia in which the accomplished horseman of a circus could arrange to have a concert given for his benefit — in the Christian church, as Schuman Cook did in 1888?[4] Is there any other country in Europe in

---

[1] *Novosti*, April, 1888.
[2] The italics are my own and are meant to emphasize Turghenieff's idea of the highest term of the climax, the *ne plus ultra* of impropriety.
[3] *Historical Messenger*, April, 1889.
[4] Cf. the *Journal Bals*, August, 1888; the *Riga Messenger*, August 1888; and the *Odessa News*, August 28, 1888, etc.

which a Minister of State, arrayed in all the gold lace and decorations of his office, taking part in the most solemn and impressive ceremony imaginable, the obsequies of his murdered sovereign, and bearing the sceptre or some such other symbol of imperial power, the cynosure of hundreds of thousands of eyes, quietly put the sceptre in one hand and with the other pulled out from his pocket a substantial sandwich which he had thoughtfully provided, and leisurely munched it while walking in the procession as naturally as if he were in the clearing of a wood on a picnic with friends.[1] It would be a mistake to treat these things as isolated facts of rare occurrence — the result of the heedlessness or eccentricity of obscure individuals. They are frequent, one may say universal, and quite as characteristic of corporate bodies and assemblies in which the collective wisdom of whole classes of the population is supposed to reside. Every year the city of Moscow organizes a public festival in aid of the Society of Christian Help. This would seem a good enough work on the face of it, but unfortunately the realization was never quite in keeping with the conception, for the festival always consisted of drinking to excess, listening to the singing of indecent songs by women who illustrated them by indecent gestures, and other equally " Christian " pleasures. Still people desirous of upholding the Society of Christian Help went and generally brought their families with them, and went home satisfied, having killed two birds with one stone. In 1888 an additional attraction was held out to the people in the shape of a pantomime for boys and girls, in which was reproduced "the life of the shady women of the *demi-monde* of St. Petersburg and the manners and morals of cooks and servant women of the capital, when organizing orgies at night with their lovers, members of the fire brigade."[2] *One* father of a family protested at last, and declared that this was not the kind of spectacle that he would like to bring his children to — the intrinsic incongruity of the thing having seemingly completely escaped his observation. The *Moscow Listok*, however, a widely read journal, ridiculed the remarks of the gentleman in question, observing that what children should be protected from is not

---

[1] This act, however, cost the gentleman his portfolio, and the usual solatium invariably given to dismissed Ministers. I refrain from mentioning his name, though I have said enough to lead to its identification in Russia. The gentleman is otherwise a very worthy man.

[2] Cf. *Novosti*, 31st October, 1888.

demoralization, but puritanical fathers; that it is a mistake to entertain ideal conceptions of what our social amusements should be, and *if one of the factors of this amusement should prove to be the delineation of light morals, etc., that in this there would be no great harm.*

This helpless inability or unconquerable repugnance to duly shape the means to the end proposed, this deep conviction that, the first step taken, everything else may be safely left to God or to chance, is manifest in every act of individuals, societies, and representatives of the nation. It strikes us with quite as much force in Siberia as in Moscow, and testifies to Russian nationality as loudly in Archangelsk as in Kieff. One is being perpetually reminded of the two simple-minded Russians who entered into conversation with each other in a railway carriage half-way between St. Petersburg and Moscow, and discovering that they were travelling in the same train though bound the one for Moscow and the other for St. Petersburg, which lie in very opposite directions, were loud in their admiration of the wonders of science and civilization, but whose raptures gave place to very sober reflections the next morning, when they both found themselves in Moscow, one of them being several hundred miles from his destination. This typical story was forcibly recalled to my mind in 1888, when reading the startling disclosures published by two respectable doctors concerning the Hospital of the Russian Sisters of Mercy in Odessa, of which they were the consulting physicians.[1] "Patients are received," we are told, "mainly in order that they should die. They are kept in narrow, moist, stinking cells, are treated in the name of mercy with a degree of cruelty that outstrips the limits of the probable; they are fed with loathsome food, are made to wait eight hours for their medicines, which are prepared in the kitchen along with the meals, being for economy's sake compounded with water instead of spirits, and put up in match-boxes and cigarette-boxes; paralytics are purged with enemas, and sufferers from typhus put in straight-waistcoats. Since the arrival of the new Superioress from St. Petersburg a new method of treatment has been superadded, and now patients are healed by charms, spells, and magical formulas."[2] There were two exhibitions in St. Petersburg during the first half of the year 1889, both of which were adaptations to a different order of things of the journey to St.

---

[1] Cf. *Novosti*, 31st October, 1888. [2] *Ibid.*, 12th November, 1888.

Petersburg in a train bound for Moscow; the one a Pan-Russian exhibition of the products of pisciculture, with specimens of fish from the far north, the extreme south, the Volga, the Vistula, and the Caspian; and the other a flower show with naiad-like lilies, royal roses, and rare exotics. Large numbers of the fish in the first exhibition were in such a very advanced state of putrescence that they were *sold* for nominal prices *for food* to the visitors, who had to hold their noses and shorten their stay. The persons responsible, when appealed to, had the fish removed, but not before they had pointed out that all the aspects of the fish industry in the Empire should be in evidence at a good representative exhibition, and that as the sale of putrid fish as an article of food was a common feature in the trade it should also figure there.[1] The finest exhibit at the flower show, a magnificent specimen of the Cape Colony *Strelitza* with gorgeous yellow-blue flowers, sent by the *Imperial Botanical Gardens*, was found to be a mere sham, a rootless flower with short stalk, temporarily stuck into the earth to deceive simple-minded visitors to the exhibition. How many other exhibits, from private as well as from *Imperial* institutions, were equally clever frauds the public had no means of judging.[2]

Conscious that these statements are the logical deductions from facts numerous enough to fill bulky volumes, I am also aware that patriotic Russians with a strongly-developed sentiment of national *amour propre* may deem, or at least declare them, exaggerated or too strongly colored. The possibility of such a line of argument, rather than any real need of further confirmation, is my excuse for quoting the opinion of a Russian *littérateur*, now living and writing on the staff of the Petersburg journal *Novosti*, who published an article in that paper in October, 1887, on the question "Are Russians Civilized?" and I am bound to say that the views which he there put forward were received with approbation by the greater part of the provincial press, which reproduced the article in *extenso* or in part.

"To begin with," writes M. Skabitscheffsky, "the most civilized of us all lead double lives: one life for our guests, when we flaunt our culture, and a totally different one in private, for daily use at home, where you can never say what enormities your most civilized man may not be committing. He may be blowing his nose with his fingers,

---

[1] Cf. *Novosti*, 12th May, 1889.   [2] *Ibid.*

licking the frying-pan with his tongue, drinking out of the bottle or milk-jug, etc., etc. It is not without cause that our proverb says: 'If you do not wish to spoil your appetite don't look into the kitchen.' Now what manner of civilization is that which exists only to be paraded before the guests like a gala uniform which is taken off after having been worn for an hour? Why, it is the fullest negation of the very conception expressed by the word — the conception of a series of customs and habits that have grown into second nature. *In the most civilized classes of society* you observe the complete absence of respect for public or private property. It needs all the watchful vigilance of the police to keep public gardens from being befouled, the trees therein from being torn up, the monuments from being broken and covered with ribald inscriptions. If you let your country house for the summer to people who are to all seeming thoroughly enlightened, with an easy conscience they allow their horses and kine to graze in your garden and to eat up the flowers in your flower-beds. I once called upon acquaintances of mine, who were also most civilized people; all the stoves in their lodgings were heated until they were well-nigh white hot, and fuel was still being added. The heat in the rooms was unbearable. 'Why do you heat your rooms so immoderately?' I asked. 'Well, how can you ask such a question?' was the reply; 'why, the wood, don't you know, is the house-owner's;[1] surely you would not have us spare it!' And it is remarkable that *in all classes of society* you see the same sottish, brutish conviction prevalent, that not only need we not save and spare what does not belong to ourselves, but that we are in a manner bound at all costs to annihilate it. It is in obedience to this instinct that we cover the tables of our lodgings with inscriptions and pour every imaginable filth upon them; that, removing from our rooms, we consider it our duty to tear off the wall-paper and if possible to damage the walls also. To reduce to rags the book we have taken from the library, to deface the margins with sottish remarks and to tear out the pictures — this also is, in due season, our sacred duty. . . . And after all this, we have the audacity to talk of Russian civilization, of the cultured class!"

---

[1] Lodgings (flats of several rooms, containing kitchen, etc.) are frequently let in Russia with fuel; the house-owner stipulating to supply all the wood required by the tenant to heat the rooms and for culinary purposes.

The lowest substratum of the Russian character which the most careful analysis can discover is irreverence. However serious the thoughts by which a Russian's mind may at a given moment be absorbed, however enthusiastic his devotion to a truly noble cause, he is always careful to leave a chink of his mind open for future irreverence, to bubble up through and swamp the relics of that faith for which he is now perhaps ready to sacrifice his life. In the height of his noble enthusiasm, like David Copperfield, when sorrow for his dead mother was most poignant, he carefully notes the most trivial incidents going on around him, and will treasure them up in his memory on the chance of their yielding him the materials for a future sarcasm against his present ideals. *Olim meminisse juvabit.* Hence the amazing suddenness with which a Russian changes his point of view, and veers round from north to south without a moment's stay at any of the intermediate points of the compass, and the picture of Dostoïeffsky, the great psychological novelist, solemnly offering up his heartfelt gratitude to the Emperor of Russia for having banished him to Siberia, to herd with the scum of creation and suffer maddening misery for acts which, if not indifferent, were positively praiseworthy, cannot be matched in Christendom, outside the walls of a lunatic asylum.

Deep-rooted faith in destiny, which is another fundamental trait of the Russian character, and is the only real faith that permeates the people, contributes largely no doubt to that peculiar frame of mind in which such fickleness is possible, such laxity of morals an inevitable necessity. "What is to be, cannot be avoided," is a proverb and a dogma of every subject of the Czar, who on seeing a murderer or his victim is always devoutly thankful to destiny that he chances for the time being to be neither; thus implying that one *rôle* is just as likely to fall to his lot as the other, neither being avoidable by any mere effort of his will. The Russian is a firm believer in the unlimited possibility not of his own active nature, but of an external power whom he indiscriminately names God and Fate, which is always actively interfering in the ups and downs of his unreal life, taking away all incentive to action, but likewise easing him of all moral responsibility. Quaint Sir Thomas Browne believed that the "rubs, doublings, and wrenches," of which most men's lives are in great part composed, and which "pass awhile under the effects of chance," need only to be well examined " to prove the mere hand of God." And the good-hearted old doctor felt the better for this conviction. In Russia, without any study or analysis, people find God's finger in every accident, crime, and intrigue, having sharpened up their sight

> "To spy a providence in the fire's going out,
> The kettle's boiling, the dime's sticking fast
> Despite the hole i' the pocket."

And the ensuing familiarity has only bred contempt, in addition to that irresistible tendency to inaction which vitiates the good beginning of so many well-meaning men and women. "The devil is now engaged in mortal combat with your guardian angel," exclaimed the prefect of some ecclesiastical seminary in Italy to a lazy student who was lying in bed, and whom he was exhorting to go down to divine service.

"What?" said the slumbering sluggard, turning over on to the other side, "my guardian angel fighting the devil on the question of early rising? Well, I have confidence in my guardian angel, who is bound to win. I will watch them both from this coign of vantage, till the fight is over. Have no fear for the result."

Now this is precisely the Russian's position in respect to the question of self-help. He lies listlessly in his place and lazily watches what he deems the finger of Fate forming and shaping the good and bad events of his own existence. With fate all things are possible and are equally probable. There is no everlasting yea or everlasting nay in the Russian's theology or philosophy. Religion shows him a hell whence there is no redemption, a heaven whence there is no fall. Science puts him in possession of truths that are unassailable, and experience gives him facts that are as certain as his existence. Yet he thinks and speaks and acts in utter defiance of them all, for down in the hidden depths of his consciousness he has a confused notion that God or fate my alter these things any day in his favor, if desirable, and that none of them are final. Finality does not exist in any shape or form for the Russian. The archangels and seraphs may yet fall from their lofty thrones, the devil has a fair chance of salvation ; the Caroline Islands may some day be shown to be in the Indian Ocean, and the earth prove the centre of the solar system ; and all this in virtue of destiny, which though almighty, whimsical, well-meaning, and mischievous by turns, is at bottom benevolent and kindly, willing to humor all desires and prepared in the next life to make things right and comfortable. His is the one active will working behind ours, moving us as puppets in the Punch and Judy show; thinking with our minds, speaking with our tongues, and living with our lives. A country where such notions are prevalent, is naturally unfavorable to the growth of Consul Bernicks, Pastor Manders, or Mayor Stockmanns — of those living pillars of society and lights of Christianity who thank God, meaning themselves, that they are not as other men. "Unto each man happens what was decreed at his birth," is one of the countless proverbs which embody that national Russian solution of the problem of free-will. Others are: "What is to be will be." "You cannot run away from fate, not even on horseback." Nor is it the merely material side of destiny, so to say, that is brought out in such bold relief in the proverbs and the conduct of the Russian people; its moral aspect is no less emphatically accentuated. "Sin and sorrow overtake all men alike." "If a dog is to be beaten, there will be no lack of sticks." "A fool shoots, but God bears the bullets." "The wolf seizes the destined sheep," etc., etc.

Hence there is no inexpiable sin, no social hell for the upper or lower classes of Russian society. How low soever a man or a woman may have fallen, he or she is never held to be irredeemably lost. They can always come back to their former places without causing "doubt, hesitation, or pain." A man who has irreparably wronged you, blasted your cherished hopes, blighted your life, ruined those nearest and dearest to you, will after the lapse of a few months seek you out and address you in the most winning way, sure that you are glad to let bygones be forgotten and renew the friendship of the past. And he is only judging you by the highest standard he knows — to which his own life more or less conforms — utterly unconscious that it implies anything incompatible with your conception of a Bayard. I could illustrate this by numerous instances, some of which came under my own observation; but I prefer to restrict myself to one or two that have the advantage of being notorious. A few years ago a well-known capitalist of Moscow, on his return home from the Exchange, became aware that a daring burglary had been committed during his absence, his desk having been broken open and a sum of five hundred roubles abstracted. Suspicion at first took no definite shape; but at last the butler suggested the name of the family physician — a man who was under innumerable obligations to the capitalist, having been rescued when a boy from abject poverty, sent to school and to the University at his expense until he obtained his medical degree, and being ever since in receipt of a large yearly salary from him for the discharge of the nominal duties of family physician. The suggestion was naturally treated as a foul-mouthed calumny at first; but the doctor was soon sent for and questioned. He began by denying the charge, but, like most Russian criminals, ended by confessing it. He pleaded necessity in palliation of the deed, and tried to prove it by saying that the money was indispensable, as he was morally bound to make a present of a costly necklace to a gypsy woman whose favors he had been enjoying for some time past. He then asked for forgiveness, and without more ado received it. And his friendly relations with his benefactor continue as if nothing had occurred to ruffle them. He is as respectable and respected as ever.[1] Another instance is afforded by the case of the notorious revolutionist, Leo Tikhomiroff, whom the present Czar lately pardoned on his expressing deep contrition and writing a recantation of all his errors. This individual returned to Russia in 1889 and called on the late Count Tolstoy, Minister of the Interior, who was so delighted with the uncompromising thoroughness of his new convictions, and was so taken with the earnestness of the man, that he actually asked him for his photograph and autographs as souvenirs. Leo Tikhomiroff is now one of the pillars of the reactionary party in Russia, one of the lights of the Moscow *Gazette*, in the columns of which paper he publishes endless diatribes against Russian Liberalism as hollow and as lifeless as a two hours' sermon in a parish church in France.

It is not surprising under such circumstances that unmerited misfortune and richly deserved punishment should be indiscriminately confounded in the one comprehensive conception of Destiny, or that disgrace and suffering coming in the guise of retribution for odious crimes have no corrective or deterrent effect upon the average Russian, whose motto is *hodie mihi cras tibi*. The Russian criminal

---

[1] *Novoye Vremya*, April 13, 1889.

is as patient and resigned under condign punishment as under wanton persecution, and his friends are lavish of their sympathies, as becomes genuine fatalists; both, mindful of one of the proverbs of which the Russian language is one vast mosaic, proclaiming that all such calamities, like spring rains and evening dew, fall alike abundantly upon good men and evil, and that immunity therefrom is the result of personal luck, not the meed of right conduct. And the most ferocious and hardened criminal is always sure of evoking a sigh of pity such as that which was breathed by the tenderhearted Adah for lost, impenitent Lucifer.

"Sleep; God will keep watch and ward for you," is a saying of the poet Lermontoff's that correctly describes the mental, moral, and political attitude of the millions of miserable human beings who dreamily acknowledge the sway of the Tsar, staggering and stumbling under the burdens of life, as in a painful half-conscious stupor. The extent to which fatalism and shiftlessness, with all the other vices of which they are the source, have eaten into the Russian character, can with difficulty be realized by those whose knowledge of the people is not derived from personal experience. Even in things that interest him most the typical Russian is strangely apathetic, and the terribly significant expression, "I waved my hand at it," meaning "I have given up all further thought of it," is daily and hourly heard from men who, at the first little obstacle they encounter, withdraw from the race within easy distance of the goal. Some idea, however, of Russian sluggishness and shiftlessness may be formed by those who have read Gontscharoff's novel *Oblomoff*, and can picture to themselves a vast empire peopled by undeveloped types of humanity welting in chaotic ignorance and misery, in various degrees of disintegration from the action of that fearful solvent nameless in the English tongue, and which Russians now term Oblomoffism. This combination of fatalism, will-paralysis, indifference, and grovelling instincts gives us a clue to the marvellous endurance of the masses, whose mode of life is at times more bleak, cheerless, and less human than that of the grazing monks of Mesopotamia described by Sozomen, whose sufferings were at least the result of choice.[1] For ages they have been taught by word

---

[1] Grass and a substitute for bread ingeniously made of the powdered bark of a tree flavored with flour is sometimes the staple food of the worst-

of mouth and by the lessons of daily experience to take no thought for the morrow; they have been trained by the Government and counselled by their Church to look to others for all things needful, to put their trust in princes and powers, visible and invisible; and the outcome of this habit is on the one hand a degree of shiftlessness compared with which Mr. Micawber's waiting for something to turn up was sublimated worldly wisdom, and on the other a lively expectation of daily miracles in which the most spoiled thaumaturgus of the Middle Ages never ventured to indulge.[1] The groundwork of the average Russian's life-philosophy is composed of two fundamental maxims, one being the Russian equivalent for Mr. Toots' favorite dictum, "It's of no consequence" (*vsióh rovnóh*), and the other an untranslateable term (*avoss'*) sometimes rendered by "mayhap," or "somehow," but in reality a sort of sacramental formula, shifting to the Fates the responsibility for the consequences of a hope entertained or an act to be performed, and challenging them to intervene and set at naught the laws of the universe, even to the extent of saving the life of him who is recklessly rushing upon destruction.

Hence the persistent refusal of the Russian to shape and vary his actions according to the objects in view, for he has a deep-rooted feeling that all his words and deeds, however incongruous or wide of the mark, are endowed with some mysterious power of righting themselves automatically, and like Vathék's sabre will do their work independently of the incompetency or clumsiness of him who uses them. "It will all be ground up fine and make excellent flour," is one of his favorite proverbs, when speaking of the tares and sweepings of life that so often mix with, and outweigh its corn, and he continues cheerfully to let things take their

---

off of these modern βοσκοί, who, when unfortunate or fortunate enough to be destitute of even this sorry apology for sustenance, have no alternative but sheer starvation, and, like the dumb, patient ox, after lowing in vain for fodder, lie down and die without a murmur. (Cf. *Moscow Gazette*, April 10th, 1888; January 18th, 1888; and the journal *Day*, 25th March, 1888.) It is astonishing, and of good augury, that in spite of the scant reasons they have for hugging life, they seldom think of passing through what Epictetus calls the "open door," and that having emulated the sect of the *Grazers* from dire necessity, they do not imitate that of the *Circumcelliones* or suicides from deliberate choice. But the Russian character is one mass of inconsistencies.

[1] That this presumptuous hope is not always vain is obvious to those who remember the details of the railway accident of October, 1888, at Borki, when, by a curious freak of chance, the Imperial family had a hairbreadth escape from death.

own course, confident that everything will be for the best at last. This childlike or childish faith is made manifest in a thousand ways, all equally hurtful to the interests of society. It emboldens him to reverse Napoleon's rule of life and leave as much to chance as is consistent with his keeping outside a prison and a lunatic asylum; thus it imparts to a railway built over crumbling embankments [1] and laid on rotten half-burnt sleepers [2] the strength it should have received from nature and engineering skill; it supports tottering railway bridges over which no sensible man would consent to forward his furniture in a goods train; [3] it encourages architects to build vast public and private edifices — like that lately erected by the merchants of Moscow — which a sudden gust of wind or the shaking of the soil by passing vans causes to fall down like the wall of Jericho at the shout of the men of Joshua, and crush to death more victims than were buried alive by their Pagan ancestors in the foundation of whole cities; it keeps them of good cheer when, as jurymen trying prisoners for grave crimes, they send one man to Siberia and let another dangerous criminal loose upon society solely because they are in a hurry to get home to supper and to bed, or because the next day is a holiday; [4] it makes them feel that they are putting their interests wholly in the hands of Providence when they send out utterly un-

---

[1] Cf. the terrible railway catastrophe at Kukuïeff, near Kursk, the victims of which were very numerous, although their exact number never was known.

[2] Cf. the Russian newspapers, during the first ten days of November, 1888, *passim*. One of the causes of the accident at Borki to the Imperial train was declared to be the sleepers, which were made of charred wood taken from a forest that had been on fire.

[3] Cf. *Novoye Vremya*, 7th September, 1889.

[4] This is not a flower of rhetoric, but a statement founded on numerous facts, of which the following is a specimen. In Borissoglebsk, Government of Tamboff, in December, 1886, a peasant woman was tried for the poisoning of her husband, the evidence being such as no British jury would convict upon. The Russian jury unhesitatingly found her guilty, and she was formally condemned to banishment from European Russia for life, and to some years' hard labor in those mines of Siberia which have lately been so vividly described. The next day that same jury, refreshed and bright after a good night's rest, spontaneously declared to the court that they had brought in their verdict, knowing it to be — incorrect, because they were very tired at the time, and that they were now desirous of having it quashed. The court accepted the statement, and decided to lay the case before the Senate. Were the jury punished, one naturally asks, for this flagrant violation of their solemn oath? The answer is to be found in the newspaper which reported the case (*Voronesh Telegraph*, 24th December, and the *Kharkoff Governmental Gazette*, 28th December, 1886 (which sympathetically concludes with this equivocal remark: "The conduct of the jury met with universal approval."

seaworthy vessels like the ill-fated *Vesta*, which a heavy sea will swallow up with the lives of all on board; and it preserves them from that momentary qualm of conscience which made even that Pillar of Society (Cf. Ibsen's play), Consul Bernick, anxious to have Rector Rörlund's absolution in one form or another before despatching the *Indian Girl;* in a word it gives the highest conceivable sanction to acts of commission and omission which nothing short of a revelation in thunders and lightnings could have justified in the old ages of theocracy, and only proven lunacy could excuse in most civilized countries to-day. In Russia these acts are not held to be criminal, and considering the intellectual and moral level of the mass of the people, it would be very hard if they were. The following case in point, deliberately chosen for its comparative tameness, will help to explain what is meant. There are about 2,500 steamers, barges, and various small trading vessels on the river Volga every year, towards the conclusion of the Fair of Nijni Novgorod, the comparative safety of which is as much the result of mere chance in the face of immense odds as is that of little children abandoned to themselves, over whom a special Providence is popularly said to watch. "Wherever you look," says M. Lender, who has written on the subject, "you find that the regulations laid down with a view to insure the safety of the shipping are continually broken through, especially at night. Here the lamps on the mast are not lighted, there a barge is lying in such a position that the first vessel that comes along must inevitably run into her. Another boat takes up its place in the very centre of the channel where all the vessels that go in or out must pass, and although the night is pitch dark the crew have not the slightest fear for their safety or for that of their craft. To their thinking it lies there quite as secure as in a garden pond. The police boat, however, approaches; the usual summons is called out, but on the barge everything is as silent as death. No one answers; no one stirs. The summons is repeated — but still there is no response. A man is sent to board the barge; he seeks for the crew and finds them stowed away in out-of-the-way places, their loud snoring the only sign of life. At last he succeeds in waking them up and a drowsy half-dressed man appears, between whom and the representative of the police the following dialogue ensues: 'Why don't you light the lamps?' 'Because all the candles are used up.' 'Well, then, why do you take up your position right in the middle of the channel that has to be kept clear for steamers? A steamer will surely run into you and smash your boat to pieces!' 'Oh, your honor, we hope not. God is merciful.'[1] A few years ago, in one of the country districts near Petersburg, one of those fires broke out which periodically destroy scores of houses owing to the inflammable material of which they are built, and to the absence of fire-extinguishing apparatus. The members of the district police, whose duty it was to go and assist in putting it out, stayed on in the coffee-house where they were, and when asked by anxious civilians where the fire was, replied, 'How do we know? Somewhere there.'"[2]

This mixture of irreligious faith and presumptuous hope lies at the root of most of the crimes and avoidable accidents of which a large part of contemporary Russian history is composed. It is rank Malebrancheism in the sphere of ethics: a belief that mere mortals are but the occasions of all their so-called acts, which are really performed by God or fate, the sole efficient cause, who can shape and form them as he pleases. "Man may walk, but it is God who leads him," is a Russian proverb which the French Oratorian might have taken for the motto of his *Recherches*. This baneful belief tinges all the qualities of head and heart which it has not actually created, transforming even virtues into positive vices.

If hospitality were, as the Talmud teaches, the pith and marrow of divine worship, then Russians might claim to be a pre-eminently religious people; for there is no other European, and perhaps no inhabitant of any other country in the globe, who will more cheerfully share his last loaf with the hungry stranger than the Russian peasant or merchant. Nor is this custom in Russia, as in civilized countries, confined to the poorer classes, whose generosity proverbially increases with their indigence. Ungrudging, genial hospitality, suggestive of that which characterized the contemporaries of Abraham, is almost as marked a feature of the higher classes as of the lower. Thus the inconveniences resulting from the absence of hotels and inns in the interior of Russia is more than counterbalanced by the spontaneous and cordial hospitality dispensed with consummate tact by landowners, proprietors and directors of factories, marshals

---

[1] Cf. also *Svett*, 12th June, 1889.
[2] Cf. *Graschdanin*, 24th August, 1889.

of the nobility and others, who practically keep open house; and if they do not often entertain angels unaware, never at least expose themselves to the danger of making awkward biographical discoveries, by putting indiscreet questions to their passing guests. Once while staying on a visit at the house of a friend in one of the southern governments — a Russian Squire Hardcastle — a day rarely passed that I did not meet at least one such traveller at table. They were generally men of some education, but of whose pedigree, antecedents, and intentions my host knew far less than history knows about those of the Iron Mask. I never saw more than one at a time, though sometimes as many as three are entertained simultaneously. They seldom stayed longer than two days, and generally only a day and night; were shown into a comfortable bedroom and invited to take their meals with the host and hostess, whom they usually endeavored to entertain with the political news of the day.

Hospitality has been aptly termed the virtue of benevolent barbarism. There are aspects of it, however, which might well be named vices, if only they who practise them were tutored enough to distinguish the boundary line where virtue ends and vice begins. And these are precisely the forms of it which one most frequently meets with in Russia, where numbers of families, lately prosperous or wealthy, are yearly reduced to beggary by hospitality as ruinous and as meaningless as that of Timon of Athens. I am personally acquainted with several noble families of St. Petersburg and Moscow, who spend on the dinners and *soirées* which they give during the season, a sum of money equivalent to their yearly income — which, it should be remarked, is not large according to British ideas. A friend of mine, a general, was wont to languish with his family for weeks on Lenten fare, in order to be in a position to give a *recherché* dinner to his friends twice or thrice a year. The wedding dinners of the merchants — often attended by utter strangers; the funeral banquets given to commemorate the death of a husband, wife, or parent; the feasting during the Carnival and in Easter week, make almost as strong demands on the purse of the host as on the health of the guests. "Help your guest till he cannot lift his food over his lip" is the popular maxim bearing upon the exercise of hospitality, which is too literally observed by the middle classes.

"Hinc subitæ mortes atque intestata senectus."

Fortunes are as recklessly squandered in this way by the Russians of to-day as they were by the Romans of the Empire. What has remained, for instance, of the princely fortunes of Prince V . . . sky, of Prince D., who has to entertain at times members of the imperial family, of the late Prince S. D., but scraps and leavings which taken all together would not have sufficed to keep Adpicius, the Roman, from committing suicide. It is no secret that a very large proportion of the noble families of the two capitals, whose brilliant *soirées* and at-homes are the talk of the press and the wonder of foreign embassadors, are living greatly beyond their income, some of them actually lacking the means of paying their men and maidservants their paltry monthly wages. Numbers of generals are well-known bankrupts, the third or half of whose salaries is monthly deducted by the Treasury and handed over to their creditors.[1] It would seem as if what Carlyle calls "the great bottomless pit of bankruptcy" were ominously yawning under this entire system of acted unveracity. But the thought, if it occurs to his mind, has no terrors for the Russian fatalist, who, like the reckless revellers of plague-stricken Florence described by Boccaccio, continues gayly to amuse himself on the brink of ruin. Every Russian, whatever his social position, his means, or his needs, beginning with the Tsar and ending with the scullion, deems it a sort of sacred duty to entertain his friends and relations on the festival of his patron saint, many spending their last borrowed coin upon these ruinous merrymakings, and, like Dick Swiveller, turning whole streets into no-thoroughfares bristling with impatient creditors.

Another of the visible effects of fatalism, to which I can scarcely do more than allude, and which created unfeigned surprise in the French, who lately had an opportunity of studying it in certain productions of Russian literature, is repentance, or rather what the Russians mistake for it, confession of guilt. "Samovar et répentir," exclaimed the French critics who sat in judgment on Ostroffsky's drama, *The Thunderstorm*, "are the two salient symbols of Russian civilization." When a Russian unburdens his breast of

---

[1] It is the privilege of Russian officers to enjoy immunity from the bankruptcy laws. When one of these cannot meet his liabilities his superfluous property is sold and part of his pay handed over to his creditors: one-third if he is married; one-half if single.

a crime, even though eager and anxious to repeat it, he feels that he has made what the Apostle Paul terms "confession unto salvation," and is authorized to begin a new score forthwith. Indeed the popular proverb, which is at bottom merely the embodiment of the popular practice, says as much: "He who confesses has repented, and he who has repented has wiped out his sin." Nothing is more striking or characteristic in the annals of Russian criminal justice than the almost mathematical certainty with which one can predict that a person arrested on suspicion, even though there be no legal proofs of guilt, and no likelihood of their ever being obtained, will take the *Juge d'Instruction* into his confidence, and glibly relate every detail of his share in the transaction. Out of sixty-five criminal cases taken at random, I find that in forty-eight the prisoners were convicted on their own confession, and in most of the remainder there was no need for self-accusation, as the criminals were caught red-handed, *in flagrante delicto*. Were it not for this, only a fraction of the criminal population now arrested and brought to trial every year would be molested by the police, who are deservedly held to be the most inefficient detectors of crime in Europe.

CHAPTER III.

SLOTH.

THERE are many ingenious explanations of the stoical contempt of death which is so marked a characteristic of the vast majority of Russians, but the most plausible of them all would appear to be that which attributes it to their fatalistic turn of mind, suggested as it is by careful observation, and confirmed by the proverbs and sayings of the people. Still it cannot be gainsaid that the galling conditions and grim surroundings of actual life are, and have been for ages, amply sufficient to account for even more desperate feelings than contempt of death; and foreigners in Russia often unconsciously repeat the saying of the Sybarite, who when he had come to Sparta and seen what a miserable life the people were forced to lead there, ceased to wonder at their valor, exclaiming, "I myself would rather rush upon a swordpoint than lead such a wretched existence." A whole string of proverbs,[1] which are in every one's mouth, go to show that the Russian's desire to die is at least as strong as the natural instinct which makes us all cling to life, and yet he lingers listlessly on, unconsciously realizing Ovid's ideal of fortitude:—

> "Rebus in adversis facile est contemnere vitam,
> Fortiter ille facit qui miser esse potest;"

and putting himself wholly in the hands of Fate, in which he is as firm a believer as Lermontoff's Voolitch who, having proved his faith in predestination by pulling the trigger of a loaded pistol levelled at his head and won the wager when it hung fire, was brutally murdered that same night by a drunken Cossack.

---

[1] For instance: "If you mourn, God will lengthen your life;" "To live is more terrible than to die;" "To live is to groan; by night in dreams, by day from suffering." This last saying recalls Job's plaintive cry: "When I say, My bed shall comfort me, my couch shall ease my complaint; then thou scarest me with dreams and terrifiest me through visions." — Job vii. 13, 14.

It is in perfect keeping with such views about life that time, the stuff that life is made of, should be greatly undervalued; and it is no exaggeration to say that it could not be held cheaper or be more wantonly wasted than by the Russians who talk and act — or rather talk and forbear to act — as if in their eyes a thousand years were as one day. The very language they speak bears witness to their incurable procrastination, making an hour signify the twinkling of an eye.[1] The ordinary term for holiday, which Teutonic nations call a "Day of Solemnity," "Day of Holiness," or "God's Day," means literally in Russian "a day of idleness,"[2] while the word week signifies in Russian that "time when no work is done."[3] And the customs and habits of the people are in strict harmony with these curious conceptions. No one is ever in a hurry in the land where *festina lente* is looked upon as the grand rule of life, even though he have the most potent incentives to despatch. A striking instance of this constitutional inability to increase the traditional creeping-pace with which everything moves in Russia, is to be found in the building of the church in commemoration of the late Emperor on the spot where he was foully murdered. It was commenced in 1881 in what seemed hot haste at the time. Eight years have dragged their slow length along since then, and yet, at the beginning of the present year,[4] the temple in so far resembled that of Jerusalem, that there was not one stone visibly standing upon another; at which state of things the present Emperor was so indignant, that he had some broad hints *à la* Dr. Francia, conveyed to certain of the parties responsible, who are now evincing a disposition to bestir themselves. Every business in life is conducted on the same principle set forth in the proverb, "The slower you drive the further you'll go." I have known foreign merchants to arrive in Russia on a Saturday evening too late to transact the very urgent business for which they had come, and having waited feverishly till Monday, discovered that it was a church holiday on which no man can work, no firm do business; and having made praiseworthy efforts to control their feelings and possess their souls in patience till Tuesday, found that it was the Emperor's birthday or name's-day, and equally sacred

---

[1] *Say tschass*, lit. = "this hour," which is often made to stretch over vast periods of time, is the common Russian word for "in a moment," "immediately."
[2] *Prazdnik.*   [3] *Niedielya.*   [4] Written in 1889.

to indolence. In a provincial city it is enough for an average funeral procession to pass along the streets for cars and cabs to pull up, tramcars to come to a standstill, the passengers to get out and gape, and traffic generally to be temporarily suspended. In all other departments of public or private activity it is the same. Judicial procedure is proverbially slow in most countries; and it would be no easy matter to beat the records of the English Court of Chancery in that respect, with its lawsuits like that of Jarndyce *v.* Jarndyce continuing from generation to generation. But even here Russia bears off the palm. The District Court of Kherson (near Odessa), for instance, has a case still before it which is older than the nineteenth century. The object of the litigation is the right of inheritance to the property of the Shidansky family, the proprietors of the great salt works. The suit was begun towards the end of the eighteenth century, and the first judgment upon its merits was delivered in 1802. Since then it has been three several times before the Governing Senate — the Supreme Court of Appeal in Russia. It is now being carried on by the grandchildren of the first plaintiffs, and lately came before the District Court of Kherson, which has again adjourned it.[1]

The post and the telegraph exist in Russia as in England or Germany, but their real significance has not yet been fully grasped by the people, who see no cause for complaint in the circumstance that a telegram reaches its destination no quicker than a letter should, and a letter frequently never reaches it at all. A friend of mine fell ill some months ago, and sent a telegram to his wife who was living with their children in the country ten miles from town. Although her country-house was only ten minutes' walk from the railway-station that telegram took eighteen hours and a-half to reach her, during which time her husband lay dangerously ill in his town-house, without attendants. And this is by no means an extreme or rare case. If you enter the chief telegraph-office of the most business-like city in Russia — Odessa — with a despatch, on the speedy transmission of which thousands of pounds, or interests still more weighty, depend, you may find the room full of people, especially if it is near two o'clock P.M., and you take your stand behind the last. Suddenly the clerk who receives the telegrams stands up, surveys the public with a quiet smile, and leisurely

---

[1] Cf. *Novoye Vremya*, 7th August, 1889.

saunters out. You wait impatiently ten or fifteen minutes, and then offer your telegram to his colleague, who is sitting at his desk, but he snappishly informs you that he cannot receive it. Where, you ask, is the man who can take it? He is gone to dinner, he tells you, and you must wait till he comes back. "'There is plenty of time,' he adds, with the air of a man who could say, if he would : "Sun, stand thou still upon Gibeon, and thou, Moon, in the valley of Ajalon." "And the public does wait," concludes the journal from which this scene is taken, "and waits half an hour, an hour, in a word until that clerk returns to his desk." [1]

On the Volga, during the fair of Nischny Novgorod, thousands of passengers are conveyed to and from the fair, whose time must be then, if ever, extremely precious, as the loss of a single hour may, and frequently does, entail the loss of large sums of money. And yet the steam navigation companies are as wasteful of time, even then, as if, like the inhabitants of Luggnagg, it was the doubtful privilege of their passengers to live for ever. The following scene which took place in the office of the best of these companies was described in a semi-official organ by an eye-witness : "'Will the boat soon be here?' asks one of the intending passengers. 'In due time,' calmly answers the clerk, who continues to sell tickets. The 'due time' arrives, but not the steamer. 'Will it soon be here?' asks voices on all sides. 'This minute; take my word for it.' But 'this minute' seems endless. An hour passes. Again questions are asked, 'Will it soon be in?' 'Immediately,' is the reply, but even this 'immediately' is followed by no satisfactory results. Two, three, four hours pass, but the steamboat is not yet come, and still the agent repeats the magic word 'immediately.' Meanwhile the steamer of another company comes in, and the passengers, weary of waiting, want their money back in order to go by the newly-arrived boat. 'That is impossible,' remarks the agent, 'but don't be uneasy; our steamer will be here immediately.' And the money is not returned. Thus, will they, nill they, they are forced to wait twelve hours before the steamboat of the 'Mercury Navigation Company' makes its appearance ; from five o'clock A.M., till evening, amid highly disagreeable surroundings on the river bank, exposed to the fierce heat of the sun, as the small rickety office could not accomodate all who were wait-

---

[1] *Odessa News*, 4th September, 1888.

ing for the boat!"[1] A short telegram might have saved the passengers this ruinous loss of time, but neither the captain of the vessel nor the company's agents, who knew that the boat would be late, thought of sending it.

In this country, where punctuality and thrift of time have become second nature, such things would not be tolerated a day. In Russia they excite neither wonder nor indignation, except among foreign residents, who must suffer in silence. No matter how serious or urgent his business, a Russian has always the leisure to turn aside from the straight road and "tread the primrose path of dalliance," as heedless of the flight of time as if his life consisted of Plato's years, each equal to 25,000 ordinary ones. Yet he does this in such a simple, natural, Undine-like way that one has not the heart to rebuke him.

"On the 25th July last, the busiest time on the Volga, the Captain of the steamer *Samolet* was walking on deck when his cap was blown off. He ran after it as quickly as he could, but it was blown into the water. Without a shade of hesitation he gave the command to stop the engines. As they could not be stopped instantaneously, when the order was executed the cap was far away. A second order was given, the steamer turned, and steered straight for the captain's head-gear, but before the engines could be stopped it was outstripped and left behind. Other commands were issued, the direction changed and the chase recommenced, but in spite of the rapidity of the vessel's movements and the dexterity of the crew, the cap was not fished up. Whenever the vessel drew near the floating head-dress and it seemed that in another moment it would be caught up by the boat-hook and restored to its owner, suddenly, as if driven of set purpose by a wilful wind it swept on further and further away. The steamer would then dash wildly after it, but the cap would again escape, to the bitter disappointment of its owner. The passengers were at first amused at the spectacle of a steamer chasing a cap, but when thirty minutes had been spent to no purpose, they requested that the vessel should resume her trip. But while the captain was standing irresolute what to do, Lebedeff, a seaman, jumped in with his clothes on and swam in the direction of the cap. He soon came up with it, caught it between his teeth and began to return to the vessel. He had to swim against the current, however, and it soon became evident that he had not strength enough to reach the vessel. He began to lose ground visibly and was being carried by the current away from the boat, when the captain threw out a life buoy which he failed to catch hold of. On this he shouted for help at the top of his voice, and a boat was lowered. After some trouble he was rescued and brought back to the steamer, but the captain's cap was never recovered."[2]

That business men in Russia, especially foreign residents, require an unusual stock of patience to bear up under the

---

[1] *Graschdanin*, 9th September, 1889. [2] *Graschdanin*, 6th September, 1889.

occasional disastrous results of this criminal waste of time, needs no pointing out here. Fancy a London city man compelled to fulfil to the letter the following formality before he could legally receive a paltry consignment of one *cwt.* of dry Swedish bread, these formalities not containing anything exceptional for his particular case, but constituting the normal rule for all.

"1. He must present the bill of lading in the customers' storehouse. 2. He must deliver it to an interpreter. 3. He must obtain a copy of the declaration. 4. He must purchase and affix a revenue stamp of the value of 80 copecks. 5. He must obtain the authorization of the director to have his merchandise examined (the examination taking place but twice daily, at 10 A.M., and at 1 P.M.), whereby he must wait till the Director arrives. 6. When the authorization has been received, he must get it entered in the books of the storehouse. 7. He must present the authorization to the storehouse board and await the arrival of the examiners. 8. He goes along with the examiners to the storehouse. 9. He has the goods examined. 10. He signs a declaration that he is satisfied with the examination. 11. The examiners signed it. 12. All return to the storehouse office. 13. The duty on the merchandise is calculated. 14. All documents relating to the matter are presented to the controller. 15. The duty is paid.[1] 16. A receipt for the duty is written out. 17. The receipt has to be presented to the head book-keeper. 18. A revenue stamp of 80 copecks has to be purchased and affixed. 19. A "talon" has to be obtained. 20. It must be handed to the customs' guard. 21. The bill of expenses of the Customs' Workingmen's Association is made out and handed to the consignee. 22. He receives a customs' ticket authorizing him to leave the Custom House precincts. 23. He must see that his cases are properly repacked; and 24. He has to hand in his ticket to the guard."[2]

The *Novoye Vremya*, from which I have translated this list of formalities without changing a word, tells us that one gentleman accomplished all this in four hours — a comparatively short time — for formalities that some people spend three days in wading through.

It would be difficult to conceive of anything so truly characteristic of Russian notions of the value of time as the keen competition that goes on in many parts of the empire between peasant carriers with their oxen or horses, and railway companies with their steam engines. Some time ago one company formally besought the Government to protect

---

[1] This is no mere formality of the *citius dicto* kind: one has often to wait twenty minutes or half an hour before the cashier finds it convenient to accept one's money.

[2] *Novoye Vremya*, 24th August, 1888. This journal has made one important omission in drawing up its list. One must set out by obtaining from the police a certificate that he who presents himself is really the person he claims to be.

their threatened interests by forbidding private enterprise to compete, as otherwise "they would lose the goods traffic" and become bankrupts.[1] In the year 1889 a firm of printers of the city of Yekaterinoslav ordered a large quantity of paper of the value of 1,700 roubles, which they had purchased in Kharkoff, to be conveyed to them in Yekaterinoslav (280 Russian versts) on floats drawn by horses, this being a much less expensive and generally more satisfactory way than getting it sent by rail.[2] In the Baltic Provinces the same phenomenon is frequent, and it is said to be yearly growing more so.[3] Between Riga and Valk, for instance, which are joined by rail, much of the carrying trade is done by private individuals, who convey the merchandise on floats and drays drawn by horses.[4] And so lively has this competition become in the South of Russia that some railway companies are, if we can believe the local press, actually being worsted in the struggle.[5]

And the weightiest interests, the most sacred considerations, go for nothing in comparison with the inherent right of the Russian to indulge in this demoralizing sloth. As soon would the inexorable order of Carthusian monks give a morsel of meat to its most valuable member — though the effect were to restore his ebbing life — as a Russian department would hasten by a single day the delivery of a document to hinder the ruin or death of scores of human beings. About two years ago I read a most harrowing account in the Russian papers of the fate of a family bitten by a mad wolf. M. Pasteur, on being informed of it, asked that they be sent to Paris at once, and on learning that they were poverty-stricken peasants, he generously undertook to pay their expenses himself. The offer was thankfully accepted, and he was informed that as soon as they received their passports they would start. In ten days or a fortnight afterwards he was told that they had been seized with the usual paroxysms and died. The authorities, it should be stated, did not refuse to deliver passports to these unfortunate sufferers, nor purposely throw difficulties in their way, they only objected to draw them up with extra dispatch, and forego any of the usual formalities. Ultimately, indeed, they forwarded passports for them all, but it was, I believe, some days after their

---

[1] The Basuntchak Railway.   [2] *Novoye Vremya*, Sept. 13th, 1889.
[3] *Ibid.*   [4] *Ibid.*
[5] *Odessa Messenger*, Dec. 1, 1888.

funeral.[1] And thus day after day, year after year, the same fatal lesson of waste of time and neglect of opportunity is inculcated upon the people, whose life might appropriately be summed up in their own proverbial phrases as "a sitting by the seashore waiting for the weather," or more happily still in the slightly modified line of Horace —

"Russicus expectat dum defluat amnis."

It is curious to watch the working of this subtle spirit of intellectual and moral sluggishness upon foreigners, at first slow and imperceptible like the symptoms of physical drowsiness, and ever more rapid and irresistible as the end approaches. A foreigner in Russia may, if he strive strenuously, keep much of his moral code intact; he may make a stand for his religious creed, if he have one, but his enterprise will insensibly slumber, his energy evaporate, and he will thereafter go about his business like one working against time, who is in no hurry to be done. And with all this there is no disagreeable struggle, no feeling of dissatisfaction, rather a sensation of pleasure. It is difficult, not to say impossible, to make it clear to those who have not lived long in the country in what this secret charm of Russian life consists, for however prejudiced one may be against the government or the officials, it cannot be denied that some mysterious spell fascinates all foreigners who have spent some years in the country, causing many who have shaken its dust off their feet, apparently for all time, to return and settle there for life. I have known enterprising young Englishmen, brisk Americans, plodding Germans, and mercurial Frenchmen, who came to Russia brimful of life and exuberant energies, resolved to do great things, to plough deep historical furrows each in his own respective field. And when a few years had passed away, I noticed with surprise what a vast change had come over most of them; their vivacity and buoyancy had gone out from them; their vast plans had dwindled down to the mean dimensions of journeymen's tasks; lethargic torpor clouded their faculties and paralyzed their will, leaving them for most practical purposes as soulless as the monster created by Frankenstein.

---

[1] I ought to say that I am narrating this story without sources or notes before me. I may have made some erroneous statements in telling it, but if so, they only affect matters of detail. I know that the newspapers at the time stated plainly that the lives of these poor peasants had been uselessly sacrificed to pedantic fidelity to the formalities of the passport system — and more than this I do not wish to convey.

Pity, and not blame or contempt, is the feeling evoked by a knowledge of the true causes of that helpless shiftlessness, bordering on hebetude, which so terribly handicaps Russians in their competition with foreigners; for they are scarcely more responsible for their helplessness than is a butterfly for the color of its wings. Well-bred boys and girls in this country and the United States are expected to do for themselves most of the things which in Russia the Government alone is qualified to perform for men and women. Indeed, the Government may be truly described as the one efficient cause of everything done or omitted, the people playing the rôle of Malebranche's "occasional causes," and remaining quite passive. Thus, to begin at the beginning, parents are not allowed to exercise their judgment or discharge their duty in the matter of their children's education. If, for example, they desire to give them a classical education, it is not enough that they have the means to pay for it, that their children possess the faculties to assimilate it, and that the schools have numerous vacancies. Besides all this, a petition must be drawn up containing a concise but complete biography of the parents, children, every member of the family, and every other person living with the family.[1] Moreover, the father must state whether he himself has enjoyed the liberal education which he craves for his son; and if not, there is an end of the matter.[2] Lastly, he must set forth in detail his profession, his yearly income, the number of rooms in his flat, the number of servants he keeps, and the profession for which he destines his son.[3] Unless the father is a man of means of the upper class of society, and of education, his children are deemed unworthy of being initiated into the mysteries of Greek and Latin, the study of which is looked upon as a sort of educational sacrament. But even if the ambitious father satisfies the Governmental demands under all these heads, he has still no better guarantee of success than before. Four hundred parents were in that condition a few weeks ago: their children were officially recognized as qualified, they were examined and passed successfully, and were then told that they could not be received, and they must now dispense with intermediate education, as this year at least no other establishments can receive them.[4]

---

[1] Cf. Circular of the Curator of the Odessa University, explaining the Ministerial Circular of the 30th of June, 1887, No. 9255. [2] *Ibid.*
[3] *Ibid.*   [4] *Novoye Vremya*, 30th August, 1889.

The difficulties in the way of choosing a profession for one's son are equally numerous and to the full as serious; for admission to the technical schools and to the universities is now become as difficult for a Russian without influential friends as admission to Mecca for an unregenerate Christian. The circumstance that the parents are forbidden to give their children the religious education which they hold to be the best seems almost reasonable and proper when viewed in the light of so many other galling and fatuous restrictions which hamper one to the bitter end. If you are an historian, the law directs your attention to various periods of history which you are invited to pass over in silence, to others which you must touch upon with painful circumspection, plentifully diluting the results of your studies with loyal fiction when setting them before the public even in one of those Cyclopean volumes which seem written for men with the lives of the Patriarchs before them. I have the authority of the late Censor General, Privy Councillor Grigorieff, for asserting that it is forbidden to publish in the newspapers or in popular books a list of Russian Emperors, *with the years of their reign*, from Peter the Great to Alexander II., because some of them having reigned a very short time the natural inference would be that they were the victims of violence.[1]

If a playwright, you have equal, perhaps greater difficulties to contend with. For here too the police step in, placing impediments in your "fancy's course," which are not "motives of mere fancy," and saying "Hitherto shalt thou come, but no further." Last season, for the first time in history, a special permission was accorded to a playwright, M. Kryloff, to have a drama represented in which the Regent Sophia[2] plays a part, the unvarying rule being that

---

[1] The editors of the chief historical reviews, MM. Semeffsky [of the *Russian Post*] and Shubinsky [*Historical Messenger*] have lately been made to feel, more frequently and more keenly, perhaps, than even editors of political journals, the heavy hand, or rather the hob-nailed boot, of a paternal government. It is a far more heroic work to edit even an historical review in Russia than foreigners imagine. Most Englishmen with a normal allowance of sensibility and *amour propre*, and no more than average endurance, physical and moral, would cheerfully take to breaking stones by the roadside or to earning their bread as dockyard laborers rather than edit a Russian journal or review — even historical — for long. Some of the most erudite and conscientious historians of modern Russia have been wantonly insulted to their faces by foolish officials, and vilified in terms of abuse which it would be impossible, even in this outspoken age of realism, to drag from the "decent obscurity of a foreign tongue."

[2] Sophia was the sister of Peter the Great, and regent during his minor-

no member of the reigning house, however long ago he or she may have been consigned to oblivion, can be introduced into a dramatic piece in Russia. Every play, tragedy, comedy, or farce, must be carefully read in manuscript by special censors, who, if they have nothing to object to themselves, pass it on to whatever other departments seem directly interested — as the ecclesiastical, for example — and even these repeated authorizations by no means guarantee that it will ultimately reach the stage. Last season a play that had passed unscathed through all these prolonged ordeals, and was at last represented — the Emperor being present on the first night — was ordered to be withdrawn the next day and never to be given again.[1]

A genuine poet's career is in truth a dim and perilous way, leading at times to disgrace, imprisonment, Siberia, as Puschkin,[2] Lermontoff,[3] Shevtschenko,[4] and others discovered to their cost; and the patriotic writers who have poured out the vials of their wrath on the unappreciative generation that made Burns an exciseman would have been astounded to learn under what unfavorable conditions Russian poetry has to thrive and flourish. A poet who is arrested for a few perfectly harmless lines, packed off to the borders of Asiatic Russia, condemned to serve there ten years as a common soldier,[5] strictly forbidden to write a line of poetry, and reduced to composing stray verses, which, with the fear of the knout before his eyes, he furtively writes in a little copy-book that he always carries in his boot-leg for fear of detection[6] — such a man might well be looked at and pointed out, like Dante, as a man who had been down *there*, had he not such a formidable number of colleagues. And what could indicate more clearly, more terribly, the depth to which the iron had entered into his soul than the fact that when this gifted and kindly bard heard the sen-

---

ity. In 1689 he deprived her of all share in the government, and imprisoned her in a monastery where she soon died.

[1] It was an Opera called the *Merchant Kalaschnikoff*, the music being by Rubinstein.

[2] The Government resolved to banish Puschkin to the Solovki Isles on the White Sea, and his friend Karamzin had extreme difficulty to get him banished to less distant or less bleak regions. He was at one time banished to Bessarabia, Odessa, Yekaterinoslav, Pskoff.

[3] Cf. Polevoi, *Hist. of Russian Literature*, 604, where the most important part of Lermontoff's life is represented by numerous full stops — the censure not allowing anything more explicit.

[4] Cf. *Sketches of the History of the Literature of Ukraine*, Petroff, 1884 (in Russian), pp. 279-368. [5] *Ibid.*, p. 324. [6] *Ibid.*, p. 323.

tence pronounced he humbly declared himself *worthy of that punishment*, and paid a tribute to the *even-handed justice* of the Tsar?[1]

A literary man's life in Russia is often incomparably worse than was that of an English bookseller's hack in the days of Samuel Johnson. Like Noah's contemporaries overtaken by the Deluge, he has to contend against the waters of tribulation from above and below; he must steer between the Scylla of poverty and the Charybdis of imprisonment and persecution, and it is no easy matter to keep clear of the one without falling into the other. The fate and physiognomy of everything he writes is absolutely dependent upon men who are no better fitted to sit in judgment upon works of literature and art than is a man born blind to lecture upon perspective. The humiliations, the disappointments,[2] the loss of enterprise and health, the long mental agony that have to be endured before a few genuine poems or a volume of honest critical or historical essays can be set before the public, compel us to look upon such books with veneration and

> "Ca' them lives o' men."

The history of Russian literature is a martyrology.

But it is not necessary to be a literary man, a poet, or an historian, to come in unpleasant contact with the watchful meddling authorities who insist on supplying you with cut-and-dried thoughts, controlling your words and regulating your actions from the cradle to the grave. Not only can you not change your church to suit your altered religious belief, but you are actually compelled, whether you are a Dissenter or an Atheist at heart, to confess your sins and receive a sacrament once a year, and to have the fact registered on the books of the Church.[3] If you prefer philanthropy to theology and wish to found a school, endow an orphanage, erect a widow's asylum, or present a library to the public, you must first ask the permission of the Government, which is often refused and never obtained until you have surmounted as many obstacles as the Baron of Trier-

---

[1] Cf. *Sketches of the History of the Literature of Ukraine*, Petroff, 1884 (in Russian), p. 320.

[2] Take this as a sample: "The difficulties (connected with the Censure) which M. Matchtet had to surmount in printing his tale (*The Prodigal Son*) which compelled him to recast the larger half of the first part, are intensified now that he is about to print the second half." — *Odessa News*, July 29, 1887.

[3] Russ. Crim. Code, § 208.

main in seeking for Gyneth, and the springs of action are sometimes dried up before you are in sight of the goal. If you retire to the obscurity of private life with the hope of indulging in the pleasures of reading, the Government is waiting for you there, and will not allow you to peruse a single printed line in Russian or in a foreign tongue until some official, probably infinitely inferior to yourself in education, judgment, and morality, has decided whether it is fit and proper that you should read it.[1] If you are tempted to pass your leisure hours in teaching poor children to read and write, who would otherwise never have learned, you have broken a law which is no dead letter, and are liable to be punished severely. If you invite some friends to your house to spend a few hours every week in reading and discussing literary works — if you formed a Russian Browning Society, for instance — you have broken the law and are liable to prosecution and punishment; nay, if you carry out the command of the Founder of Christianity and call together your own servants to read to them the Gospel, you will be treated as a malefactor or a felon.[2] If you wish to visit the theatre and see one of the best plays of the season, you cannot dispense with the services of an intermediary: you must first sit down and indite a petition to the Theatre Board, setting forth your desire, stating the day you would like to go, the seat you would like to engage and enclosing a stamp for a reply,[3] after which you again relapse into your normal state of expectancy. You may in time receive a reply briefly informing you that there are no places vacant, and leaving you to find, when it is too late, that there are many; or you may not be vouchsafed any answer whatever until you personally apply for one. When you do get inside the theatre, if it is in the provinces, the authorities, who are unceasing in their solicitude for you and yours, lay down rules for your conduct which any one but a Russian would resent as insulting. In Pereyasslav, on the 1st August, 1889, a play was given by the Little Russian Dramatic Company,

---

[1] Cf. Censure Laws, §§ 187, 182, and *passim*.

[2] Even University professors, like the late O. Miller, have been forbidden to read privately in their houses with their students, no matter how harmless or praiseworthy the object in view might be. For the crime of reading the Gospel to their servants, Colonel Paschkoff and Count Korff are exiled, just as if they had offended like Prince Krapotkin or Stepniak.

[3] It should be stated that all the theatres are not provided with this Bureau, and tickets can be had in the others in the same way as in France or England.

of which M. Sokoloff is the Director. The theatre bills printed and published on the occasion contain the following paternal admonition: "In virtue of articles 152 and 153 the District Police Superintendent requests the public not to be noisy; to refrain from talking in a loud tone of voice, and not to interrupt or hinder the conclusion of the piece. Disputes, wrangling, and free fights should be avoided."[1] You sometimes cannot obtain even medicine for your children without petitioning the Government, and even then your request may be coldly refused. I know a gentleman who even exerted himself for weeks to obtain permission to order some bottles of Bromure de Potassium de Henri Mure, a medicine strongly recommended to his child by one of the first physicians of Paris — and all to no purpose. If it would have saved the child's life she would have had to die or else leave the country, and this not because the medicine is alleged to be hurtful or even useless, but because the Medical Council think it superfluous. You cannot enter or leave a city or town in the Empire without reporting yourself to the police like a ticket-of-leave man;[2] you are forbidden to extend the hospitality of your roof to your friend or neighbor for a single night without first informing the police of your intentions and sending them your guest's passport;[3] whether you are a Russian or a foreigner you can no more spend a night in an hotel or change your lodgings even for twenty-four hours without communicating with the police and sending them your passport, than you can bespeak rooms in the Winter Palace.[4] Nay, whether you are a Russian subject or a foreigner you cannot possibly subsist a week without a passport, which is such an essential part of your being that Russian lawyers have not inappropriately defined a man as an animal composed of three parts — a body, a soul, and a passport. This passport you must have renewed once a year, unless you are a noble or an ' honorary citizen, and the process is as tedious and painful as moulting is to birds. A voluminous correspondence, and a pile of documents with copies, petitions, and fifteen supplements, was the result of the attempt of a man named Dudinsky in the Government of Smolensk, to renew his

---

[1] *Graschdanin*, 2nd September, 1889.
[2] Cf., for instance, Art. 61 of the Penal Code for Magistrates.
[3] *Ibid.* Art. 59. Cf. also Penal Code, § 958.
[4] *Ibid.* The only exception in practice is in favor of houses of ill-fame.

passport two years ago. And yet his papers were in order, his conduct irreproachable, and his right to have his passport renewed was not even called in question.[1] These obstacles and irritations make one's soul weary of life; and explain why it is that in the course of one year in St. Petersburg alone 14,799 persons were arrested and imprisoned for not having complied with the passport laws. Many of these wretched creatures may be now on their way to Siberia.[2]

Whatever you do yourself, whatever others do to you, the accidents you meet with, and "visitation of God," are all valid motives for the interference of the police, who take cognizance of everything, and direct you how to demean yourself under the rapidly changing conditions of life. They come into your home and look after the morality of your children, keeping a watchful eye the while on your own occupations and those of your friends; they dog your steps in the streets, open your letters, cross-examine your hall porter who is *ex officio* one of the eyes of autocracy; and their constant meddling in your private life is almost as maddening as the noise of the Chinese drums to the wretch condemned to die of want of sleep. Last year the Police Prefect of Petropavloffsk actually forbade all the inhabitants of his district to leave their houses after ten o'clock P.M., not on political grounds, real or alleged, but simply in the interests of what he considered propriety.[3] Some few years ago three or four young ladies were upset in a boat when crossing the Neva. The current being pretty strong there,[4] there was some difficulty in rescuing them, and when they were taken out of the water, it took nearly ten minutes to row them ashore. The weather was bitterly cold, and the ladies were shivering when they landed. Here, however, instead of being allowed to drive home as quickly as they could and change their clothes, they were compelled to walk to the station, where a detailed account of the accident (called *protocoll*) was drawn up and carefully read over to them, and it was only when they had signed this that they were at liberty to go. One of them was ill for six weeks afterwards.[5]

---

[1] Cf. *St. Petersburg Gazette*, 29th August, 1887.
[2] *New Review*, July, 1888.
[3] Opposite the Gagarin Quay at the Vyborg side.
[4] The press mentioned it at the time, but I am narrating from memory. I spoke to one of the young ladies at the time.
[5] *Novoye Vremya*, 28th August, 1889.

It almost requires the credulity of an Orgon — rare in England — to believe that the law of the Russian Empire solemnly lays down the rules of spelling to be followed in writing or in giving citations from the Little Russian language, and very strictly enforces the decree! Yet it is perfectly true, though it is one of those truths which are stranger than fiction, as men like P. Kulisch, Professor Antonovitch, Krapovnitsky, the playwright, and many other contemporary *littérateurs* have learned to their cost. I possess, however, the text of the law in question, the second paragraph of which is as follows: "Are forbidden in the precincts of the Empire original works and translations in Little Russian, except (*a*) historical documents, (*b*) literary productions, on condition that they keep to the orthography of the originals, and *that there be no deviations from the commonly accepted Russian system of* SPELLING, and that the authorization be accorded only after the manuscript has been examined." Signed, Grigorieff, Director of the Central Board of Censure. 18/30 May, 1876. Now it is proposed to forbid in the length and breadth of the Russian Empire the printing of works in the Polish tongue, unless they are written with Russian, instead of Latin, letters; and according to the laws now rigidly enforced, no tradesman can print an advertisement or handbill without receiving the authorization of the police.

It is not to be wondered at, under the circumstances, that the Government has become in the eyes of the people a fetish, to be conciliated, feared, obeyed — the embodiment of omniscience and omnipotence, whose word is law to nature as well as to man. Hence they come to the authorities in all the difficulties of life, asking for spiritual bread, and invariably receiving a stone. If an earthquake is feared, a war expected, an inundation apprehended, they hasten to the nearest representative of power for instructions how to receive the impending calamity. Four years ago, for instance, when the Russian press predicted a destructive storm in certain parts of the country, the like of which for violence had never yet been experienced, the police stations were crowded with men and women anxious to learn the why and the wherefore. Here is a specimen of what daily took place at that time, which I literally translate from a local organ of the press. "May I make so free as to ask your honor," says a peasant who has come afar *ad hoc*, "when this here storm is to burst?" "What storm are you talking about? Get away from here and don't bother." "Three days ago, your honor, our Nick Safronitch came home from town and told us that the papers printed all about this same storm. I don't believe it myself, but my wife says, 'Go,' she yells, 'and ask the authorities — the police, that is, for they know everything, because they know the high authorities and the regulation of things' — and the neighbors all over the place are talking about it too." "Get away with your storm; go to your wife and neighbors, and say that the authorities have not sent us any orders yet concerning the storm. We know nothing about it." "All right, your honor. I'll tell my wife and neighbors that there is no ukase about the storm in Odessa; that it must be untrue."[1] So strong is this feeling of abject helplessness on the part of the people, so incapable are they of walking even to destruction without being led thither by the hand, that thieves and pickpockets cannot always pursue their calling to their satisfaction without appealing for the "moral" support and guidance of the police. This seems a paradox; but the annals of criminal justice for the last twenty-five years yield a harvest of cases that go far to establish in such matters the connivance and active complicity of the police and other authorities as the rule rather than the exception. As for the common people, they do not hesitate to ask the authorities in whom they live, move, and have their being, for assistance in the commission of crime. It is only a few years ago since some peasants of the village of Stryscheff, district of Rybinks, lacking the funds necessary to purchase liquor and drown their cares, decided that the best way to raise the money would be to rob the country-house of a certain Madame Syroyeschin, which was not inhabited at the time. They went to work systematically, broke open the door, dragged out the furniture, mirrors, etc., into the adjoining wood, and proceeded to divide the spoils. But they could not satisfactorily solve the problem. They disputed, quarrelled, shouted, fought; but to no purpose. At last they cooled down, and agreed to decide the matter calmly, reasonably, equitably; and went off in a body to the nearest representative of law and government, the *starosta*, in whom they showed their confidence by requesting him to divide the booty among them, "according to the dictates of his conscience."[2] The semi-official organ from which this

---

[1] *Odessa Messenger*, Sept. 18, 1887.   [2] *Graschdanin*, Aug. 26, 1889.

account is bodily taken, commenting in its following number
upon the comparative statistics of education, from which it
appears that Holland, Saxony, and England spend more
money upon the education of their subjects, and Russia less,
than any other European nation, jubilantly exclaims, "And
'glory, glory be to God that it is so!' we cry out in sincerity
of heart and full of love for our native land. This place of
honor in the statistics of national education has been purchased by Germany at the price of the colossal development
of socialism and atheism."[1]

No man, were his faith in the future of humanity never so
robust, can contemplate these things without a feeling of
sadness akin to despair; for eighty or ninety millions[2] of
human beings, with blunted faculties, palsied will, distorted
views of life, the divine fire within them being deliberately
and diabolically quenched and stamped out, are, in sober
truth, one of the saddest sights of the nineteenth century.
And the tragic effect of the situation is heightened, not
transformed, by the fatuous pomposity and conceit with
which the masters of these uncomplaining serfs, instead of
taking pity on their helpless victims, prate about their lofty
mission to diffuse light and culture and political liberty
among the Slavs of Europe and the Mahometans of Asia.
Philanthropic Mrs. Jellyby, neglecting home and children to
sweeten the lot of the unregenerate natives of Borrioboola
Gha, was a paragon of good sense and modesty in comparison. No doubt the Government is and always has been
composed, not of angels and saints translated beyond the
sphere of evil influence, but of men with the same nature,
subject to the same temptations as the millions whom they
lead. Moreover, where the reciprocal action and reaction
of governors and governed is so complex and difficult to
analyze as in Russia, it is extremely easy to err on the side
of exaggeration in attempting to allot to the authorities their
fair share of the joint responsibility. But whether much or
little is of no practical importance, seeing that it is the misfortune of the masses to have to pay dearly for the folly of
their rulers after having fully expiated their own. It is
hard to suppress a sigh of pity for a generous people dragged

---

[1] *Graschdanin*, 8th September, 1889.
[2] The difference between this number and the total population of Russia
is the large margin for exceptions which it is wise to allow in a country of
ten millions of Nonconformists, many of whom would bear comparison
with the choicest spirits of Western Europe.

down by those whom they support in luxury, to the level of the beasts of the field ; for men who are serfs in everything but the name, who toil and moil from childhood to old age, creating riches that elude their grasp, and who can still affirm in a proverb in which is embedded the crystallized history of ages : " Our soul is God's, our body the Tsar's, and our backs belong to our masters."

CHAPTER IV.

DISHONESTY.

"I BEG to tender my heartfelt thanks to M. Rudzky, tradesman of this city, for having restored me my watch, which I inadvertently left on the counter in his shop a few days ago. When I offered him money as a token of my gratitude, M. Rudzky refused to accept it, saying that he had only done his duty. This is an example worthy of imitation!— Signed, Madame Karasteleva."[1] This pithy pæan, curiously characteristic of the country, was published in one of the principal papers of one of the principal cities of Russia about a year ago, and must have made M. Rudzky feel as if his originality bordered on suicidal mania or some equally dangerous form of eccentricity. Neither such spontaneous testimonials, however, nor the absence thereof, are needed to prove that Russia can boast of numbers of obscure but upright men whose sterling honesty will bear comparison with that of the noblest characters described in history or besung in fable. It would be indeed sad were it otherwise. No society, however rude, is wholly destitute of these pioneers or survivors of a higher stage of social life, without which it could no more exist than falsehood lacking a grain of truth to leaven it. What this outburst of gratitude really implied, and what few foreigners who possess no special knowledge of the country would willingly take for granted, even on the word of the most trusted ethnologist, is the great paucity of such moral giants as Rudzky. It is estimated that there are in Russia about thirteen millions of Dissenters all told, considerable numbers of whom belong to rationalistic sects such as the *Molokani*, the *Stundists*, and others — chaste, veracious, honest Puritans, whose theology is pure morality, and whose dealings with all men are regulated by the principles of the strictest justice. But

---

[1] The first sentence is quoted from memory; the others are taken from the *Novoye Vremya* of the 30th August, 1889. The paragraph appeared in the *New Russian Telegraph* (Odessa) about the 25th of that month.

the sectarians scarcely amount to the eighth of the entire population, and the rationalistic sects are but a fraction of the sectarians. The great bulk of the Russian nation not only does not associate dishonesty with criminality, sinfulness, or ethical deformity, but holds it to be rather a meritorious employment of heaven-sent gifts which it would be sinful to let rust for want of exercise. At the root of all the dealings of the people among themselves, and of all the commercial relations of the nation with foreigners, like the serpent gnawing at the root of the tree Yggdrasil, lies ineffable contempt of the practice of common honesty, which is held equivalent to hiding in the earth those talents of worldly wisdom which it should be man's first object to increase, reaping where he sowed not, and gathering where he has not strewed. And it is upon this view that they shape the conduct of their lives with all the persistency of which a feeble-minded, fickle, nerveless people are capable.

It would be a mistake to call this degeneration. It is merely stagnation, arrested development; for the Russia of to-day, when stripped of the outward hull, which is varnished and modern, will be found to differ in no essential respects from the Russia of the Middle Ages. The German Hanseatic cities, which strictly forbade their merchants to give Russians goods on credit, to lend them money[1] under any pretexts, or even to borrow of them, under pain of speedy punishment,[2] are now mere memories of the past. Reval, which was equally careful about guarding itself from the consequences of dishonesty, has lived to become a flourishing city of the Russian empire. But the characteristic traits of the people are still what they were; and the frequent complaints of the Germans and Belgians of the fourteenth century, that Russian traders put lying brands and false trade-marks on their goods; that light weight went hand-in-hand with bad quality, heavy bricks being freely added to consignments of adulterated wax;[3] that sham furs were so

---

[1] *Liev. Ehst. und Kurländisches Urkundenbuch nebst Registern;* Reval, 1852–1864. II., 576, 583.
[2] *Urkundliche Geschichte des Ursprunges d. deutschen Hanse;* Hamburg, 1830. II., N. ix., p. 27. It would be wrong to imagine that the Russians did not complain on their side of occasional dishonesty on the part of foreign merchants. It is nowhere recorded, however, that they found it so frequent or so ruinous as to justify them in "boycotting" Germans or Belgians.
[3] Cf. for ex. Lievländ, *Urkunde*, VI.; Aristoff, *Russian Industry in Ancient Times*, p. 213 (Russian).

common that foreigners ceased to buy any furs, good or bad, wherever Russians traded; that enormous sums had to be distributed in bribes to the Russian authorities before the Germans could get these evils diminished to a point at which trading was possible; these and countless other complaints of long-forgotten times would, if published without mention of persons or dates, pass with the student of contemporary Russian history for cuttings from the newspapers or extracts from consular reports of to-day. Russian merchants are no longer permitted, as in the seventeenth century, to pawn their kith and kin, their wives and children, whom they were supposed to love and live for; but they still cheerfully sacrifice whatever they are allowed to pledge: good name, friendship, honor, with the same frequency with which their great grandfathers used to let their wives and children be sold, prostituted, enslaved for debts that they could have easily discharged;[1] and if the average merchant of the present day were to set about following the advice of the Roman poet, to wrap himself up in the mantle of his own integrity, it would prove no better protection from the cold blasts of a wintry world than the Italian beggar's coat, which was described as being made mostly of fresh air. On the other hand, the Russian merchant may be said to be living almost as well up to his lights as his colleague the German or the Englishman; it is not his fault if these lights are just sufficient to intensify the gloom about him. He has been brought up to deceit and trickery from his childhood; he has sucked it in with his mother's milk, he has inherited it from generations of dishonest ancestors, it is the lesson daily, hourly taught him by his government and his church; and if in the teeth of all this he were to stand out in strong contrast to his fellows, an honest, straightforward, veracious man, we should be safe to regard him as a genius, a monster or a sectarian.

But merchants and traders, though they have more frequent opportunity for its cultivation than others, have no monopoly of dishonesty. It is universal, Pan-Russian. According to a popular writer who had a life-long experience of his countrymen, studying them from various coigns of vantage, as bureaucrat, governor, author, journalist, and suspect, "roguery is one of the forms of social life,"[2] and it is

---

[1] *Collection of State Documents*, III. N. 60.
[2] Schtschedrin, *Well-Meant Discourses*, p. 29 (Russian).

Hobson's choice; he who is not hammer is anvil. "If you manage the estate of another," complains this same writer, "and forbear to take advantage, to the detriment of him who trusts you, of what is called your 'opportunity' to enrich yourself, it is hard to be told that you are green — ah, yes! very green."[1] You are made to feel in such cases that you have been guilty of a social sin, of something not far removed from treason in thus swimming against the current, and every man's hand is straightway raised against you for refusing to raise yours against any man. It is difficult under such conditions for a Russian who has outwitted a friend that implicitly trusted him not to feel as flushed and as happy as the self-respecting Fijian of a few years ago after swallowing the last morsel of a savory enemy. One of the truest patriots Russia ever possessed and one of the most acute observers of the age has given us a series of masterly life-like sketches, illustrative of what is meant by saying that roguery is one of the common forms of social life, from which I subjoin one or two.

"On the perron of a solitary house (in a country town) unprotected even by a yard, two men were sitting dressed in morning attire, smoking cigarettes, and chatting together before retiring for the night. 'Well, you know that Kharin lost that suit of his?' one of them said. 'You don't mean it!' 'Oh yes, no doubt about that. He's a fool and so he lost it.' 'How so?' 'Doesn't everybody know that the deceased lost the use of his hand before his death. Why, the whole town is well aware that Margaret Ivanovna forged the will the day after his death. Aye, and that the Archpriest wrote it, too! Oh yes! no doubt at all, she forged the will; the Archpriest himself, when half-seas over, blurts it out often enough. But for all that Margaret Ivanovna is now the owner of a cool million, while Kharin has to shoulder a beggar's knapsack. And all because he's such a fool!' 'No mistake, he is a fool, but still'— . . . . 'Oh! he's a fool, and that's the long and short of it. Margaret Ivanovna offered to compromise the matter: "Take twenty thousand," she said, "and joy be with you." Why didn't he accept? since he knows that he's a fool? Then he had another chance: the father Archpriest and Ivan Therapontitch also made him offers; "Give us ten thousand apiece," they said, "and we'll make a clean breast of it in

---

[1] Schtschedrin, *Well-Meant Discourses*, p. 29 (Russian).

court as witnesses: we'll speak according to our consciences; we'll say we signed the will from lack of circumspection, and there will be an end of it." Why didn't he close with that, since he knows he's a fool? Margaret Ivanovna, she didn't want to be asked twice, I warrant. She accepted fast enough. She whipped out the money and handed it over in a twinkling. But he was as obstinate as a mule. And if they had asked him for the hard cash, there would be some excuse for him, but no — all they wanted was an I. O. U. Why couldn't he have given it and then later on think better of it and lead them a pretty dance for the money? He might say that he had not signed it, or that it was not given for value received. The unmitigated fool.'"[1] Macaulay once said of Italians that so perverted was their moral sense of right and wrong in the matter of cunning and deceit, that if Othello were represented before an Italian audience, the entire sympathy of the public would be with Iago, while his dupe would come in at most for their contemptuous pity. This is emphatically true of Russians, though, strange as it may seem, far from engendering universal distrust, it coexists with a degree of credulity that borders on the miraculous. The following is another of these typical conversations preserved by Schtschedrin, which throws more light on the social and moral conceptions of modern Russians than volumes of statistics :

"'Nay, but do listen to the way he fooled the German. He bought 1200 roubles worth of timber from him, had it brought home, and then told the German to call on him for the money. He came, was made much of, treated to refreshments, champagne and all the rest. "Now," he says, turning to the German, "you write your receipt, while I'm getting the money ready," and with this he began to count the notes. The receipt being drawn up in a moment, he took it, glanced at it, found it in order — a legal receipt for 1200 roubles — and then clapped it and the money into his pocket. "You have acknowledged here, Bogdan Bogdanovitch," he said, "that you have received the money in full. I don't see that you have anything further to wait for." Ha! ha! ha! That, brother, was a stroke of business. Oh, how we did laugh! I thought my sides would split. But listen to what's coming. At first the German looked as if he did not grasp what was the matter, and then when it

---

[1] *Well-Meant Discourses*, p. 31.

suddenly dawned upon him, he cried out, "You are a thief!" "All right," was the answer he got, "you Germans invented, they say, the ape, but here am I, a Russian, bringing in one moment all your contrivances to naught." Bravo! No, but you should have seen the German's phiz, frightened and incredulous, his hands feeling his pockets the while — wasn't it rich? Germans are still greenhorns in such matters; they're fools and nothing else.'"[1]

These pictures are not overdrawn, they do not even do full justice to the subject. Take up any daily paper or monthly review, or printed book with the stamp of contemporariness upon it, and you will be struck by the close resemblance between the life therein described and the scenes depicted by Schtschedrin. Open any of the monthly magazines, and read their realistic descriptions of the ethical conceptions and practical maxims of the average Russian, and you will ask yourself in wonder whether it is a question of wild anarchical tribes in Central Africa or the backwoods of Brazil, or of a people ruled by a government alive even to its own paltry interests. The *Northern Messenger*, which I take up almost at random, describes for example, in detail, how a whole company of peasants in Manuilovka split their sides (or, as they themselves picturesquely put it, tore their intestines) with genuine, hearty laughter at the recital of how a hay merchant cheated a poor woman, selling her the same load of rotten hay three different times.[2]

The relations of capital and labor, which are rapidly developing into the relations of governors and governed, are hopelessly vitiated by duplicity, breach of faith, downright roguery, with which no amount of Draconian legislation can successfully grapple. A few years ago laws were made empowering landowners and farmers to hire laborers for several years' service, and enacting a long list of severe penalties for breach of contract. In practice these laws have proved as efficacious as a gossamer veil spread out to stay the fury of the hurricane.

Every autumn and winter the newspapers are filled with descriptions of the harrowing scenes enacted in the country districts between the men who raise the corn and those who take it. Agricultural laborers of both sexes taken on by the year, or by the five years, frequently run away, leaving their

---

[1] *Well-Meant Discourses*, p. 34.
[2] *Northern Messenger*, N. 7, 1888, p. 54.

masters in the lurch at a most critical time, when there are no other laborers to be had to replace them, and think no evil of it.[1] In the government of Tamboff, for instance, farmers and landowners, taking time by the forelock, secured a band of laborers in advance, at what seemed a fair rate of wages under the circumstances. The men eagerly accepted the terms, and a portion of the wages in advance as earnest money; but they seem to have felt no obligation to come and work when harvest time came round; and the employers were left lamenting. Complaint was made to the magistrate, and warrants taken out to bring the delinquents to justice, and very likely many of them may have been punished; but that was cold comfort for the landowners whose corn was rotting in the rain and whose affairs were going to ruin.[2] Similar tales reach us from the south, north, and east of Russia, where the people are suffering the effects of their own dishonesty, while they grumble—if at all—only at fate.[3] In one place we read of all the ponderous machinery of the law being brought to bear against the defaulting peasants, with the result that matters were left just where they were before. The fugitives were discovered by the police and restored to their masters by force, after the harvest to be still more severely punished, but in three days they arose again, and, shaking the dust off their feet, went away, saying "This time no man shall find us." Nor were they discovered, in that classic land of passports and police supervision.[4] If in all these cases the employers played the melancholy part of victims, the presumable explanation is that the conditions were unfavorable for their assuming that of oppressors. They were indignant, like Bill Nye with the Heathen Chinee, at the success rather than at the iniquity of the proceeding. The great majority of such employers take the utmost advantage of their legal position; cheat their workmen, starve them, grind them to grist like the corn in their mills, and then jibe and jeer at them, as rustics poke caged bears with sticks. The Moor has done his work, the Moor can go, is their device. Thus we hear of bands of laborers in the fertile, smiling Crimea, weak and emaciated as if recovering from typhus or dying of consumption, who, working like helots, are fed "upon something which is not bread, but a black, nauseous mass, the indigestible ingredi-

---

[1] *The Don Speech*, N. 91.
[2] *Tamboff Governmental Gazette*, N. 78.
[3] Cf. v. g. *Odessa News*, N. 1042.
[4] *Odessa News*, N. 1030.

ents of which no man can determine."[1] Others are duly hired at the uniform rate of four roubles a day during the entire season, and when they arrive on the scene of their labors and have worked some time are told that they will receive but two roubles a day.[2] In Samara a numerous party of agricultural laborers were hired at five roubles and a half per *dessatine* (about 2¾ acres), and having journeyed to the district where they were wanted at their own expense, were informed that on consideration the employer could only pay them somewhat less than half that sum (two roubles and a half). They returned at once in disgust and spent their last coins on the road.[3] In other places whole companies of harvest laborers come home as poor as they went, without a copper coin in their pockets, because the landowners keep back a third, or even a half of each man's earnings, relying on the reluctance of the men to undergo the loss of time, the trouble, and the worry of suing for their wages through the law courts.[4] Numbers of such famishing wretches, returning from their harvesting, roam despairingly about the streets of the towns and cities on their way, begging for bread to keep them alive, and asking for alms to take them home, and having asked in vain, they seize upon as thieves what was denied to them as beggars.

The pursuit of trade, properly so called, as a means of livelihood, requires in Russia no special training of the individual as in other countries. Inherited racial aptitude, mother wit, natural shrewdness, and inborn unscrupulousness are deemed amply sufficient. It is scarcely to be wondered at that men with no more varied mental and moral outfit should have transformed trade and commerce from powerful instruments of civilization into a labyrinth of "ways that are dark," a very quicksand of deceit and chicanery. The most heartless trickery, covered over with a frank childlike look and a voice clear as an echo from the well of truth, passes current as easily as a counterfeit coin. The average trader makes no bones about over-reaching his customers, native or foreign, and of swearing to the truth of the most audacious falsehood ever invented, with all the cheerfulness of a man performing a pleasant duty, and easing his mind. For his chief business maxim is that he may, nay, must —

---

[1] *Crimean Messenger*, N. III.
[2] *Gazette of Samara*, N. 155.
[3] *Ibid.*
[4] *Yuschny Krai*, N. 2591.

"Stamp God's own name upon a lie just made
To turn a penny in the way of trade;"

though he often does it for less even than a penny. If caught in *flagrante delicto* and convicted of downright roguery, he is no more abashed than if it were a question of his hair growing grey; and eying you with all the tenderness he can infuse into a look, he will say: "I must live somehow, your honor; if not by washing, then by mangling, as the saying is. I could have dealt with your honor without lies or cheating, but then your honor is not everybody — indeed, I might journey on foot from here to Kieff and not meet with your equal." The perfect ease with which he shuffles off the weight of his ill-doings, as a goose shakes off drops of rain-water, forcibly reminds one of Wainamoiren, the Ancient Truthful One of the Finnish Epos, who advances the most deliberate uncalled-for lies, and, when convicted thereof, with astonishing simplicity, makes answer: "Well, I did lie somewhat," and conscientiously proceeds with the previous question. "If you don't lie, you won't sell," is a proverb, for which the Russians can scarcely put forward an exclusive claim, though it must be admitted that they act upon it as no other people, ancient or modern, have dared to act. "In the way of trade," said a Russian Orthodox priest of forty years standing, in conversation with me on the subject some months ago, "a Russian would sell his soul to the Evil One and then pledge it to the Lord; and if an angel from heaven were to tell him that he had swerved somewhat from the path of virtue, he would smile incredulously and continue to transgress."

The evil has been frequently discussed and explained in Russia, but the explanations are one-sided, incomplete. The press is inclined to attribute it to the overmastering passion for gold and to the Russian's proverbial impatience to grow rich, in order that he himself may spend the money he has collected.[1] This account of the matter is partially true, but only partially. Russians are open to a charge of rapacity, to insatiable cupidity, but not to anything savoring of niggardliness. He loves money far less for its own sake or for the advantages it can procure him in future than for the opportunity it affords him of playing the king. He can no more hoard and pinch and stint than an average Bush-

---

[1] "In all things," says the *Novoye Vremya*, "the specific quality of the Russian mind is unbridled lust of sordid gain." — 29th September, 1889.

man can play the part of Beau Brummel in the London of to-day. He regulates his budget as behooves a firm believer in the doctrine that it is more blessed to give than to receive; scatters money lavishly to the right and to the left, giving away his last hundred roubles as royally as if he had a Fortunatus' purse to fall back upon. There are scores of needy wretches in want of a dinner, who once were rich men, in St. Petersburg, Odessa, Moscow, Kieff, who built up their own fortunes almost in a night, and then scattered them to the winds as if they were all mere gold of Tolosa. There used to be a Scotch beggar in London who attributed his poverty to a single miscalculation. He began, it appears, at the age of thirty-five to spend a fortune of £20,000, unexpectedly left to him, at the rate of £1,000 a year, living in ease and idleness the while, in the belief that his span of life would not exceed sixty years; and after the rapid flight of some twenty-two or three years was stupefied to find himself healthy and a beggar. None of the Russian spendthrifts whom I ever saw or heard of could with truth allege that they entertained any, even the most slipshod, calculations before frittering away a fortune.

On the other hand it cannot be denied that hot haste in the pursuit of riches is a characteristic of the Russian merchant, and does much to intensify that spirit of improbity which it did not create. Many merchants are so impatient to do business that they cannot even wait till their customers enter their shops, but must needs sally forth, lay violent hands upon them, and drag them in. This is at bottom the same kind of ardor that the mythical Lien Chi Altangi observed in the London shopmen of last century, only duly intensified and Russianized. "'There,' cries the mercer, showing me a piece of fine silk, 'there's beauty. My Lord Suckeskin has bespoke the fellow to this for the birthnight this very morning; it would look charmingly in waistcoats.' 'But I do not want a waistcoat,' replied I. 'Not want a waistcoat!' returned the mercer; 'then I would advise you to buy one. When waistcoats are wanted, depend upon it they will come dear. Always buy before you want, and you are sure to be well used, as they say in Cheapside.'" You are certainly very ill-used at times if you do not buy before you want in Russia, where brute force so often does duty for persuasion. A friend of mine walking for the first, and last, time in his life along the streets in the *Apraxin Dvor* — a sort of miniature city composed of the shops and stores of the genuine Russian chapmen, whose manners, morals, and mercantile methods have been admirably painted by the playwright Ostroffsky —was forcibly drawn into a ready-made clothes shop, his coat slipped off and another fitted on in the time it takes to tell it. He pleaded, protested, threatened; the assistants alternately bullied and cajoled him, but after a long struggle released him amid a shower of picturesque epithets. He had not had time enough to collect his scattered senses, when he was lifted bodily into a trunk store and shown a capacious trunk. "But I don't want a trunk, not even gratis," he apologetically pleaded. "Well, this is gratis, or nearly so, only fifteen roubles." "But I assure you I do not" .... "Oh! you think it is not the best of its kind. Well, sir, God is witness that you won't get a better trunk in all Petersburg, nor a cheaper. You are not used to bargaining? We like honest men of your stamp, take it for ten roubles.". "Let me go; I will have none of your trunks." "Not till you have seen some more. Ivan, take the gentleman upstairs and show him all the trunks we have. Take your time, sir; a trunk is bought not for a day or a way, it's for a lifetime, sir." But my friend, who preferred a money loss of ten roubles to unknown and possibly more serious sacrifices, paid the money, had a droschky called, and drove away.

The newspapers have been constantly full of complaints of the same description. "Moscow knows," says the *Russian Courier* of Moscow, "what the Knife Row is, and St. Petersburg realizes what the Cerberi of the Apraxin Dvor are, how they fight among themselves over a customer, how often a whole squadron of them fall foul of a passer-by, drag him into their shop and violently force him to buy something. The police-courts in Petersburg, where a long series of prosecutions have arisen from attacks on the public in the Apraxin Dvor, treat the merchant Cerberi with all the severity of the law."[1] Laws in Russia, however, are seldom efficacious for long and we find the Police Prefect of Warsaw ordering all merchants in that city to bind themselves over to cease in future from dragging passers-by into their shops and warehouses, and threatening them with all the rigors of the law if they break their promise.[2] Such violence is not always visited on the purchaser only. At

---

[1] *Russian Courier*, July, 1887.   [2] *Odessa Messenger*, 27th July, 1887.

Saratoff the other day a gentleman entered the shop of a fish salesman named Krynkin. While he was making a selection, a fishmonger a few doors off, entered, seized the inoffensive customer by the throat and dragged him into his own shop. Krynkin expostulated, but was knocked down and severely beaten by his rival, who then returned to serve the unhappy man whom he had dragged along the street like a shark. There were a number of people looking on, but they only took a speculative interest in the proceedings. The strokes of business that are daily done in those stores and warehouses by the shaggy-bearded, inoffensive-looking barbarians would prove a revelation to Ah Sin himself. The following sketch is taken from the journals, and can be vouched for as characteristic. A middle-class state functionary enters a ready-made clothes shop to purchase a suit of clothes or a coat. When trying it on he notices in one of the pockets an article of value (a watch, silver cigar-case, etc.) put there designedly by the tradesman. The intending purchaser covets the watch as well as the coat, and keeps his own counsel. He pays the price demanded almost without haggling, such is his anxiety to leave the shop. The tradesman charges twice as much as under ordinary circumstances, and having received the money, stops the happy purchaser who is rapidly gliding from the shop, with the words, "I beg your pardon, but I forgot to take my watch from your pocket," and having removed it, adds, "You may go now, many thanks." The other day a certain N. went into one of these shops to purchase an overcoat. He was exposed to the above described temptation and succumbed. Seduced by the massive silver cigar case stuck in the pocket, he paid £2 12s. for an article worth £1 10s. at most, and at the threshold of the door he was relieved of his prize and left the shop meditating revenge. A few days later he returns to the same store, treats for a morning coat, puts it on, and feels the inevitable cigar-case. Having hastily substituted a tin cigar-case silvered over for the genuine bait, he haggled a little to save appearances, declined to buy, and went his way. When the theft was discovered the tradesman was *naif* enough to bruit it abroad and to inveigh against the rascality of the St. Petersburg public;[1] forgetting that dishonesty is less the monopoly of any one profession than a talent lying latent in all his countrymen,

---

[1] *Novoye Vremya*, 18th August, 1888.

waiting only for the occasion, like the Æolian harp for the caressing breeze.

If the Russian public were alive to its own vital interests, nothing less than force would cause it to consume many of the articles of food that are sold in the shops. When such an article as pepper is adulterated to the extent that a pound of that condiment contains but two ounces of real pepper, and a *pud* (about thirty-seven pounds), which sells for twenty-four roubles, costs the vendor only three, one can form an adequate idea of the proportions assumed by adulteration. Four years ago a correspondent of the *Moscow Gazette* interviewed a well-known Moscow wine-merchant, whose piety is equal to his business qualifications. This is what they said to each other : — " How is business ? " " We can't complain, thanks be to God. Last year I sold no less than 80,000 bottles of Madeira alone." " Where did you get such a large quantity of that wine ? The island of Madeira produces altogether 10,000 barrels (?) of wine, of which only 3,000 come to Europe." The wine-merchant smiled and answered, " God sends it. What do you suppose I pay a chemical expert 3,000 roubles with board and lodging for ? And what profit could I make if I sold mere wine ? It would cost me from $4\frac{3}{4}$d. to $5\frac{1}{4}$d. a-bottle ; I might sell it for 8d. or 9d. If I were to conduct my business like that I might just as well throw the beggar's sack over my shoulder at once. It's a vastly different thing if out of this wine you fabricate Madeira, and a bottle of it costs you 9d. or 1s., while you sell it for 3s. or 4s. ; that's what I call business." " Yes, but that is adulteration, falsification," I objected. " Now you're a man of ' education,' " said the merchant, " and yet you call my Madeira an adulteration. Do you eat beetroot ? " " Yes." " And is sugar made of beetroot ? " " Undoubtedly." " Well, and do you call sugar a falsification. And when the confectioner makes sweetmeats from sugar, is that adulteration ? " " No doubt confectioners' sweets are at times harmful and even poisonous ; but your sherries and Madeiras, with their noxious ingredients, are extremely common, and you are seriously injuring the health of those who consume them — sometimes you poison them outright." The merchant smiled and answered according to his piety : " If God does not send death, you may drink any stuff you like, and you will be safe and sound. ' And if you drink any deadly thing it shall not hurt you.' Do you know whose words these are?

If you know you are bound to believe. You may drink water without praying over it and sicken."[1]

Occasionally the police, dissatisfied with their share of the spoils, make a raid and seize on a hogshead or two of alcoholic poison, or a chest of sand called tea, and prosecute the public poisoner. But long before the unwieldy machine of the law can be brought to bear upon him he again makes friends with the mammon of iniquity, and the "wine" and "spirits" in the casks carefully sealed up by the law officers, mysteriously changes to pure water or evaporates. In such cases, says an Odessa journal, either the *vodka* completely disappears from the vessel, which was sealed with the seal of the Revenue Office, or at the very least it changes to water.[2] Adulteration of food is common to all countries, and even in England people are slow to realize the extent to which they are imposed upon by unscrupulous speculators. The special features of the Russian practice, however, are its universality, openness, and the impunity enjoyed by the merchants whose profits are dependent upon it. Coffee bought in Moscow in April, 1887, for 1s. 6d. per pound was analyzed. It was fine quality to look at, and had a delightful aroma. Many of the berries, however, appeared less bright-looking than the others, and when taken out and examined by the analyst of the university were found to consist of clay mixed with chicory, without a trace of coffee.[3]

Turning to banks and counting-houses, we find that they have become a byeword in Russia. It is but a short time since that a new law was launched against the sharp practices of some of the best-known and apparently respectable banks of St. Petersburg[4] — a law which will prove as

---

[1] *Moscow Gazette*, October, 1887; cf. also *Saratoff Gazette*, 23rd October, 1887.

[2] Cf. *Odessa News*, 20th June and 4th July, 1888, where cases of transformation and evaporation are described in detail.

[3] The following is taken from an official report on teas supplied by well-known firms: — Green tea, 14s. a lb.: Of poor quality; contains boiled tea leaves, and is largely colored with ultramarine. Black tea, 4s. 4d. a lb.: Contains very little tea, mixed with boiled tea leaves and willow herb, colored with burnt sugar; 27 per cent. of sand. Reddish tea, 4s. a lb.: 60 per cent. of boiled tea leaves and 12 per cent. of sand. Black tea, 3s. 9d. a lb.: *Contains no tea;* is made of boiled tea leaves, elm and willow herb; 40 per cent. of sand. Black tea, 5s. 5d. a lb.: 50 per cent. of willow herb and elm leaves. Black tea, 6s. 6d. a lb.: 50 per cent. of boiled tea leaves, and others of a plant unknown; colored with logwood; 7 per cent. of sand. — *Warsaw Diary*, 16th April, 1888.

[4] Cf. *Journal de St. Pétersbourg*, 26th September, 1889. *Graschdanin*, 26th September, 1889. *Novoye Vremya*, 26th and 27th September, 1889, etc., etc.

efficacious as the feather of a young humming bird employed to tickle the side of a healthy rhinoceros. Within the eight years most of the "best" banks in Russia have stopped payment, and tens of thousands of peasant farmers, clergymen, widows and orphans who put their trust in these establishments approved by the Government were turned adrift on the world to beg from door to door. The horrors of war have been many a time described with realistic vividness by artistic pens in prose and verse. It would require a masterly hand to depict the wailing and the weeping, the cries of anguish, the looks of despair, the suicides, the robberies, the hideous crimes and heartrending sufferings that ensued upon the failure of the banks of Skopin, Kozloff, Orel, wherein were swallowed up millions of roubles laboriously scraped together by the thousand of units within whom, in spite of all their inborn recklessness, stirred a faint perception that providence and thrift might after all be worth a fair trial. The tale of wholesale, cold-blooded spoliation that was unfolded during the trials of the galaxy of swindling bankers who have reduced thousands to beggary during the past eight or ten years, might well cause any but the most sanguine patriot to despair of the future of Russia.

Men can never wholly escape the influence of their age and country; and it is to be regretted rather than wondered at that enlightened physicians, men of science, whose education and mission would seem to give promise of better things, should compete with professional swindlers in this inglorious race for ill-gotten wealth. Last spring a wealthy gentleman called upon a well-known and "respectable" dentist of Moscow, reputed to be a brilliant light in his profession, and ordered a complete set of teeth in gold. When it was ready his expectations were fulfilled to the utmost in all but the color of the metal. "Excuse me, doctor," he said, "but is this pure gold?" The scientific light blazed out angrily: "How can you doubt it? For whom do you take me, sir?" on which the gentleman felt ashamed of himself and left. He went straight to a chemist's laboratory, however, and had the usual tests applied, when it was made evident that the metal was copper without a trace of gold anywhere.[1] "Our hydrotherapeutic establishments," says one of the principal organs of the St. Petersburg press, "under cover of philanthropic advertisements, announce

---

[1] *Novoye Vremya*, 13th April, 1889.

that they charge, say, twenty-five roubles for a course of treatment. A patient of scanty means believes and begins the course, and it is soon made clear that he has been lured into a swindling trap. They charge him for everything as extras, and, instead of twenty-five roubles, exact forty-five or even fifty. The patient, not possessing the means of defraying these unforeseen expenses, is first stripped of everything of which he can be relieved, and then turned out when half the course is over. He is thus fleeced of his money, gets no benefit in return, and sometimes incurs positive harm by abruptly breaking off a drastic water-cure."[1]

It would be no easy matter to point out a trade, a profession, a calling followed by genuine Russians, in the code of which elementary honesty has a place. It is not merely the unwritten law, the vague, shadowy borderland of sharp practice that lies between mere infamy and the more palpable terrors of stone walls and iron bars, that is daily encroached upon, but the Rubicon of the Penal Code is continually passed with a calm tranquillity that guaranteed immunity from mere human penalties could scarcely justify. The bland simplicity with which wholesale robberies are carried on for years within the knowledge of the public, the priests, and the police, amazes even travellers who have lived long in China. That light weight, now as of yore, should be eked out by heavy stones,[2] that trade-marks should be forged; food adulterated; goods despatched to distant purchasers which are infinitely inferior to the samples that elicited the orders, is no doubt highly reprehensible, but might still, perhaps, be glossed over as venial errors by a moralist willing to make allowances for exceptional human weakness under strong temptation. But notorious vulgar robbery, propped up with perjury, forgery, and every conceivable form of chicanery, and raised to the dignity of one of the recognized methods of trade by representative men of good standing, who can yet be religious without blasphemy, and edifying without hypocrisy, would seem in sober truth to imply a standard of ethics specifically different from that of civilized nations.

---

[1] *Graschdanin*, 18th September, 1889.
[2] Take as a typical instance the firm of Messrs. Weingurt, of Odessa, who received from the factory with which they deal and sold to their own customers without having previously verified it, sugar in which to nine cwts. of sugar there was one cwt. of stones (*Odessa News*, 7th December, 1887).

There is a curious class of discount booksellers in Russia who thrive and prosper while the fate that continually threatens and often overtakes the publishing firms whose works they trade in is insolvency and ruin. Vast palatial buildings that yield a handsome yearly income prove that they drive a brisk trade in books, and give the lie to the saw, that honesty is the best policy. Their method is simple: they usually fee young apprentices of the principal publishing houses to steal whatever books are in demand, and to deliver to their own boy-apprentices, who are also members of the conspiracy, as many copies of them as may be required by their customers. That the consciences of these tradesmen give them no uneasiness needs no more convincing proof than the fact that some of them are bringing up their own children to the business. Nor could it well be otherwise. Trade is held high in esteem by men of all countries, classes, and confessions, and to their thinking trade is merely the art of robbing your neighbor without exposing yourself to his vengeance. The first part of this definition is tersely expressed by the proverb, "Wherein one deals, therein one steals," while the moral blamelessness of robbery could scarcely be proclaimed with greater force than in this other proverb: "Why not steal, so long as there's no one to hinder it?"

Another of these booksellers, we are told, did a thriving little trade, in addition to the sale of books, in wax candles made by the monks, in accordance with the canons of the church. He obtained the candles in the same way that he came by the volumes: the little boys who were assisting the monks to sell them being paid to steal them. "*He was often detected*, and occasionally threatened with the legal consequences of his acts." It was on these occasions, we are told, that the religious principles to which he always tenaciously clung buoyed him up and bore him safely out of danger. "I say, Masha!" he would cry out to his wife, who was sitting in a little parlor inside, "take a wax candle, a good thick one, mind, and run off and light it before the *icon*."[1] And his faith was strengthened by the knowledge that his fervent prayers for a way out of the difficulty were always heard and granted. A less pious colleague was proportionately less fortunate, and once had to stand his trial. He made up in sharpness, however, for what he lacked in

---

[1] *Novoye Vremya*, 21st October, 1888.

piety, and "wriggled out of the accusation in a truly masterly style." Chatting after his acquittal with his neighbor, the man who had prosecuted him for the theft, "What a greenhorn you are, to be sure!" he exclaimed. "If, when you caused the raid to be made on my shop, you had only looked under the counter, you would have found all the stolen books there. But it's evident that, to punish you for your litigiousness, God turned your eyes away."[1]

To some readers the curious combinations of religion and rascality, friendship and treachery, without the cement of hypocrisy, which are so conspicuous a feature of the Russian character may seem vastly amusing. They undoubtedly have the charm of novelty and are as real as they seem improbable. They suggest to our mind's eye the picture of an unimagined community, the antipodes of Plato's Utopia, and compared with which Lamb's imaginary Sydney[2] was a colony of stern Fabricii —

"Scorners of all-conquering gold."

But the phenomenon has also its serious sides, which constitute the only *raison d'être* of its delineation here. What, for instance, could be more terrible than the position of the boys who serve as apprentices and have to sell their souls to their masters, sometimes against their will? "Not to mention," says a publicist who has fully discussed this subject, "the boys who are in the service of the discount booksellers and are initiated into all the secrets of a swindling trade and systematically demoralized, youths who serve their time to respectable, orderly and honest publishing firms are in a very sad plight: first frankly tempted to steal one volume from the warehouse, if the boy yields, abstracts a book and sells it to the discount bookseller, he has thereby delivered himself into his clutches for all time. He is ever afterwards receiving orders to steal popular works, and, if he demurs, is threatened with public exposure."[3] This has been going on for years — nay, from time immemorial, and to-day it is the broad rule, not the exception. "It was proved in court," the St. Petersburg press remarks, "that the practices of Semenof (a bookseller tried a few months ago for theft) represent the usual procedure of our discount booksellers."[4]

---

[1] *Novoye Vremya*, 21st October, 1888.
[2] "And tell me what your Sydneyites do? Are they thieving all day long? Merciful heaven!"
[3] *Novoye Vremya*, 21st October, 1888.
[4] *Ibid.* 24th May, 1889. For another curious case of robbery by a bookseller see *Novoye Vremya*, 4th October, 1889.

There are probably more beggars in Russia alone than in all the rest of Europe taken together, a goodly number of whom are men of considerable means who might live in absolute comfort, but prefer to lead a wandering life, putting by from 8s. to 10s. a day;[1] while healthy men and boys are deprived of their eyesight, horribly mutilated and barbarously deformed by monsters called "leaders," with whom they conclude a business compact before exposing themselves in the markets, fairs, and bazaars of their Empire to the gaze and pity of the people.[2] There is quite enough real poverty and misery in the country without simulating more. Famine for instance, like cholera in India, is perennial, killing off as many wretches as any epidemic. The peasants bestir themselves to alleviate the suffering they cannot remedy — the Government never does — but at the same time they actively assist scheming speculators to balk their own humane intentions, and they shake their shanties with homeric laughter at the cleverness of the trick. Thus an enterprising sharper who contracted lately with the Sarapulsky *Zemstvo* to distribute to the needy peasants a fixed quantity of corn for seed, of which he actually possessed but a fractional part, distributed what he owned many times over, getting it back each time, and keeping it for himself in the end, satisfying the easy-going peasants and realizing a considerable sum of money by the operation.[3] For the key to conduct of this kind we need not look further than cupidity on the one side and hebetude on the other; there are thousands of cases, however, which seem psychologically explicable only on the assumption of inherited kleptomania, a theory frequently relied on by Russian medical experts, and still more frequently by Russian juries. It would certainly seem to cover the conduct of the public who visit and read in the library of Samara, who are publicly accused in the local press of shamelessly stealing whatever books they can lay hands on. The remedy proposed by the aggrieved Director seems to favor that theory and is evidently based on the view of theft embodied in the proverb cited above, for he requests the visitors to the library "to spy upon each other," in the interests of all.[4] The same distressing ailment, inherited from their parents, doubtless drove the band of volun-

---

[1] *Messenger of the Volga*, 22nd June, 1888.
[2] *Yaroslavsky Governmental Gazette*, October, 1888.
[3] *Novoye Vremya*, 9th August, 1888; *Messenger of the Volga*, August, 1888.
[4] *Gazette of Samara*, December, 1887; *Novosti*, January 1st, 1888.

teer thieves of the district of Slavyanoserbsk — many of whom were in affluent circumstances — to execute all the robberies traditionally associated with successful fairs, markets, and bazaars;[1] nor need one ask for any more satisfactory explanation of the extensive thefts that were lately committed at the Kieff flower-show, numbers of "respectable" visitors stowing away the "rare and beautiful flowers in their cylinder hats and dress improvers."[2]

The Government, which contemplates these unerring symptoms of moral paralysis with a contented eye, has nevertheless had striking proofs of the practical inconveniences which it is calculated to cause in times of great national crisis. Thus the colossal web of knavishness and villainy, spun by the lords of high places during the Russo-Turkish war, in which the meanest soldiers were caught and had their life-blood sucked out by the bloated human spiders for whom they were recklessly risking their lives, was within an ace of occasioning a national disaster. Such conspiracies of the shepherds against their sheep are as common in Russia as snowstorms in winter. They pass unnoticed in foreign countries, or if spoken of are "semi-officially contradicted" by the *Journal de St. Pétersbourg*, and people not knowing whom to believe shrug their shoulders and pass on. Who in England paid any attention to the extensive frauds on the Treasury and on special funds reserved for benevolent purposes, committed by high functionaries of State, on the discovery of which the late Minister of the Interior, M. Makoff, wound up his accounts with the world by shooting himself in his chambers one night? Yet the diamond necklace fraud was a joke in comparison. The Grand Railway Company of Russia, "sanctioned by the Most High," as the Tsar is officially described, is affirmed by the principal newspaper in Russia to have defrauded the public during several years past of twelve million roubles.[3] The *Novosti* informs us that the Volga Steam Navigation Company have been giving large dividends to shareholders, thanks to the frauds which they have been practising upon the Government for several years past, and which now amount to several millions.[4]

From the days of the Hansa down to the present, Russia's commercial and political reputation among foreigners has

---

[1] *Northern Messenger*, January, 1889.   [2] *Ibid.*
[3] *Novoye Vremya*, 28th August, 1888.   [4] *Novosti*, 9th May, 1889.

lost nothing only because it had nothing to lose. A certain limited, working confidence based upon obvious mutual interests, without which all social intercourse would be impossible, has necessarily been exhibited by foreign merchants and governments from time to time. But even this shadow of a good name has been repeatedly realized to the last farthing, until the word Russian is become synonymous with qualities subversive of everything implied by relations of trade, commerce, and friendship. Examples abound. Russian kerosene, for instance, is looked upon by English purchasers with "misgivings," as we learn from the Russian Consul at Hull,[1] whose countrymen found no better way to retrieve their lost reputation than by damaging that of a competitor, making thousands of tin cans in all respects identical with those used by American firms, filling them with wretched stuff and flooding therewith the markets of Central and Southern Europe, where they were bought, sold, and condemned as first-class American kerosene.[2] In Brazil Russian canvas for sails is being "boycotted," while the French and English material is eagerly purchased, because "conscientiously" prepared.[3] In Belgium Russian timber has no chance in the competition with Norwegian, Swedish, Hungarian, for the same reason.[4] As to flax, any quantity of it would, we are officially assured, be accepted gladly, if only honestly sorted and sold. "At present, however," adds the Russian representative, in his latest report to his government, "in the cases containing flax from Russia you can *almost always* find stones, old ropes, etc., which add greatly to the weight and spoil the quality of the merchandise. It is owing to this *fraud that Russian flax fetches only half the price of the inferior qualities of the Belgian article*."[5] Official complaints on this head have been received by the Russian authorities from Lille, Leeds, Dundee, and other European cities, much as they used to be received from the Hanseatic cities of the fourteenth century. Even Russian eggs in

---

[1] *Report of the Russian Consul in Hull,* 25th March, 1889.
[2] I have reason to believe that a complaint on this subject was addressed to the Russian authorities by the United States Government.
[3] *Report of Russian Legation in Brazil;* Rio de Janeiro, 25th February, 1889.
[4] *Report of M. Ratmanoff of the Russian Legation in Brazil.*
[5] *Ibid.* The Russian Department of Agriculture admits that "Archangel, in consequence of the distrust entertained towards it by foreign manufacturers, has lost all importance as an export port for flax." — *Journal of Kazan,* 9th November, 1887. The same fate, adds that journal, is sure to overtake Riga.

England fetch forty per cent. less than eggs from other countries of the Continent, merely because, being Russian, they are believed to be everything else which this fatal word implies.[1]

But the staple export of Russia as an agricultural country is corn, of which Great Britain is a purchaser to the extent of about six millions sterling. Yet the manipulations to which that corn, excellent by nature, is subjected before it reaches this country would seem incredible were they not vouched for by the most trustworthy authorities in Russia, and evident to all corndealers of the world. It is no easy thing to believe, and yet we have it on the undisputed authority of all parties concerned, that the corn-exporters of the city of Liban had the coolness to request the authorities of the Public Corn Warehouse of Yelets to sell them the sweepings that remained over after the sorting of the oats, which consisted " of earth, husks, unripe grainless ears, fine tares, and pigweed," in order, as they honestly explained, to mix them with the oats to be exported to England. The Warehouse authorities refused to be a party to this fraud, but the exporters, who insisted and based their request on the obstinate "refusal of British importers to purchase oats without the admixture of compost," obtained elsewhere about one hundred thousand poods (about 2,500 bushels) of what the official corn-broker and representative of the Government terms "unadulterated manure," with which they humored the fabulous caprices of their English customers.[2] According to a Russian expert, who has lately published his views on the matter, the net gain to the complaisant exporters on this commercial operation was one hundred per cent. He assures his countrymen that this practice goes on at all times and places in the Empire, "otherwise," he explains, "our corn export offices would not be found everywhere in such a prosperous condition."[3]

The official agent of the Russian Ministry of Finance in London timidly informs his chief that the quality of Russian oats is "so inferior to the samples that the importers are

---

[1] Cf. *Official Messenger of Finances*, N. 19. Article entitled "The Egg Export Trade."
[2] *Declaration of the Correspondent of the Ministry of Finances of Graschdanin*, 12th April, 1889. All the Russian papers have discussed this subject *ad nauseam*. Last winter the demand for this manure to make the blend so agreeable to Englishmen was so great that prices rose to 8d. a bushel.
[3] *Novoye Vremya*, 11th September, 1889.

compelled to cut down the covenanted price as much as 9d. a quarter, and that this deduction is often increased to 1s. 6d. a quarter."[1] In 1886 some of the largest importing firms of England consulted together and resolved to avoid as much as possible purchasing barley from Russia, on the ground that in the consignments of barley sent from Odessa to England, a large quantity of earth was added.[2]

This is the highway of Russian commercial practice, of which the driest of official documents are the milestones. Whither it leads seems to interest least the persons whom it most nearly concerns. Lack of faith in Russian honesty, lack of trust in gaseous promises explains why so many foreigners have themselves gone to Russia to develop the resources of the country; why the linen and cotton of Poland are driving those of the Moscow factories even from the home markets; why the timber trade is managed by Englishmen, and the kerosene trade has fallen into the hands of a Swede and a foreign Jew. But even in Russia the shrewdest foreigner, assisted by native talent, is not always able to avoid falling into the innumerable snares spread on all sides of him. The laws are usually as powerless to help him as if they were written in dust or on the sand of the ebbing sea. The following typical instance of what traders — native and foreign — have to expect will astonish only those who have practically no knowledge of Russia or the Russians.

In 1889 the Berlin Timber Company floated down the Dnieper-Berg Canal an immense quantity of timber purchased for £30,000. It was overtaken by the frosts of winter and remained imbedded in the ice. The company were compelled to wait till spring, and meanwhile their agent, Herr Kuntze, came up periodically to inspect it. The first time he saw it he found everything in order; the second visit was equally satisfactory; but the sight that met his eyes when he arrived the third time made his hair stand on end: the timber, he found, belonged no longer to his company, but to a few obscure and utterly indigent Russian Jews. Herr Kuntze appealed to the authorities, consulted with the lawyers, but all of them declared, having been made acquainted with all the circumstances of the case, that the timber had slipped from the hands of the Berlin

---

[1] *Report of Agent of Ministry of Finances in London*, 6th April, 1889.
[2] Cf. *Kazan Newsletter*, 9th November, 1887.

Company and would never legally return to them. What happened was this: The logs being marked B., a famished creature named Begoon profited by the accident of his name also beginning with that letter. He simulated a quarrel with a beggar friend, to whom he pretended he owed 100,000 roubles. They referred the matter to a mock arbiter, and then asked the District Court to enforce his decision — namely, that B.'s property be sold and the proceeds given to his creditor. The order was made with unusual promptitude by the court, and the creditor having pointed out the frozen timber as portion of the Jewish beggar's property, it was forthwith sold for trifling sums to some friends of the two starvelings.

"Herr Kuntze was as pale as a sheet," says the sympathizing publicist, "his advisers excited, and the Crown lawyers sympathetic, but as, according to our law, there was neither crime nor criminal, no earthly power could avail to have the timber restored. One issue there is, and only one: Herr Kuntze might take a civil action and after endless delays might obtain judgment against the paupers for £30,000 and costs; but then he himself, found guilty of injuring the reputation of Begoon and his friends, who are legally innocent of any crime, would have to go to prison in consequence." [1]

Fraudulent bankruptcy is as much a recognized institution in Russian trade as credit, the Russians belonging to that class of persons whom Sir Philip Sidney described as "delighting more in giving of presents than in paying their debts." Most traders look upon it as the haven of safety into which they may run from stress of hard times; and even creditors, whose point of view is naturally quite different, regard it as a necessary evil and treat defaulting debtors accordingly. Thus it happens that a man who has performed what he deems his duty to himself and family by deliberately refusing to pay his creditors more than a few pence in the pound, sets up in business the day after it has been accepted, and is soon again trusted for considerable sums by those very persons whom he lately victimized. Thus some time ago a man named Liever — a wholesale colonial merchant — suddenly disappeared just when pay day arrived and his creditors sent in their bills. It was supposed that he had been foully murdered or had met with an accidental death. As it turned out afterwards, he was taking his ease at one of the railway stations, whence he opened negotiations with a view to bring

---

[1] *The Week* (*Niedielya*), 27th August, 1889; *Novoye Vremya*, 28th August, 1889.

about an amicable arrangement with his creditors, and when satisfactory results rewarded his perspicacity and duplicity, he returned to Odessa and began anew. That this did not hinder him from receiving credit again is plain from the statement of the *Moscow Gazette* that he had just failed once more for one hundred thousand roubles.[1]

It would require a volume rather than a review article to convey anything like an adequate idea of the singular methods employed by Russian merchants to supplement the proverbial slowness and meagreness of trade profits. They would seem to exhaust the possibilities of naïveté and criminality, nothing being too grotesque, nothing too dangerous to tempt their cupidity. A well-known merchant of Kieff thought it merely a clever stroke of policy to bribe all the telegraph messengers to bring him every telegram addressed to the business men in whose speculations he was interested. He paid one rouble per telegram, and having read, copied, and resealed them, he sent them to the consignees and used the information thus acquired for his own ends. He profited by this trustworthy source of information for two years, and would probably have continued to profit by it till his death, had the conspiracy not been discovered — by the merest accident.[2] The Exchange Committee of Odessa — a body of men obliged by the trusted position which they occupy to be above all considerations of a sordid nature — was found to quote the fluctuations of Russian funds so inaccurately as to cause bitter complaints to be made by the press as well as by the representatives of commerce. A year and a-half ago an official request was addressed to the persons responsible reminding them that their duty is "to announce the quotations correctly, *irrespective of the consideration whether anybody's interests are affected thereby*."[3] "The main evil of Russian society," says one of the Government organs, "is that it suffers from complete, absolute dissoluteness, recognizes no moral discipline, and has practically emancipated itself from duty."[4] At the trial of a railway servant for robbery, the prisoner — as is usual in such cases — confessed the facts rather than his guilt, and stated frankly as a thing of course that all the railway servants robbed, and that robbery

---

[1] *Moscow Gazette*, 2nd February, 1888. For another curious case, see *Novoye Vremya*, 1st March, 1880.
[2] *Kieff Word*, 17th April, 1888.
[3] Odessa newspapers *passim*, 10th, 11th, 12th June, 1888.
[4] *Graschdanin*, 6th October, 1889.

was thoroughly organized along the line, some stealing only manufactured goods, others leather wares, and others again corn, and so on, the rules of honor forbidding those who devoted themselves to the robbery of one species of property to encroach upon the domain of the others.[1]

The universality of these lax views of the rights of property, which in Russians are not identical with what we are wont to understand by criminal dishonesty, explains, though it does not justify, the feeling at one time freely expressed by the Austrian and, I believe, German press, that certain of the official representatives of the Empire must be as typical of the shortcomings of their countrymen as they obviously are of their good points. Now such vague and general arguments are apt to break down when subjected to serious criticism, and should never have been relied upon to support the sweeping accusations brought, for instance, against the present Minister of Finance, especially by the Austrian press, which reproduced strange rumors, dragged long-forgotten stories to light, and vamped up old anecdotes verified by no one, as soon as his nomination to the post he occupies was made known. The circumstances that M. Vyshnegradsky rose from the ranks like many great and good men, that pedagogy, his calling, is one of the least remunerative in Russia, that he changed irksome poverty into abundant riches rapidly, mysteriously, as by a magician's wand or an Aladdin's lamp, have no direct bearing on the question. Nor are the most circumstantial stories of shady practices conclusive evidence in Russia, where a good name is as superfluous as the qualities elsewhere needed to acquire it. More important than all this, though not by any means a clinching argument, is the undeniable fact that some years ago the doors of certain of the ministries were ignominiously closed to the man who now represents the finances of the Empire. I am personally acquainted with high officials who, without laying claim to exclusive or singular integrity, felt it incumbent upon them to deny him admittance to the departments under their direction, in the interests of the Government, its servants, and public integrity. Whatever species or degree of commercial cleverness this fact may imply is all that this writer can, with justice and truth, allow to be imputed to the present Minister of Finance.

These things, which need no commentary, throw a light on

---

[1] *Novoye Vremya*, 26th November, 1888.

the manners and maxims of the Russian people, which, were it not the direct outcome of undisputed facts, would seem too lurid to be credible to any but their staunchest friends or most malignant enemies. Nothing less convincing than a knowledge of these and similar facts — which are legion — could hinder an unprejudiced foreigner from largely discounting such sweeping statements as those made by Professor Kitarry, who in his lectures on commerce thus characterizes his countrymen: " Extortion and fraud have become the flesh and blood of the Russian trading class — to such an extent indeed, that an honest man *cannot remain* in that calling; he will be inevitably seduced in the long run, and little by little will himself become a model for others." [1] One of the latest of many curious exemplifications of the second portion of this assertion occurred a few months ago, when the salt of the earth, as it were, lost its savor. No one needs to be told that no more honest people than the Finns breathe the air of Europe. Yet the Russian Press unanimously informs us that the exemplary Finnish Railway Company of St. Petersburg-Halsingfors has lately been detected using false weights for the purpose of cheating the public who forward goods by that line, and that up to the time of the discovery, last April, they had succeeded in thus wrongfully appropriating 30,000 roubles.[2] So true is it that, as the Arabic proverb expresses it, he who passes through the onions or their peel will surely smell of them.

At the same time it should be remembered that there are whole communities in Russia, religious bodies separated from the Orthodox Church, but composed of genuine Russians, which are characterized to a man by the strictest integrity, whose word is a bond, and whose commercial dealings with their fellow-men are dictated by profound respect for the altruistic precepts and counsel of the Gospel. Take, for instance, the so-called *Sarepta Brotherhood*, whose head-quarters are in the Volga district, and who do a large business in St. Petersburg in the mustard, yarn, and woollen trades. These people are to Russia, in respect of honesty and single-mindedness, exactly what the Society of Friends was and still is to England and America. The same thing may be said of the thousands, nay, of the tens of

---

[1] *Memoir presented to the Minister of the Interior by order of his Majesty the Emperor concerning the Jewish Question*, p. 33.
[2] *St. Petersburg Leaflet*, 12th April, 1889; *Novoye Vremya*, 13th April, 1889; *Graschdanin*, 19th April, 1889, etc.

thousands of sectarians, called Molokani, Stundists, Pashkovites, behind whose yea and nay one need never trouble to intrude, and to whose promise alone one may tender a receipt. To trade with such men is a genuine pleasure, and to proclaim their existence — which is little less than heroic in Russia — a highly agreeable duty.

No man with the interests of humanity at heart will hear without profound regret, be he Christian or Atheist, that the religion which has effected this almost miraculous change in the Russian character is systematically proscribed and persecuted by the Government. Fortunately, Russian laws, which are calculated to render life an intolerable burden, are not generally obeyed nor strictly enforced. The people, adopting Frederick the Great's magnanimity towards the press, would say of their Government, that " it may say and write what it likes, on condition that we *do* what we like," and thus religious sects founded on the Gospel of Christ are rapidly increasing, and with them the number of men and women who put honesty above sordid gain and the momentary gratification of petty malice.

Chief among the oases of honesty consisting of Dissenters, naturalized foreigners, Russians educated abroad, and others, one naturally expects to find the intellectual class of the population, the natural Pillars of Society. Russia, however, is the country of surprises, and even these leaders of men, when weighed in the balances, are found sadly wanting. Thus, one of the best known litterateurs in Russia, a frank, wordy writer of independent judgment, whose name at times is not unknown to some of the readers of the *Fortnightly Review*, owes his first introduction to the Republic of Letters to a daring theft which he committed on one, of its presidents. As for the representatives of the Press, no characteristic of them which satisfied the exigencies of truth would fulfil the conditions of credibility unless the grounds for the opinion were first set forth in detail. The most popular newspaper in Russia is the *Novoye Vremya*, and its proprietor and irresponsible editor, M. Suvorin, has with impunity been made the subject of accusations which in any other country would either brand his name with infamy or send his accusers to prison.[1] In Russia it has done neither.

---

[1] *Odessa Messenger*, 22nd February, 1887; cf. also St. Petersburg *Novosti*, February, 1887. It is fair to say that personally I believe that if the case were tried in a Russian court of justice, M. Suvorin would be unhesitatingly acquitted of the charge.

The following illustration of the honesty of scientific men is too suggestive to be withheld. The eighth edition of a complete Dictionary of 115,000 foreign words incorporated into the Russian language was lately published in St. Petersburg. A gentleman bought it and counted the words. There were only 20,681, or less than one-sixth of the promised number! He then continued his researches into the history of the work, compiled by MM. Bourdon and Michelsohn, and dragged the following curious facts into the light of day. *All the editions* of this precious dictionary, which is the standard work on the subject, are revised and enlarged. It came out in 1873 for the *first* time as the *fifth* edition, promising the explanation of 30,000 words for 2¼ roubles. A year later the *fourth* edition was published, in which 32,000 words were said to be etymologically interpreted for the same price. In 1875 the sixth edition appeared, and the price was reduced to 1¾ roubles, while the number of words remained the same. In 1883 the ninth edition saw the light, and was sold for 4 roubles, and finally the last and best edition, namely the eighth (after the ninth), was brought out in 1888, in which 115,000 words are said to be analyzed and explained for 5 roubles, whereas in reality only one-sixth of the promised number is to be found, and one-third of the number said to be explained in the cheapest edition that cost but 1¾ roubles.[1]

Compared with such extraordinary doings, plagiarism, far from unknown even in Great Britain, sinks to the level of a mere peccadillo. Still Russian plagiarism would seem to belong to a different species from that prevalent in other countries. In England, for instance, the thought, passage, description appropriated without acknowledgment, but seldom without modification, is to the whole work in which it appears as a dew-drop to the ocean. In Russia whatever is plagiarized is rarely transformed, being usually offered, with its merits and blemishes just as it stands, for whatever it will fetch in the market. In 1888 Dr. Von Cyon, late Professor of Physiology in the Medico-chirurgical Academy of St. Petersburg, and a friend of the late M. Katkoff, published in Berlin a complete edition of his works,[2] among which is to be found an interesting research on the influence of change of temperature upon certain nerves of

---

[1] *Novoye Vremya*, 10th June, 1888, etc.
[2] *Gesammelte physiologische Arbeiten;* Berlin, 1888; pp. 138-143.

the heart, written, not by him, but by a M. Tarkhanoff.[1] "I
do not," says the real author in a letter to the Press, "set
any great value on this investigation as distinguishing it from
my other scientific works; but I have no right, I think, to
pass over this act of Dr. Cyon's in silence, considering its
important bearing upon the picture of contemporary scientific morals."[2] A similar "accident" happened in 1889
to M. Tolmakoff, who, according to the *Moscow Gazette*,
stole exactly ten-elevenths of his dissertation on the *History of Apiculture*.[3] Another case occurred a few months
previously of so extraordinary a nature that some of the
daily newspapers actually alluded to it in anger. "The
Russian professor," says the *Svett*, one of the organs of the
Slavonic Society, "works in the field of science just enough
to obtain his degrees, to seize upon comfortable positions,
lucrative chairs, and remunerative tuitions, and then lives
jovially ever after, teaching anything and anyhow. Hence
it comes to pass that, although our universities are provided with hundreds of professors, we have extremely few
genuine workers in the field of science. Lately a revolting
instance of this exploitation of science occurred in the St.
Petersburg University." It then goes on to relate how
Professor Morozoff published a book on the history of the
Russian drama, the best portions of which were surreptitiously taken from the rare work of a Moscow professor,
whose name he deliberately ignored. For this production
he demanded the degree of Doctor, and was on the point
of obtaining it, when the fraud was discovered. "What
are the students to do now?" asks the journal in conclusion. "Will M. Morozoff remain in the university, as professor, and how will his colleagues look upon the plagiarism?"[4] Professor Morozoff has remained at his post, and
is still there, contributing according to his lights to bring up
the young generation in the way they should go. His colleagues are mortal, and as such liable, like him, to err;
"instead therefore of casting the first stone at an erring
brother," one of them said to me in conversation at the
time, "each of us can say with a feeling of humanity —

"*Nihil humani a me alienum puto.*"

---

[1] *Novoye Vremya*, January, 1888, and *St. Petersburg Journal* (Russian), 25th January, 1888.   [2] *Ibid.*
[3] *Moscow Gazette*, 5th August, 1889; *Novoye Vremya*, 7th August, 1889.
[4] *Svett*, 1st November, 1888.

Russian lawyers as a body have not the shadow of a claim to be considered as exceptions to the general rule; they are emphatically of their age and country. In the report issued by the Council of the St. Petersburg bar for the year ending in March, 1888, consisting of 113 pages, eighty-eight are taken up with the enumeration of the disciplinary pains and penalties inflicted *en famille* upon members of the bar for misconduct. If we ask in what this misconduct consists, the report answers " in irregularities in money matters between them and their clients; in insults offered to them, their opponents, their colleagues; in the breach of the professional duties of a lawyer; in *desertion to the side of their clients' opponents;* in acts of fraud, such as abuse of confidence, operations injurious to the financial interests of their clients' creditors,"[1] etc., etc. I translate the following case, chosen by the press as most typical of these reprehensible doings, not adding a word nor excising an expression:—

"The Libau Romensky Railway Company were condemned to pay M. Z. 735 roubles damages for bodily injuries, and a monthly pension of fifteen roubles. The lawyer appropriated these sums to his own use, on which the client's wife appealed to another lawyer, M., entreating him to persuade Z. to hand over the sums in question. M. acquitted himself of this mission with success, but as it was afterwards proved, on the hearing of Z.'s suit, knavishly seized upon twenty roubles (£2), his alleged expenses for a journey to Moscow — a journey which he never made. It would be difficult to discover a sorrier piece of fraud, which *not* even *every* salesman would perpetrate. And yet the Council passed a resolution merely to administer a caution to this petty knave among lawyers."[2]

The following scene in a law court cannot fail to prove interesting to English readers, as characteristic of various things and people besides Russian lawyers:—

"A lad accused of stealing a cow endeavored to secure the services of a lawyer to defend him, and in the course of the negotiations admitted that he did commit the theft, 'accidentally somehow.' The lawyer named the fee for which his services were to be had, and higgled with the lad a long time before they both agreed upon seventy-five roubles (about £7 10s.). The day of the trial arrived. The accused appeared in court guarded. The counsel for the defence, knowing that his client was heretofore at liberty, was somewhat surprised at this, but accounted for it by supposing that the court had later on ordered him to be kept in custody. The court, however, turning to the prisoner, asked, 'Accused, why are you guarded?' 'I was caught in the act of stealing.' 'What! Before being acquitted of one theft you have already commit-

---

[1] Cf. *Novoye Vremya*, 10th May, 1888.
[2] *Novoye Vremya*, 10th May, 1888.

ted another?' 'What was I to do, your Excellency? He — the counsel, I mean — demanded seventy-five roubles for defending me. Where was I to get this money from?'"[1]

One can never guard too carefully against the strong temptation to generalize with which every writer upon nations and classes has to contend, and it is in the nature of things that accusations levelled against numerous corporations of men should be received with caution. Here, however, it is not a question of accusing individuals, much less whole classes of men; if anything, it is rather an indirect attempt to excuse them. It would be singularly exceptional, however, not to say miraculous, if a corporation, recently and accidentally called into existence in a society which has never stratified itself like other European communities, should profess and practise a system of ethics radically different from that adopted by the great bulk of the nation. The facts already detailed go far to prove the truth of this thesis. That these, of which they are but a specimen, are equally conclusive, is evident, among other things, from the following characteristic of Russian lawyers deliberately given by the most patriotic (in a Pan-Russian sense) and most popular newspaper in the Empire:—

"Perpetually occupied with money matters and financial interests, though completely lacking all respectability and moral footing, the contemporary jurisconsult of the corporation of lawyers falls more quickly than a prostitute strolling through the streets. . . . In need of profitable practice, of which there is a dearth just now, the modern jurist makes up for want of practice either by masked robbery, the levying of blackmail, or by forgery of financial documents."[2]

Magistrates, who in Russia discharge certain of the functions reserved in this country to judges, are on the whole the most high-principled men in the Empire. Their position is as difficult as a suspicious public, a distrustful Government, exacting and unscrupulous patrons, and frequent penury can make it. That they are not all as spotless as was Andrew Marvell under greater temptations, is natural; that so many of them have kept clear of open venality deserves far more credit than it has heretofore received. The following sketch represents one of those magistrates who scorn to lay themselves open to the charge of corruption, and yet in the

---

[1] *Diary of Saratoff*, November, 1887; also *Novoye Vremya*, 12th November, 1878.
[2] *Novoye Vremya*, 30th August, 1889.

interest of self-preservation would fain act upon the proverb which says that "Unless you stoop, you cannot gather mushrooms." It is taken from a St. Petersburg Government journal: —

> "A day never passes that this magistrate's district vassals do not bring in their offerings. But Ivan Yeroffeitch [1] is guided in such cases by thorough disinterestedness. For instance, a peasant brings him a wether. The magistrate exclaims proudly, 'I accept nothing gratis. Sophia (to the housekeeper), pay him 4½d.' Ten ducks are presented to him, and he instructs his Sophia to pay 3d., and the transaction is blameless in the eye of the law." [2]

In the Kratoyaksky district (government of Kharkoff) the entire Court of Appeal was brought up for trial some time ago on a charge — which was substantiated in court — of organizing trumpery cases against the railway company, drilling the witnesses and inducing them to commit perjury, and on the basis of that evidence pronouncing unjust judgments against innocent persons of means, for the sake of a paltry two hundred pounds to be divided among all the members of this numerous conspiracy.[3] M. Franzia, magistrate of the Ooglitch, who is also a publican, had no scruple to prosecute a rival publican, for some imaginary offence, and to try the case himself. The depositions of the witnesses, although favorable to the prisoner, did not prevent this publican-judge and plaintiff from condemning his rival to three months' imprisonment, or from artfully compelling him to sign a document in which he waives his right to appeal.[4] M. Volkoff, President of the Court of Appeal of the first instance, in Vinnitsa (government of Podolia) made a profession of selling justice — or injustice — to the highest bidders. His secretary kept by him a sheaf of receipt forms for loans, ready signed, and whenever a lawsuit arose that seemed to give promise of profits, this gentleman would call on one of the two parties, and having received what he considered a fair sum of money, would write a receipt for it then and there, setting forth the date and the sum received. In spite of these and innumerable other instances, however, it would be impossible to find a less corrupt body of men in Russia, and in seeking the explanation of this curious

---

[1] An imaginary name, but a real person.
[2] *Graschdanin*, 29th August, 1888.
[3] *Novoye Vremya*, 5th December, 1888. Cf. also *Svett*, 12th December, 1888.
[4] *St. Petersburg Russian Journal*, 21st October, 1887.

phenomenon, it would be extremely ungracious to lay too much stress on the abject poverty of the vast majority of suitors in the magisterial courts or on the indifference of the press to any but the most signal cases of glaring corruption.

The reputation of the rural courts for integrity leaves far more to be desired than that of the magistrates' courts, though even here the scale of judicial decisions is conducted with a certain rude dignity which excludes that higgling and bargaining which is of the essence of all commercial transactions in Russia. "In the public-house," says the *Graschdanin*, "justice is administered, or rather sold, and the court purchased. . . .' If you have recourse to the rural court without treating the judge to *vodka*, were your case incarnate justice and as spotless as the driven snow, it will become as black as a coal. Right will be found on the side of the gallon of spirits."[1]

It may be permissible to apply to the Courts of Orphans in Russia the strong but well-merited epithets used of the house of prayer in Jerusalem, and describe them as dens of thieves. The thefts committed in the Orphans' Courts, however, are explicable, excusable, almost justifiable; they are certainly quite as much a constituent part of the salary of the officials as *pourboires* are of the perquisites of the unsalaried waiters in large Continental hotels. The head of a department, for instance, whose office is permanent, who gives all his time to the work, and is practically precluded from seeking other sources of incomes, receives a very paltry salary for one through whose hands pass hundreds of thousands of roubles yearly, and who is compelled to pay fancy prices for food, lodging, fire-wood, etc. This salary is 8s. a month. His assistants receive about 4s., all told. No one will therefore be surprised to hear that these paltry shillings are made to go as far as the loaves and fishes of the Gospel miracle; they purchase comfortable lodgings, excellent board and clothing for a numerous family, Government scrip, country houses, and a competence in old age.[2]

No boy can pass through any of the Government grammar schools, or such high schools as the Lycæum, Law School, or Corps des Payes, without purchasing the goodwill of his masters and frequently of his directors. I know

---

[1] Cf. also *Svett*, 20th March, 1889, in which the curious ways of selling justice in open court are described.
[2] Cf. for instance, *Graschdanin*, 25th January, 1889. This, however, is a notorious fact, admitting of no manner of doubt.

scores of children whose parents pay yearly bribes to a little army of pedagogues, and I am acquainted with some parents who will never cease to rue the day when they resolved to set their faces against it. The Russian army has been praised by all the nations of the world, and deservedly so, and yet mere knowledge can no more qualify you to pass the examination for a commission than an Englishman's abstract right to become a member of Parliament can procure him a seat in the House of Commons. A friend of mine, whose intellectual gifts were as brilliant as his means were limited, set about entering the army a few years ago. He proposed to pass his examination loyally, not to purchase immunity — to imitate Arago, whose profound knowledge compelled the respect of hostile examiners. He confided his intention to a friend of his, who was an officer and an examiner, from whom, however, he received but cold comfort. No exception, he was told, could be made in his case, the utmost he could expect was to receive a considerable reduction in the prices. He was presented with the tariff containing these reductions, the literal translation of which is as follows:—[1]

Subjects.	Price. Roubles.	Subjects.	Price. Roubles.
Artillery	300	History[2]	
Fortification	200	Chemistry[3]	
Tactics	200	Christian doctrine	60
Topography	150	Statistics[4]	
Administration	25	Mathematics	200
Military Law	250	Foreign languages[2]	
Trigonometrical survey	25		
Russian language[2]	—	Signature ———	

Far more significant, however, than whole volumes of illustrative instances is the view taken of them by public opinion. Is dishonesty indignantly condemned? are those guilty of it rigorously excluded from such society as there is, their names gibbeted as a warning to others, and the application of legal pains and penalties applauded? Or do

---

[1] The original of this *naïf* document is in the possession of the editor of the FORTNIGHTLY REVIEW.

[2] As the teachers of these subjects were not military men, special arrangements had to be made with them.

[3] The examiner in chemistry was above bribery, nothing but genuine knowledge passing current with him. He made many heroic — and almost Quixotic — efforts to suppress the bribery system; but it would have been as feasible to suppress autocracy itself.

[4] For statistics nothing was demanded but an inkling of the subject.

people look upon such offenders with pity tinctured with that selfish *hodie-tibi-cras-mihi* foreboding with which old men receive the news of the death even of a stranger? Public opinion is practically non-existent in Russia. As the Empress Catherine truly observed to Princess Dashkoff in one of Landor's *Imaginary Conversations*, "Russia has no more voice than a whale." Still such unmistakable indications as do exist leave no doubt whatever that the average Russian is unconscious of anything criminal in dishonesty and double-dealing, and would feel it a hardship were he hindered from indulging therein. In a former paper we saw that robbery, aggravated by burglary and envenomed with the worst kind of ingratitude, was treated by the victim as a sort of practical joke which could not be permitted to come between him and his friendship for the thief. We have seen that the public press and the authorities have nothing worse than a good-natured smile for the story of wholesale robberies committed by the Courts of Orphans, as long as they do not attain the dimensions of a national scandal; and we have also seen that the Council of the Bar of St. Petersburg considered a fraternal caution punishment enough for a colleague guilty of embezzlement under circumstances which in this country would have caused him to be speedily disbarred by the benchers and imprisoned by the magistrates. The annals of every Russian court of justice abound in similar instances. A postman burns thousands of letters in the course of several years for the sake of the few stamps he steals from them. He is arrested, tried, and he confesses. But the jury acquit him. In 1888 T. Tschentsoff, a lackey in whom his master had unbounded confidence, realized his reputation for honesty by abstracting at various times during the twelvemonth 30,000 roubles, and losing them at a card-table in one of the clubs. He was tried on the 4th of April of the following year, when he pleaded guilty, confessing the details of the theft. Yet the jury found him innocent.[1] On the 26th of June, 1889, in the enlightened city of Kieff, a woman was tried for robbery. The case was simplicity itself. She had been arrested red-handed, with the objects in her possession. She was known, moreover, to be a notorious professional thief. Yet the jury saw so little that was reprehensible in

---

[1] *Graschdanin*, 5th April, 1889; cf. also other Petersburg newspapers of same date.

her acts, that they unhesitatingly declared her innocent. In Odessa another woman, also accused of theft under circumstances that left no loophole of a pretext, and upon evidence that no body of men outside Russia would refuse to convict upon, was as unhesitatingly acquitted by the jury.[1]

An equally clear indication is afforded by the press and the morals of its most accredited and trusted representatives, which must necessarily seem inexplicable to those Europeans who treat journalism as a priesthood, requiring a special vocation and calling into play the noblest qualities of head and heart. Such persons' sense of the fitness of things must receive a very severe shock at the thought that a vulgar thief, who emerges from the cells of a filthy prison, where for a twelvemonth he has herded with the scum of the earth, at once joins the ranks of this modern priesthood, is received with open arms, and forthwith sets about ministering to the spiritual wants of his fellow-men, letting that light shine before them which was so long under the bushel of a prison. In Russia such a spectacle is neither striking nor incongruous. Nay, such a journalist is as great a stickler for his honor as if he were a spotless Bayard.

"The correspondent of the *Odessa Messenger* at Orgheïeff, we read, S. Goldberg, described as having been frequently tried and found guilty of theft, is about to enter an action for libel against the editor of the *New Russian Telegraph*. M. Goldberg is desirous of proving publicly that he did not steal the goloshes of M. Trikolitch, and that he was not *frequently* found guilty of theft, but only once, for which he was imprisoned for eleven months and twenty days. Moreover, M. Goldberg threatens to publish a series of letters in his organ, the *Odessa Messenger*, to show that he was on the staff not only of the *Messenger* and of the *New Russian Telegraph*, but also of several other journals."[2]

Now, if this were an isolated fact, it would nevertheless imply a degree of ethical slovenliness in the representatives of the Russian press which could scarcely co-exist with the general prevalence in the nation of universally accepted views of morality. But it is not an isolated fact, but one of daily occurrence. Another journal published in St. Petersburg, discussing the morality of the Russian press and the antecedents of its representative men, remarks, "There are vast numbers of cases in which the editor is perfectly well aware that a certain member of his staff is a thorough-going

---

[1] Odessa papers of the 15th October, 1887.
[2] *Graschdanin*, 25th January, 1888.

rascal." "Why do you not dismiss him?" you ask. "He is a man of talents," you are answered. "But he is not an honest man," you insist. "What's that to me! I am not going to baptize children with him."[1]

Nothing is more significant, however, than the manner in which courts of justice condone, if they do not positively encourage, theft. We have seen with what indulgence Russian jurors treat it, as if they feared that this precious national characteristic were in danger of disappearing, and that their sacred duty was to preserve and develop it. The following instance took place in a court where there are no jurors, but only judges. Two young men of sixteen and seventeen years of age broke into a village shop one night and abstracted cakes, sweetmeats, nuts, and liquors, to the value of about 15s. to 16s. Part of the good things they consumed themselves, the remainder they hid away in the hay, bringing them forth when occasion required, to treat the lads and lasses. When brought to trial the president of the court asked them if they admitted the charge. They replied affirmatively. He then inquired whether they were possessed of sweet teeth. They laughed heartily, repeating the words "sweet teeth." They were then acquitted.[2]

It may be urged that some allowance must be made in such cases for Russia as a country that has not yet succeeded in shaking off the moral and intellectual fetters of barbarism, as a community holding views upon many questions of ethics as of politics diametrically opposed to those of European nations, and that under such peculiar circumstances this indulgent way of treating thieves, this justice that comes disguised in the form of encouragement may, after all, be productive of better effects upon men who are not malicious criminals than the cast-iron rigor of the cut-and-dried law of the West. All this may be granted — must indeed be granted, seeing that it is vouched for by undisputed facts; but then this is but another way of declaring the level of Russian morality, in the matter of honest dealing, of veracity in action, to be several degrees lower than that of the rest of the civilized world.

Nor can it be suggested that the juries who thus freely scatter certificates of morality, the judges who pass off robbery and burglary as a joke, the corporations and editors

---

[1] *Minute*, 23rd October, 1887. *Odessky Listok*, 29th October, 1887.
[2] *Northern Messenger*, January, 1889, p. 43.

who amicably associate with thieves, would modify their views, if they themselves had directly suffered from the dishonesty of those whom they thus take under their protection. Such personal considerations would not be permitted to have the slightest weight in modifying conceptions that are universal forms of thought rather than the result of a chain of reasoning. Of a hundred persons who have been robbed in Russia, though all might be equally eager to recover their stolen property, no more than twenty, if indeed so many, would wish to see the thief punished; and only very few even of these would go to the trouble of actively contributing to the realization of this object. They prefer to curse the thief, wave their hand fatalistically, and continue their way as before.

"In Saratoff on the Volga," says an eyewitness, "the steamer *Alexander II.* was about to start. It was crowded with passengers. All the first and second class tickets were sold, and in the third class there was no room for an apple to fall; the passengers, so to say, sat upon each other. After the first whistle the assistant captain, hurrying through the crowds of third class passengers, was suddenly stopped by a peasant. 'Your honor, the money has been found,' he said. 'Found! Where?' 'Sewed up in that soldier's mantle. I went over there to search for it, and sure enough there were forty-one roubles and a twenty-copeck piece,' said the peasant, brandishing a chamois-leather purse as if it were a war trophy. 'Where's that soldier?' 'There he is, asleep.' 'Well, he must be handed over to the police.' 'Handed over to the police! Why to the police? Christ be with him. Don't touch him, let him sleep on,' he repeated naïvely, good-naturedly adding, 'the money is found; it's all there.' And so the matter ended."[1]

But this perversion of moral sense is considerably emphasized when transferred from the offender's person to paper. The Russian is so hearty, so good-humored, so intensely human, that dishonesty seems in his hands only a distracted virtue. You catch him in the act, overhaul him, unabashed he confesses, sees nothing very objectionable in the deed, and is ready to sacrifice all his gains to put you in good temper. This trait of mere criminal *bonhomie* in all his dealings with the World, the Flesh, and the Devil should never be overlooked in estimating a Russian's character. He is no distressing moralist clamoring for a stringency in public opinion which he will do his best to evade; he asks no greater laxity than he will allow; and playing the game of life with cards in his own sleeve, he would only laugh if you are detected in a similar fraud.

[1] *Graschdanin*, 30th August, 1889.

Nowhere is the indulgence with which the people regard the gravest forms of dishonesty — robbery and burglary — so clearly, so unmistakably manifested, as in their solemn consecration, their elevation to the dignity of religious ceremonies, in the celebration of one of the most impressive popular festivals of the year. The feast is called Kuzminki, in honor of Saints Cosmus and Damian. It is usually celebrated on the 1st November, by a number of quaint ceremonies ending with a copious refection, in all of which only unmarried girls take part. In order to get together the refreshments which constitute an essential element of the feast, all the girls of the place rob and steal without exception. And not only do they steal from their parents and relations, but they extend the operation to perfect strangers, whose money, fowls, and movable property generally, they seize upon with that contempt of consequences which befits apostles of a religious cause. "The feast of Kuzminki," says a special writer on this subject, "is *wholesale robbery*. The lads also steal for it, giving the booty to the girls. They have no hesitation about using violence to all who resist."[1]

It has been pointed out more than once in the course of this book that there is a numerous minority of honest men who are neither sectarians nor Jews in this vast empire of dishonesty — men who deserve great praise for fortitude, and greater still for perseverance amid almost irresistible temptations, whose standard of morality is higher than the average standard in England, who would as soon think of cutting out their tongue as of telling a gratuitous or malicious lie, and who would die of starvation rather than defraud friend or enemy. It should not be disguised, however, that even they bear upon them unmistakable signs of the influence of the society in which their lot is cast; and while their own conduct may be in strict accordance with the highest principles of justice, their views of the differently shaped actions of their fellow-countrymen are determined by considerations wholly foreign and even hostile to all accepted theories of right living. "I have often conversed," says a Russian writer in a journal approved by the Government censure —

"I have often conversed on the subject of theft with men who are absolutely honest; but even they never once expressed that repugnance to lying which characterizes the way of thinking of civilized people.

---

[1] *Northern Messenger*, 1888, No. 12, pp. 61, 62.

An epically calm tone, smiles and laughter at the description of thievish conduct and at what they consider the ludicrous position of the victims of the theft, and a rapturous raising of the voice when detailing the deftness of the robber — that is all that I have observed during such conversations."[1]

This inconsistency is apt to puzzle the logical mind. But inconsistency, and even the simultaneous play of diametrically opposed tendencies, is to a much greater extent the basis of the Russian character than at first sight seems possible; and a noble deed is often the outcome of an irresistible and sudden impulse felt and acted upon the very instant after the will had deliberately approved and resolved upon a base treason.

This picture of millions of men and women wallowing in an ocean of moral ooze, wildly stirring up the muddy depths of unimagined baseness, while fighting life's battle on a false issue, is well calculated to evoke profound sensations, to leave lasting impressions. Those whom it moves to self-congratulation or to contemptuous pity would do well to reflect that the frequent back eddies of their own superior civilization are often mighty enough to be confounded for a time with the main onward current. The spirit in which these gaping sores of the Russian people are pointed out to the gaze of the curious world is identical with that which impelled the despairing and dying soldiers of Napoleon's army in Joppa to display theirs in all their disgusting nakedness — in the hope of touching the hearts of those responsible for such horrors, and inducing them to adopt some measures with a view to effecting their cure.

---

[1] *Northern Messenger*, 1889, No. 1, p. 49.

CHAPTER V.

RUSSIAN PRISONS: THE SIMPLE TRUTH.

THE views of that section of the British public which possesses, or thinks it possesses, the right to hold any respecting the advantages and the evils of the Russian prison system have, within the past few years, touched every extreme of admiration and loathing, and are now waiting, like Sacculinæ in search of crabs, for new facts to cling to. First we were treated to the views of an English clergyman, named Lansdell, who, after having rushed rapidly through a long stretch of country which he was credibly informed was called Russia, wrote several volumes on the land and people, breaking out into lyrism whenever he alluded to the prisons of Siberia. Then came Mr. George Kennan,[1] who, having taken the trouble to study the subject before writing upon it, has been engaged for over a year in piling agony upon agony, exhausting the resources of the English language in his search for words adequate to express his horror and indignation at the inhuman cruelty with which convicts in Siberia are treated, and which is erroneously supposed to be restricted chiefly to political prisoners. Lastly, we have an official representative of Russia[2] solemnly assuring her countrymen and the civilized world generally that the only trait in the Russian prison system calculated to astonish Englishmen is the excessive indulgence with which Russian convicts are treated — the kindness with which they are brought up by hand, as it were. No wonder that the bewildered British public is at a loss what to believe, and is desirous of unearthing some fresh facts, unvarnished by political prejudice and uncolored by personal feeling, from which it may be permitted to draw its own conclusions.

The object of this paper is to furnish them.

---

[1] Prince Krapotkin, who spoke *en connaissance de cause* and whose scientific accuracy and objectivity is beyond praise, was considered too deeply interested to be listened to with more than idle curiosity.

[2] Madame Novikoff has lately been appointed a member of the St. Petersburg Prison Board.

Like Mr. G. Kennan, I have been put in possession of ample, interesting, and trustworthy information about the latest phases of the so-called "horrors" by Russian friends, many of whom were at one time, and others of whom still are, exiles in Siberia. It is my intention, however, to withhold all such accounts, because their existence, vouched for by a person or persons unknown, might be denied or their significance belittled, as that of very exceptional incidents, by the Russian Government, with the ease and assurance with which Mr. Kennan's statements were contradicted; and the confusion would only be worse confounded.[1] Instead I have determined to rely solely on the authority of facts which will pass current with Russians themselves, because vouched for by loyal Russian officials who, occupying responsible positions in Siberia, or sent out there for the purpose of investigating the subject, have devoted years of unremitting labor to the study of the prisons, have drawn up reports, not about exceptional instances or "horrors" that occur once a year, or to one class of prisoners only, but concerning the general working of the entire system. These reports have lately appeared in print, with the sanction of the Government, thus becoming invested with an authority the value of which can scarcely be exaggerated.

Before proceeding, it may be well to clear the ground still further and say a word about motives. I am not one of those optimists who believe that diplomatic interference in the internal affairs of Russia, if possible, would be productive of any more good than could be effected on a vicious rhinoceros by painting its hide with jod. And even if it could, I confess I am not sufficiently in love with that rank Pharisaism which seems to be one of the main ingredients of the moral atmosphere of these islands to encourage Englishmen to monopolize the task.

---

[1] In the *Review of Reviews*, May, 1890, Madame Novikoff is represented as having explained away the so-called "Siberian horrors" by the phrase, "Every private blunder which deserves to be regretted and investigated is puffed up into a systematic and normal plan of action on the part of our administration" (*Review of Reviews*, p. 406). This magniloquence seems very nearly akin to that which made a Russian Slavophile, writing last year in the *Pall Mall Gazette*, during the Abyssinian expedition of the "Red Sea Cossacks," describe as "saintly sisters of charity, who were brutally fired upon by the French," certain women of very loose morals who attached themselves to Aschinoff's lawless marauders, and shocked the untutored Abyssinians quite as much as the harridans who accompanied the Christian warriors at the siege of Acre scandalized the Mohammedans. Surely better samples of saintly feminine virtue can be found in Russia than these.

Lastly, I would venture to point out that the almost exclusive attention paid in these questions of prison treatment to the hard lot of political prisoners, whom in Russia it is often difficult to distinguish from ordinary criminals, has the effect of narrowing the issue to an extreme degree, and making us entirely lose sight of the extent and the root of the evil. Moreover some allowance should surely be made for that peculiar irritation which the government of an autocracy must necessarily feel towards political conspirators who threaten its very existence, and who, before embarking in such unpromising ventures, may be taken to have carefully counted the cost. No state, ancient or modern, republic, monarchy, or theocracy, has ever shown much consideration for its political prisoners, and from the days of Darius Hystaspes, who tells us in his off-hand way how he mutilated and chopped up the malcontents who disturbed his peace of mind, down to the present year which has witnessed the death by flogging of Madam Sihida, there is little to choose in the way of clemency. For this reason I have thought it advisable not only not to restrict my remarks to the treatment experienced by political prisoners, as has been done by most of the writers on Russian prison life, but to treat the latter merely as a part, and a not very considerable one, of the vast army of criminal and innocent people of all ages and both sexes who are always brutalized and often tortured to death in the prisons of Russia.[1]

---

[1] If we can credit an extraordinary statement to which currency is given by the *Review of Reviews*—a periodical which apparently thinks that nothing can interest English readers more than detailed accounts of the sayings and doings of obscure Slavophiles—Madame Novikoff has publicly asserted in a Russian periodical that the sensational accounts of the treatment to which Russian political prisoners are subjected are based on deliberate, wanton falsehood; journalists, travellers, Members of Parliament, and Englishmen generally being condemned by tyrannical public opinion to lie in a gross, unjustifiable manner whenever they take to describing Russia or the Russians. A gentleman named de Windt, however, is one of the few just men who dare to shame the devil and speak the truth. This gentleman wrote a book in 1889, entitled *From Pekin to Calais by Land*, in which Madame Novikoff contends he has refuted "nearly all the Siberian horrors which at present ornament the pages of the principal English journals. Accustomed to English ways (in England people are hanged, almost every week), he cannot understand [I am quoting the *Review of Reviews*, May, 1890] *why Russians should show such compassion as they do to convicts*." Now the Siberian horrors have all reference to the sufferings of *political* prisoners, and turning to Mr. de Windt's book, p. 363, we find him saying plainly about them the very opposite of what is here attributed to him. He calls their prison, Kara, "a hell upon earth,"

"Our systems of prison organization and penal settlements," says a specialist of many years' experience, in a most interesting report on Russian prisons drawn up for the behoof of the members of the International Prison Congress now assembled in St. Petersburg,—

"our systems of prison organization and penal settlements are now passing through the third period of their evolution. The theory of brutal retaliation found expression in the damp and dark casements of the kingdom of Muscovy, in the torture, the splitting of nostrils and the quartering of prisoners; its influence, preserved in an epoch very nearly approaching our own, was manifested in slavery, branding, the knout and the *plète*.[1] Our present houses of detention and convict prisons are the embodiment of the theory according to which noxious members of society should be cast out and no further care taken of their lot."

There are four categories of prisoners recognized by Russian law, and it is to meet the requirements of these that the prisons are supposed to be constructed and maintained: 1. Those who are charged with having committed a crime, but may prove to be perfectly innocent of it (*slédstvennye*). 2. Persons detained "administratively," viz. (*a*) "political misdemeanants" not condemned by any court of law, but whom the authorities deem it desirable to deprive of their legal rights and to punish as convicts; (*b*) the members of tax-paying societies, such as the *Mir*, who have been ex-

---

Whenever he does express himself in favor of Russian prisons he expressly excepts political convicts and says, "Be it understood that I speak of criminals and not of political prisoners or Nihilists, to whom, notwithstanding all that ardent Russophiles may say, *Siberia is a veritable hell upon earth.* The Russian 'criminal' is exiled to colonize; the Russian Nihilist (*in most cases*) to die." The writer who defines this to be a "refutation" of the "Siberian horrors" would surely object to the commonly received definition of veracity. Whether Mr. de Windt's praise of the admirable treatment of common criminals in Russia is better founded than Captain Cuttle's keen appreciation of the worldly wisdom of the Bible as embodied in what he thought were Bible aphorisms, the reader will be in a position to judge later on.

[1] It may be well to give Mr. de Windt's description of this instrument, which he admits is still used: "It is a lash of twisted hide about two feet long, terminating in thin lashes a foot long with small leaden balls at the end; it is a terrible instrument, and one which, if severely wielded, often results in the death of a prisoner. From 25 to 50 strokes are usually given, but if the prisoner have friends they usually bribe the executioner to make the blow a severe one. A skilful flogger and one who wishes to make the convict suffer, draws no blood, for this has the effect of relieving pain. Commencing very gently he gradually increases the force of the blows till the whole of the back is covered with long swollen wales. In this case mortification often sets in and the victim dies. The *plète* is only used at Kara, Nicolaieff, and Sakhaliern, and then only very rarely and on the most desperate criminals." *Op. cit.* p. 415.

pelled by their fellow-members and handed over to the Government for deportation to Siberia, without being accused of any definite crime; (c) persons who have never been accused or suspected of any crime or misdemeanor whatever, but who are being forwarded to their native place at the request of relatives, guardians, or the authorities. 3. Convicts properly so called who are being deported in virtue of a legal sentence condemning them to live in Siberia, to colonize it, to serve their time in convict battalions, in penal servitude, or in a central prison. 4. Criminals who are undergoing incarceration as an independent species of punishment, to which they have been sentenced by the law courts for crimes ranging from common assault or larceny up to a wilful murder.

In theory, Russian prisons keep these four classes of persons quite separate from each other, and humanely provide for treatment varying in rigor in proportion to the degree of the prisoner's guilt. In reality the more brutal and casehardened a criminal is, the more consideration he receives at the hands of his jailers; the more savage and beastly his instincts, the greater his opportunities to gratify them.

"Everyone is familiar with the *ostrog* (provincial prison), the sight of which plunges one's soul into a sea of melancholy, and which is almost always the first thing that meets your eye when you enter a provincial city. This building is destined to serve as the temporary place of confinement for all gangs of prisoners that pass through the place; it has also to accommodate untried persons who may prove to be innocent of the crimes laid to their charge; and it is likewise the place in which are incarcerated all local criminals for the short periods of imprisonment to which they have been condemned. Hence each prison should be, and is in theory, provided with three separate sections corresponding to these three classes, in addition to which it is supposed to be divided into a male and female half. Lastly, the letter of the law requires that there should be a special wing for members of the privileged classes"[1]—

(nobles, tschinovniks, merchants, and ecclesiastics). Such is the theory, fair and humane, if somewhat complicated and artificial.

Simplicity is unfortunately the only merit that can be predicated of the reality, which is utterly at variance with the theory. "Provincial prisons are in the majority of cases so small and their financial resources so slender, that the

---

[1] Cf. "Report on Russian Prison Organization drawn up for the behoof of the International Prison Congress." *Law Messenger*, 1890, No. ii., p. 331.

more you divide them into partitions, the more each room looks like a dog-kennel in Naples."[1]

The most important functions of all are exercised by the so-called "Forwarding prisons" (*Peressylnye*), which have been aptly likened to prisoners' hotels, where meetings between the members of the entire criminal world are continually taking place. In any one of them you will find, especially during the period of winter confinement, representatives of all the peoples and tongues of the Russian Empire, men guilty of all categories of crime, and stained with every degree of guilt, convicted, suspected, untried, notoriously innocent.

A short summary of some of the official data published by the Russian Government in 1885 will enable us to form a more correct idea of the life that throbs within these terrestrial hells than any rhetorical description. During the year ending in 1885, in addition to the 94,488 convicts who remained since the previous year, no less than 727,506 prisoners arrived in the various places of detention in the empire. Of these 116,998 were deported convicts; 324,807 were criminals on their way to their respective destinations; 11,631 were prisoners of other categories, and "administratives," and 52,904 were of their own free will accompanying the convicts. That same year 722,021 were taken off the list, of whom 103,453 were exiles deported; 319,375 were being forwarded to various destinations; 10,939 were "administratives," and 50,054 were, of their own free will, accompanying their relatives, who were convicts. Consequently during that year there passed through the *étapes* and the various forwarding prisons of Siberia 506,340 prisoners.

When we reflect that a large proportion of this army of half a million criminal nomads — about 300,000 — are every year being sent backwards and forwards, we can form some idea of the difficulty of the problem which a humane Russian government will sooner or later be called on to solve. To regulate the conduct of legions of desperadoes who are here to-day and gone to-morrow is a task for the execution of which something more than good intentions combined with brute force is indispensable. The Central Prison Board, it should be said to its credit, has endeavored to induce the

---

[1] Cf. "Report on Russian Prison Organization drawn up for the behoof of the International Prison Congress." *Law Messenger*, 1890, No. ii., p. 331.

government to take some measures to mitigate the evils of the present system, and has among other things given strict orders that every forwarding prison should contain separate sections for convict families, much as zealous young country doctors occasionally insist upon an indigent patient purchasing beefsteaks and port wine, forgetful that he has not the wherewithal to buy even a platter of porridge or a meal of cold potatoes. There is not a prison in Siberia that does not contain from twice to four times the maximum number of prisoners for which it was constructed.

The effects of this overcrowding are far more horrible than anything that can be realized by readers who have never seen prisons on the associated system moderately filled. It is the cause of inconceivable human misery; the rooms are transformed into loathsome cesspools, hotbeds of every species of disease, physical and moral; the stench of the noisome air is intolerable; the clammy, clinging vapors which poison the body seem to eat into and dissolve the very soul; and to all these miseries is superadded a torture akin to that the mere anticipation of which seemed to Shelley's Beatrice a more terrible hell than any that priests or prophets ever conjured up to terrify guilty consciences with; the hated presence of human fiends, who are killing the souls as well as the bodies of the majority of the prisoners.

Internal prison control on the part of the authorities is a fiction; inspectors and inspected strike up an agreement in virtue of which the forwarding prison becomes, for the winter, a semi-independent oligarchy governed — or misgoverned — by a few desperate villains amongst the worst class of the so-called tramps.[1] These few ringleaders, resolved to live as comfortably as they can till marching time begins again, take the reins of government in their hands, organize and put in motion all the complicated machinery that takes every prisoner in hand and shapes his life and slightest actions, and, turning the prison into a hell, enjoy the rights and privileges of devils.

Their first step is to get storehouses in which all their contraband property is hidden whenever a sudden search is made, and the remarkable success which they usually attain in disguising these secret strongholds is due to an amount

---

[1] Tramps (Russice, *Bro-dyágh1*) are frequently the most desperate criminals of Siberia who have escaped and persistently refuse to give their names or disclose their antecedents. The law calls them tramps and treats them as desperate cut-throats.

of energy and inventive power which one seldom sees employed by free men engaged in the ordinary callings of life. A "good" prisoner is able, in a perfectly empty room, which has just been repaired, swept out, and put to rights, to stow away spirits, tobacco, tools, and even arms, and to hide them so effectually that their discovery can only occur as the result of treachery or of pure chance. Whole window-sills are taken to pieces, stone walls (when they exist) are scooped out to an incredible depth, planks in the floor are deftly removed, the posts that support the plank beds are drilled and made hollow — and all this is done so thoroughly, so artistically, as almost to defy detection.

"Thus in the Sterlitamak prison, in the year 1880, a convict named Sookatsheff *hid a live horse*, which he had unyoked a short time previously from the cart on which flour had been conveyed to the prison. All attempts to find it were fruitless. At last at the request of the inspector, Sookatsheff himself undertook to 'search' for it. He 'found' it, its feet tied together in the loft of a two-story house, the door of which was locked with the inspector's own lock."[1]

The next care of the members of the prison oligarchy is to establish regular communications with the outer world, mainly in order to smuggle in spirits, cards, tobacco, tools, and "materials." In this matter the warders and the sentries who guard the prison from the outside render them inestimable services. Wares that are not very bulky are brought directly into the prison, in spite of the circumstance that persons coming in are always searched; large objects are thrown over the wall at a place agreed upon beforehand, spirits being poured into tin vessels, which are rolled up in straw or rags and flung over. *Maidans*, or prison clubs, are founded for the sale of greasy cards, wet tobacco, and poisonous spirits; "common" fund is formed — always for the sole benefit of the oligarchs — from the monthly subscriptions, something in the nature of the "garnish" levied in old English prisons before Howard's time, which every prisoner who receives food-money is compelled *nolens volens* to pay, and from the exorbitant tributes extorted by barbarous methods from the unfortunate wretches who pass through the forwarding prison on their way elsewhere. One, and not by any means the worst, of these inhuman practices consists in compelling all new comers, even though they pass but one night in the prison, to pay *three roubles* (about

---

[1] *Law Messenger*, 1890, No. iv., p. 634.

seven shillings) for the use of the *parasha*, or night vessel.[1]
The oligarchs select a complete staff of officials to carry on
the work of "governing": "elders," "bakers," "cooks,"
"guardians of the *parasha*," etc., etc. Immorality is practised on a scale unsuspected in the very worst of over-civil-
ized European countries, and contemplated only in the penal
code of the Old Testament.[2] Were it otherwise one might
feel shocked enough to learn that not only do the prisoners
succeed by means of bribery, cunning, or violence in gaining access to the female half of the *ostrog*, but they also
organize, wherever possible, a Persian harem. Not only are
these things connived at by the authorities, but the prison
officials frequently outbid the convicts in unnamable immorality.

Lastly, a prisoners' committee of safety is formed — an
institution which, in some respects, reminds one of the
redoubtable Vehmgericht of the Middle Ages, terrible by
the absolute, uncontrolled power it wields, by the Venetian
suspiciousness with which it regards most men, and by the
inexorable cruelty with which its decrees are executed. The
life of every prisoner is in its hands. For acts which convicts call "light crimes," and free men term indifferent, seeing that they are devoid of moral guilt or merit, they are
beaten with knotted handkerchiefs; for treachery or even
neglect in executing commissions the penalty is death, and
the sentence is immutable as the laws of the Medes and the
Persians, and as sure to be carried out as a decree of fate.[3]

The so-called "Central" differs completely from the forwarding prisons — among other things, in that it is a strictly
"cellular prison." Judging by its results it might be aptly
termed a "soul-extractor"; it utterly destroys human per-
sonality. "All the customs, the personal characteristics, the
traits that distinguish a man from other men, are all annihilated after he has spent some time in the Central Prison,
where he becomes a mere thing, a number."[4] He is not
even so much —

"as a beast of burden, which is fed in order that it may work. In most
cases he has no work to do. He sits, or as the prisoners themselves
express it, 'he lies,' and this weight of idleness crushes him down infinitely more completely than the most grinding forms of penal servitude.
I saw many hardened criminals, who cared not a rush for their wives,
weep like little children when the latter refused to follow them to Sibe-

---

[1] *Law Messenger*, 1890, No. iv., p. 634. [3] *Ibid.*, 1890, No. ii., p. 324.
[2] *Ibid.* No. ii., p. 324. [4] *Ibid.* No. iv., p. 635.

ria.[1] I have also frequently seen prisoners who had served their time in the 'Central' and had recently been released: they were mere shadows, mannikins, automata wound up once for all — men they were not."[2]

When a prisoner, condemned for a long term,[3] has spent the third part of it in the "Central," he is deported to Sakhalien, which, bad as it is, is considered a most attractive place in comparison to the prison he leaves. There these "stupid living ruins" are left to their own devices, and expected to earn a livelihood by their own unaided efforts. It is scarcely surprising that they should rapidly develop into tramps.

"I have known cases of men condemned for short terms of imprisonment in the 'Central' exchanging their names with men under long sentences, allured by the outlook of passing but a third of the long sentence in the terrible 'Central' and of being then sent on to Siberia. Thus a man condemned for seven years (this is called a short term in Russian law), which he must spend at the 'Central,' willingly exchanges his identity with one sentenced to fifteen years, because he will have to spend but a third in the 'Central' and the remainder in Siberia."[4]

The following two typical cases may be taken to illustrate the working and the injustice of the system: Ivan and Peter commit equally grave or perfectly identical crimes, and both are sentenced to six years' penal servitude.

"Ivan happens to be married and his wife volunteers to accompany him to Siberia, in consequence of which, having worked hard for three years, say in the prison of Srednie-Karinsk, he continues to work at the same mines but not in prison during the second half of the sentence, living in a convict colony with his family. The unmarried Peter goes to the 'Central' and undergoes his sentence there; and if he survives it, is released with his soul crushed out of him and his body diseased, and is sent on to Turukhansk or some such place where there is absolutely nothing for him to do but steal and enter the criminal army of tramps."[5]

Such are the broad lines on which prison life in Russia is organized. If we now turn to the daily existence of the inmates of the forwarding prisons, in so far as that is the work

---

[1] An unmarried convict, or a married one whose wife refuses to follow him, and is therefore *ipso facto* divorced from him, is sent to the Central instead of to the mines.
[2] *Law Messenger*, No. iv., p. 635.
[3] If the term is a short one, viz., not more than for seven years, he spends the whole of it in the Central.
[4] *Law Messenger*, iv., p. 636.   [5] *Ibid.*

of their own hands, the spectacle that meets our eyes is one that would have sent a thrill of horror to the soul even of a Jefferies.

The *Maidan*, or club — and some prisons are provided with several — has a canteen attached, in which tea and sugar, cards, spirits and tobacco are sold at exorbitant prices. All the news is reported and commented upon in the *Maidan*, all questions of interest to the prisoners are discussed and solved there, and always in accordance with the wishes of the omnipotent oligarchs. The prisoners have numerous amusements in which they indulge by order of these ringleaders, and more barbarous, filthy, hellish pastimes it would be difficult to imagine. They cannot even be darkly hinted in a Russian review read only by specialists, and which publishes things which cannot be alluded to in this country. Among the few prison games that are not of this kind may be mentioned the " Belfry," which consists in the prisoners getting up on each other's backs in two rows, and every four such hauling up a fifth by the beard or by the hair of the head, and swinging him about like the tongue of a bell, crying out the while, " Bom ! bom !"[1] Another popular pastime is " Horse selling " : a convict is hoisted upon another's back and carried round the room, being mercilessly beaten with knotted handkerchiefs all the time. He often suffers quite as much from this amusement as from a sound flogging by the executioner. " The Prisoners' Oath " is a pastime which in cynical blasphemy outdoes all the others: it cannot be described. " The Sewing of the Caftan," by its obscenity and the exquisite torture it inflicts on the victim, has nothing else to match it."[2]

It is not necessary to have incurred the serious displeasure of the oligarchs to be subjected to these kinds of punishments. For " serious " offences death is the penalty, and the executioners do their bloody work with perfect impunity. In the prison of Tsh . . . . ski I saw a young man for whom they had " sewn the caftan " the day before, and I shall never, as long as I live, be able to blot out from my memory the image of that martyr's face ! He shortly afterwards died of the results.[3] " As a matter of course, the investigation that ensued brought nothing to light."[4]

If in the course of this or any other investigation a pris-

---

[1] *Law Messenger*, iv., p. 627. [2] *Ibid.*
[3] *Ibid.*, p. 628. [4] *Ibid.*

oner should say too much, if his reticence or his admissions compromise his fellows, if, generally speaking, he is of a talkative disposition, or a boaster, he is set down as a "heathen," and is mercilessly persecuted, beaten, tortured. If he informs on his colleagues, death is his portion, and the authorities are powerless to save him.

"No matter how well a spy is screened and protected in secret cells, his fate will overtake him sooner or later. The greater the injury he inflicted on the convict corporation, the crueller their vengeance. I was acquainted with a convict condemned to deportation to Eastern Siberia, who, for the sake of lucre, had informed on three of his companions. Thanks to the efficient measures taken to screen him he got as far as Moscow and in the Kolymashny courtyard was interned in a secret cell. That very night the lock was picked by some person or persons unknown and the spy beaten within an ace of his life. After several months of careful medical treatment he recovered and was forwarded on. In Kazan, in the forwarding prison he was tortured and would have been killed outright had he not been torn out of the prisoners' hands in time. Put in hospital under the doctor's care, he was poisoned and his life was with difficulty saved. He then feigned madness and was placed in the Central Hospital for the Insane, where, thanks to his extraordinary ingenuity, he succeeded in remaining for about a year. Sent on along with the first spring gang of convicts, he reached the forwarding prison of Tiumen, where he was crushed to death 'by persons unknown.' This is by no means an exceptional instance and the most horrible feature of such executions is that they sometimes take place on mere suspicion."[1]

One has no difficulty in understanding the reluctance of prisoners, under such circumstances, to complain of the pain and misery inflicted upon them by their brutal colleagues, who really rule them. They are as little disposed to complain of the abuses for which the authorities are directly responsible, some few of which it may be well to point out.

If in the first place we glance at the buildings — the *étape* prisons — we find that they are the most miserable lodgings any class of human beings has ever yet been housed in since the Troglodytes took to dwelling above ground. This perhaps is natural, seeing that the maintenance of the prisons is entrusted to unscrupulous petty speculators who receive from £35 to £45 a year for the work. One contractor will often include five or even more prisons within the sphere of his operations, receiving £45 for each. His part in the transaction generally ceases here, for he immediately cedes the contract to some still less scrupulous and more grasping

---

[1] *Law Messenger*, iv., p. 628.

village speculator, to whom he pays £5 per prison, thus gaining £200 without putting himself to the slightest trouble, or from whom he sometimes receives as much as £300 for ceding the contract.

" For it is a very lucrative occupation, the money being earned in two ways, by not carrying out the very moderate conditions of the contract, and by engaging in illegal business with the prisoners, selling them spirits, cards, tobacco, tea, sugar, needles, thread, meat, and the sinful human body. In one of the *étape* prisons of the Mamadyshevski District in 1882 there lived two cheap enchantresses. Generally speaking, everything is dear at the *étapes, except the human body.*" [1]

These *étape* prisons are horrid holes, utterly unfit for human habitation, and unworthy to serve for the housing of brute beasts. These words have the ring of exaggeration about them, and yet the idea which they are capable of suggesting to a civilized reader will prove but a pale shadow of the dread reality. When speaking of Russian prisons and Russian convicts, ordinary expressions fail to convey the meaning intended. Nor is it a question of mere intensity, but of kind. The song has to be transposed into a wholly different key. The dry matter-of-fact report from which I have been hitherto quoting speaks of the prison buildings in the following terms : —

" Nearly all the *étapes* of the Government of Astrakhan are filthy mud hovels, heated only during two months of the year, and then insufficiently and only with the roots and branches of a shrub called tshilishnik. Scarcely a single prison is provided with a female section, and when this section does exist it is a dog-kennel, a stable, a black hole — anything but a place to live in. The prisons themselves are at best mere dark, low hovels built to accommodate from five to six men, the cost of erecting them amounting to no more than from £10 to £15 each. The only place where I saw good prisons was in the Sterlitamak district. The prisons of the district of Tshistopol and part of the Laisheff district are well built, but kept in a disgustingly filthy state. The Podlessensky *étape* (district of Ufa) was a complete ruin, its stove crumbling to pieces, its roof fallen in, the earthen floor burrowed to such an extent by pigs that these animals came in freely from the streets to the prisoners' rooms. This was duly reported to the authorities, and when, several years later, I was again passing through the village of Podlessnoïe, I yielded to my curiosity to examine it. There were some traces of improvement; the roof had been repaired with tree bark, the stove, which had only been recently put up, smoked terribly, and the pigs of the place went on with their destructive work as before." [2]

It is no easy matter to realize fully what is meant by the words " insufficiently heated," that one meets with so often

---

[1] *Law Messenger*, No. ii., p. 343. [2] *Ibid.*, p. 342.

in these reports. "In the winter of 1882," says the same authority —

"in the Salikhovsky *étape* prison (district of Ufa) I was shown a barrel of water destined to be drunk by the prisoners; it was covered over with a large piece of ice that had become detached by thawing a little at the edges, and was five and a quarter inches thick. This barrel, I should mention, is *never* taken out of the room in which the prisoners live. This prison, like so many others, is only heated a few hours before the arrival of a convict party, and sometimes not even then, and when heated the stove yields more smoke than heat. The prison floor there was so rotten that one of the planks broke under me, and it was not without difficulty that I got my foot out of the deep hole that resulted. It was on this floor that the prisoners had to sleep, with absolutely nothing under them, for there were not even any plank beds. The 'Elder' of the convict party complained of the weakness of the bolts, etc., and, with two fingers of one hand twisted and bent with ease the *tin* bars on the windows."[1]

"On the premises of the Tshookadytamak *étape* (near Belybay) the prison warder lives with his family, and he uses the common room in which the prisoners sleep, eat, drink, and live as a *sheep-pen;* early in the morning, before the departure of the convicts, I myself saw that while the convicts were still sleeping on their plank beds, there were thirty head of sheep and goats quartered immediately under the plank beds.[2] The *étape* of the wealthy village of Alexeievsk (district of Menzelinsk) is situated in an underground cellar. The Uslonsky *étape* near Kazan is a mere wooden cage $19\frac{3}{4}$ feet square. It has no sections or partitions whatever, not even an ante-room; the floor is earthen. In March, 1882, a convict gang of twenty-seven prisoners and fifteen Cossacks arrived; the Cossacks were billeted in the neighboring huts, while the twenty-seven prisoners, thoroughly fagged out after a day's journey of 30 versts, carrying their effects along with them, were shut up in this dungeon."[3]

It is difficult to read the calm, matter-of-fact account of how these miserable wretches passed that terrible night without a shudder.

"They lay stretched out on the planks; they sat on their heels on the plank beds and under them; they stood up shoulder to shoulder on the ground from 7 P.M. till 8 A.M. A portion of the planks broke down; the windows had to be smashed in order to let in a blast of cold air; there was no fire in the stove, and the common night-vessel was standing in the room, but it was utterly impossible for any one to get near it."[4]

"It is not my intention," the writer significantly adds, "to give even an inadequate picture of some certain kinds of prison horrors. A glance at the official documents in the

---

[1] *Law Messenger*, No. ii.
[2] *Ibid.*
[3] *Ibid.*
[4] *Ibid.*

offices of the military commanders of the eight Volga Governments would be rewarded by the discovery of materials enough to fill up the outline."[1]

A Russian gentleman named Ptitsin was sent some time ago in a purely official capacity to Siberia, where he acquitted himself in a most conscientious manner of the difficult mission with which he was entrusted, carefully examining the prisons, many of which Mr. Kennan never saw. He drew up a lengthy report, which was duly pigeon-holed, as such reports usually are, part of which he recently published with the permission of the authorities, accorded with a very bad grace. This unimpeachable document is a complete confirmation of the report inserted in the *Law Messenger*. Notwithstanding the statistical brevity and lack of consecutiveness which characterize the style of both these documents, a few extracts from them is better calculated, I believe, to convey to Englishmen a correct idea of what prison life in Russia really is than the most vivid description given by the most impartial of their countrymen.[2]

All along the Yakootsk tract, M. Ptitsin virtually tells us, the Government really does nothing, or next to nothing, for the prisoners. Thus the cost of forwarding the convicts along this immense tract falls directly upon the peasants, who are as poor as country mice. It is they, indigent as they are, who have to build the prisons at every post station, and keep them in repair. That they fail, lamentably fail, to discharge these duties is natural, nay, inevitable; but, whoever is to blame, the victims are always the wretched prisoners. Take, for instance, the forwarding prison of Katschoog (236 versts from Irkutsk); the rooms there, M. Ptitsin affirms, have only single windows, although in the streets the mercury registers at times 79 degrees of cold (Fahr.), with the result that in one room built to accommodate forty men at most the temperature is 39° Fahr., even when one hundred persons are passing the night there. In Verkholensk prison, we learn from the same authority,

---

[1] It is very curious, that in the face of these things known and proclaimed even in Russia itself, men, and Englishmen, who know nothing of the language and customs of the country and, if possible, still less about its prison system, should solemnly assure us that "on the whole there is no doubt that the Russian Government treats its prisoners far better than we in England are inclined to give it credit for."— De Windt, *op. cit.*, p. 411.

[2] M. Ptitsin's account was published in the December issue of the *Northern Messenger*, a Russian monthly magazine which appears in St. Petersburg.

there are but two rooms, very low, eight arsheens (20 feet) long, and six arsheens (15 feet) wide. The prisoners receive fifteen copecks a day to live upon. They complained to M. Ptitsin that the jailer who purchased for them the bread on which they lived gave them a very bad quality, while the governor of the prison — a brutal peasant — beat them and their guards likewise most mercilessly in his drunken fits.

The Tiumen forwarding prison, a low hut constructed for the accommodation of twenty convicts, frequently contains eighty. Some of the prisoners whom M. Ptitsin found there *had no clothes*, nothing but their linen, and this in the month of February (1883). Thus he mentions the convicts Goosyeff and Goltakoff by name, whom he found in this pitiable plight. The authorities, questioned on the matter, informed him that they had sold their clothes; the convicts, on the contrary, assured him that they had been stolen from them. When the stove was heated many of the prisoners were asphyxiated, and were with difficulty restored to life.

The Karkinskaïa prison is a low unheated hut built for twenty men, but occupied by parties of from eighty to a hundred, who arrive every week. The convicts declared the Ponomareffsky prison a magnificent place by comparison, and yet they were squeezed together there like herrings in a barrel. To avoid death by asphyxiation the door was left open all night, although the thermometer registered 25° below zero (Fahr.).

From Gruznovsky Station (the seventeenth from Irkutsk) to the town of Kirensk on the Lena, an extent of 540 versts, there are no prisons, the convicts being quartered on the peasants. The forwarding prison of Ust-Kutsk has but two cells almost dark, which can accommodate three men each at a pinch. They do not possess a stove or other heating apparatus. There are generally five, sometimes, though rarely, ten men in each room, who remain at times as long as fifteen days. *No food whatever is allowed them, nor money to buy it. Every second day the jailer leads them to the village to solicit alms. What they get in this way is their only means of supporting life.*[1] When the prison can hold

---

[1] It is instructive, or ought to be, to note the light in which an Englishman, who could, had he wished, have studied the subject before writing upon it, puts this same fact mixed up with some fiction before his readers. "The criminals (as distinguished from politicals) have no complaint whatever to make as to food and clothing; each man has two pounds of black bread, three-quarters of a pound of meat, and a small allowance of quass

no more, the prisoners are quartered on the peasants, but as the latter discuss and deliberate, and squabble among themselves in choosing their prisoners (chiefly by their looks, each one anxious to obtain a convict who is comparatively harmless), the wretched exiles are left freezing in the open air, it may be *six hours* at a time, till some decision is taken.[1] In one party there was a woman with child. She was delivered in the cell. There was no help near and she died, leaving three small children, an old mother and her husband, all bound for Siberia.

It would be misleading were I to omit to state that at some places in the mines life, for the non-political convicts at least, is tolerable, almost human, by comparison with this, although they are compelled to work on Sundays and holidays.

The Sookhovsk forwarding prison, M. Ptitsin informs us, consists of two cells "almost pitch dark," made to accommodate ten men. *The majority of the prisoners live on alms alone.* The same story is told by the author of the report on the prison system which appeared in the *Law Messenger*. To begin with, we there read:—

"The prisoners *have no clothes to put on* them. I examined their linen, clothes, and boots in scores of provincial prisons, and I was always struck by impracticability in the conception and dishonesty in the manufacture of these articles of necessity. The underclothing was always old, torn, and with very faint traces of having been washed. The cut of it was invariably absurd: the drawers, for example, are sewn out of two pieces of cloth into a perfect triangle, so that unless you rip it up, it is impossible to get inside of it or put it on; the legs below the knees are uncovered; the shirts, not meeting at the collar even on the slenderest neck, leave the entire chest and the arms below the shoulders unprotected. The boots are mere slippers as shallow as goloshes. The clothing for the most part consists of one tunic, a parody on the Biblical tunic, which buttons nowhere, and in which no man can work. It is true that in the convict battalions cloth trousers and jackets are given, and convict gangs on the march are supplied with short overcoats and ear-coverings; but, on the other hand, it should be borne in

---

daily. This, it must be remembered, *is what the Government actually allows him* [italics mine]. He may make what he can on the road in addition to this by soliciting alms from travellers and caravans. . . . Imagine a convict travelling from Portland to Dartmoor being allowed to beg at the railway stations!" — De Windt, *op. cit.*, p. 411.

[1] "No travelling is done in winter," Mr. de Windt assures us. Now this is a very grave mistake. In Europe and Siberia they cease travelling during the wet season, which lasts from three to eight weeks. But in the interior of Russia, as well as in the interior of Siberia, convicts continue to journey on foot *during the whole winter*. Cf. for ex. the *Law Messenger*, No. iv. p. 638.

mind that the majority of prisoners in district and provincial prisons, both in the interior of the *ostrog* and outside of it, work in a frost of 58° Fahr.[1] And thus at last it comes to pass that a compromise is agreed to between the prisoners and their jailers; the convicts dress themselves, and the prison inspector continues to send in his accounts for the mending, washing, and repairing of clothing and linen which are really never repaired, washed, or mended."[2]

Concerning the question of food, the same authority writes : —

"I can safely assert that of the 100,000 inmates of Russian prisons *less than one-third live on prison rations.* Estimating at 10 copecks a day the money value of the food of each of the prisoners, this one item alone gives us more than two million roubles a year that are taken from the Crown and go to people who have no right whatever to appropriate it. In most of the prisons visited by me the rations are distributed as nearly as possible in the following manner: *to two-thirds of the total number of convicts nothing whatever is given.* On two-thirds of the quantity of food actually doled out only about one-fifth of the prisoners are fed. The remainder of the rations falls to the convict-bakers, cooks, tramps and other oligarchs. It can scarcely appear surprising under the circumstances that the ordinary prisoners (or *tsheldoni*), as distinguished from the ringleaders, have to make the best they can of hot water in which a grain or two of corn and a rag of cabbage are swimming about."[3]

In the Krassnoyarovsk forwarding prison, M. Ptitsin reports, "*one third of the prisoners receive absolutely no food*"; they live solely on what they receive in alms from the peasants, who are very little better off than they are themselves. The peasants bitterly complain of this, and also of the terrible responsibility that weighs upon them; for if a prisoner dies while he is the "guest" of a peasant, the latter has to pass through no end of circumlocution offices, leaving his work and incurring serious trouble and expense before the inquiry can be brought to a satisfactory issue. "There are often as many as twenty sick persons in a gang, but the peasants, apprehensive that they should die on the way, hoist the invalids into the tumbril and hurry them off to the next station, no matter what disease they may be suffering from;"[4] typhus fever, smallpox, or rheumatic fever.

"The Kirensk prison (974 versts from Irkutsk) is a wooden building surrounded by a palisade. It is so old and dilapidated that were it not propped up with wooden supports it would tumble down immediately. A convict stuck his finger into the wooden wall, into which it entered

---

[1] *Law Messenger*, No. iv. p. 625.
[2] *Ibid.* [3] *Ibid.* p. 626.
[4] Cf. M. Ptitsin's Report, *Northern Messenger*, December, 1889.

as into butter or soft snow, so rotten was it. The ceiling fell down in 1883 and buried a prisoner, who was fortunately dug out alive. The inspector complains that since 1882 the convicts receive no prison garb, no socks, no warm goloshes, *no clothes of any description, so that they can neither work nor walk.* The prisoners complained of the overcrowding of the rooms, so that they frequently have to sleep not only on the ground but *under* the plank beds: thus in room No. 1 six convicts slept *under* the plank beds; in No. 2 five; in No. 3 nine; in Nos. 4 and 6 eleven. There is no hospital; the sick are located in the civil hospital, which is described in the Governmental report as surpassing in filthiness anything that was ever seen or heard of even in Siberia. The floor of the corridor through which the patients have to pass to the water-closet is covered with a thick coating of ice which is soaked through and through with the foul liquids that flow from the watercloset, which is never cleaned. The sick and dying lie generally on the floor which is so thickly strewn with them that there is no passage through the room. There they lie crying and wailing, and complaining of their specific sufferings and of the cold — for they are almost naked and have not wherewith to cover themselves. The visitor standing in the room with his furs on and his head covered found the cold barely tolerable. One room was occupied by male and female syphilitic patients thrown together indiscriminately, and under a table in a corner of the room two small children, about two or three years old, were crawling about like little puppies. There was no room for them elsewhere. The convicts who come here have to remain in this corridor, as there is no accommodation for them in the rooms."[1]

On the 17th February, M. Ptitsin found 120 prisoners from Irkutsk there, of whom seven, down with typhus fever, were in the throes of death and three were frostbitten. They were all laid on the floor of that corridor. One of the party from Irkutsk died from the cold.[2]

The food supply, at all times insufficient, ceases altogether at times for several hundred miles at a stretch, which may mean some weeks, or even months. At Ulkansky, Krasnoyarovsky, and other stations, complaints were made to M. Ptitsin that convicts were sent up without warm clothes,

---

[1] *Northern Messenger*, December, 1889.
[2] Cf. M. Ptitsin's Report, *loc. cit.* In the light of the above it is entertaining to read the following: "Personally I would very much sooner undergo a term of imprisonment for a criminal offence in Siberia than in England." — *A Journey from Calais to Pekin*, p. 448. If the example of these two gentlemen, Messrs. Lansdell and De Windt, does not put the British public once for all on its guard against glowing accounts of Russian prisons, finances, universities, or other institutions, it richly deserves to be kept in that gross ignorance of everything Russian in which it has helplessly floundered so long. One cannot but regret the unjustifiable way in which a portion of the English press, working in the interest of cant, contributes to perpetuate this lamentable ignorance about Russia. Thus this morning's *Standard* (19th June, 1890), in a telegram from St. Petersburg, informs the British public that the International Prison Congress now sitting at St. Petersburg has proved a complete success!

and also without food or money to buy them. Nearly all convict parties from Kirensk to Wittim are forwarded *without any food supply whatever*. They live as best they can on alms.[1]

No wonder that the miserable men thus treated strip themselves almost naked, and part with their clothes to their fellow prisoners for a ridiculously small sum, and purchase food or temporary oblivion with the proceeds. This is frequently practised in the depth of a Siberian winter, when the mercury is at the bottom of ordinary thermometers, at depths undreamt of in England. The men who do this form a numerous class known as the "Naked People." M. Ptitsin met hundreds of them in Siberia; the peasant, he tells us, who has to take a number of convicts a certain distance on the way to their destination, is always in great dread lest the naked people should freeze to death while under his charge, so he throws a coat or a horse-cloth round them, puts a wisp of hay or straw next their skin to ward off the cold, and drives them in post haste to the next station, where, if he delivers them up with signs of life still discernible, he breathes freely once more, for the burden is then shifted on to another peasant. At Skokinsk and Rischsk, M. Ptitsin saw many such "naked people," who had sold their clothes and purchased food or drink, or both. In Ust-Kutsk, he assures us, "there are always several of them in each party who dispose of their clothes for money, get a few rags to hide their nakedness with, and put hay next the skin to keep the cold out."[2]

Between Gruznovsk and Kirensk, on the Lena, one is continuously meeting "naked people," dressed only in their shirt and drawers. If we bear in mind that the thermometer often registers as many as 35° below zero, and 67° below freezing point (Fahr.), we can understand why it is that some people die of cold. The old coat or horse-cloth which the wary peasant lends to the naked convict, he takes off him at the next station, leaving it to the peasant to whom he delivers him up to cover him up temporarily as best he may, and so the "naked convicts" are hurried along on tumbrils from station to station, till they arrive at Kirensk, where if delivered alive, they are soundly flogged for being without clothes.[3] In Surovsk and Diadinsk the same harrowing spectacle of naked wretches shivering from

---

[1] *Northern Messenger*, December, 1889. [2] *Ibid.* [3] *Ibid.*

the intense cold, some frostbitten, others perhaps dying, met the eye of the St. Petersburg official. "In the Su-. khovsk prison," he informs us, "by far the greater part of the convicts live solely upon alms." In the Potapovsk forwarding prison they receive neither money nor food, and each gang as a rule includes from four to ten sick men, besides many "naked people."[1]

Men and women, many of them as innocent of crime as babes, undergoing torture of this description, would be more or less than human if they failed to snatch at any opportunity that offered of drowning, even for a short time, their misery, and forgetting themselves and their environment, even though they should drift thereby into nameless crimes and hopeless insanity. The prospect of transitory oblivion is enough to buoy them up under the greatest conceivable hardships. "Generally speaking," says the matter-of-fact report published in the *Law Messenger*,

"prisoners and their jailers become reconciled to all imaginable privations and extortions, so that they be allowed to do just what they please. . . . The forbidden fruit of the prison (the *vodka* with its foul-smelling fusel oil) is transformed by their imagination into a heavenly nectar, and it must be admitted that Russian prison life is in the last degree desolate and weird for people with sober brains. At first the money given for food (whenever money is given) is spent in the purchase of spirits, afterwards the prisoners' clothing is disposed of, and then both guards and convicts go begging for alms. . . . Thus the day is spent and night draws nigh, and the *étape* prison is metamorphosed into a terrible hell upon earth. The poisonous fumes turn every one's head. Neither age nor sex is recognized or respected in the wild glutting of brutal instincts. Every attempt at resistance is speedily overcome by dint of blows of the fist and strokes given with the butt end of rifles. If during the scuffle a convict runs away, on the morrow a general hunt is organized, *and the wretch when caught is beaten to death. It also comes to pass, as in Orenburg in the spring of 1881, that when those who run away are not overtaken, one or more of those who remained behind are deliberately killed, and a report drawn up setting forth that 'three ran away, shots were fired at them, and one of the three was killed, while the other two escaped.'* "[2]

---

[1] *Northern Messenger*, December, 1889.

[2] "Accustomed as he is to English ways," says Madame Novikoff approvingly of Mr. de Windt (I am quoting textually from the *Review of Reviews*, as I have not been able to procure the journal in which that lady wrote her article), "he cannot understand why Russians should manifest such compassion as they do for criminals." Quite so. If they murdered a few thousands more (of the most wretched) every year and put them on the list of prisoners shot while attempting to escape, they would not be laying themselves open to an accusation of deeper immorality than at present, and they would assuredly have a somewhat stronger claim to be termed compassionate.

"During these nocturnal orgies the manager of the *étape* is occasionally attacked for his extortions or for cheating at cards, and the frightful scenes that occurred in Alexeïevsk are rehearsed."[1] Sometimes skirmishes, or rather real battles, occur between prisoners and soldiers, the latter laying siege to the *étape*, and many are wounded, mutilated, killed, as happened at Alexeïevsk. "I visited this prison a week after this had occurred (it was in 1883), and I saw all the traces, still fresh, of a regular siege."[2]

But are there not such institutions, one may ask, as Prison Boards? Are there not humane prison directors in Russia, where only one year ago men like Galkin-Vrasky were exhausting the resources of a rich tongue in eulogies of John Howard and of Venning, and were discussing with scrupulous minuteness the application of the very latest discoveries of science to the amelioration of the unhappy prisoner's lot? The answer to this pertinent question, in so far as it is not implicitly contained in the foregoing, may be given in the unimpassioned words of the specialist, whose report appears in the *Law Messenger*:—

"The Prison Board belongs to the number of those collegiate institutions which exist solely on paper, and the members of which, to use a popular expression, are strollers. The members of this Board, each engrossed by his own private affairs, meet together at a fixed time on the days on which the Secretary has prepared the reports, drawn up without previous consultation or discussion. . . . They then hastily sign these dry documents, and hurry away each to his own concerns."[3]

Another great impediment to prison reform, if the Government were seriously minded to undertake it, is the reluctance of the prisoners to utter a complaint against their jailers, who often treat them like vermin, or against their fellows, who

---

[1] *Law Messenger*, 1890, No. ii. p. 344.

[2] In 1883 there was a battle, or rather a series of them, between convicts and soldiers at the prison of Alexeïevsk; it was stormed at last after a regular siege. Are these things usually reported and commented upon in this country by zealous travellers anxious to spread among their countrymen the truth about Russia?

[3] *Law Messenger*, No. ii. p. 334. This being so, one is at a loss to understand why certain English journals were lately so ecstatically jubilant on learning that Madame Novikoff had been appointed a member of the Prison Board of St. Petersburg, seeing that she has so little opportunity for ventilating her humanitarian views. At the same time it seems doubtful whether and to what extent Russian prisons would benefit by the application of the ideas of a lady who, knowing her own country as she does, is yet profoundly convinced, that compared with the treatment of prisoners in England, that of convicts in Russia sins on the side of leniency and tenderness.

can maim, wound, torture, and kill them with perfect impunity. "It is a Herculean feat," we read in the report which has been largely quoted,

> "to prevail upon any one to utter a complaint in prison. The prison inspectors connive at much, and allow the 'oligarchs' to do just what they think fit with the ordinary convicts (Tsheldoni). And thus it happens that while these fellows are eating to satiety, smoking, playing cards, and drinking till they fall helpless to the floor, and have free access to the female section, the unfortunate man who will be set free perhaps to-morrow (and is not a convict at all), has to endure the pangs of hunger and cold, to go about almost naked, and to live worse than any beast of the field."[1]

Every inmate of a Russian prison is well aware that to prefer a complaint would not only not have the effect intended, but would not fail to work woe to the complainer. The Prison Board, it is true, has imposed on the Police Superintendent, or the Ispravnik, on the local doctor, the assistant procuror, and the justice of peace the duty of visiting the prisons, in addition to which the governor and the procuror go whenever they feel disposed and see for themselves.

But whenever any of these personages is about to visit the prison, his intention is known beforehand, and " both prison authorities and convicts combine to hide all signs and traces of the scandals that are continually taking place among them, 'so as not to make fools of themselves.'" To this course they are impelled by admitted solidarity of interests, and so they hide not merely the *vodka* and cards, but even the teapots, the cups, nay, their own shirts and other harmless objects. The mutual dissatisfaction of jailers and prisoners is smothered for the nonce, and "'We are all well satisfied with everything, your nobility,' is the unanimous cry with which the humane visitor is greeted."[2] A prisoner foolhardy enough to introduce a discordant note into this sweet harmony would soon lose his voice and his life to boot. Positively inhuman tortures beyond anything here described are needed to rouse up the prisoners and make them stand up in their genuine shape and form and give expression to some of the thoughts that are crowding their minds.[3] "The Governor of Toblosk," we read in the *Novoye Vremya*,

> "lately made an inspection of the district cities and volosts, and rumors of his intended visit reached the parties interested as early as January (1890). The administration of the district was up and doing. For

---

[1] *Law Messenger*, No. iv., p. 626. [2] *Ibid.*, No. ii., p. 334. [3] *Ibid.*

weeks before the time fixed for the visit, messengers and couriers were unceasingly rushing about on horseback from the district cities to the volosts and back again, delivering the most stringent orders, and directions about the clearing of the streets, etc., and, *above all* (this was the chief burden of their message), *commanding that under no circumstances should any petitions*, requests, or complaints about the administration be allowed to reach the ear of the highborn visitor." [1]

That complaints when made, inquired into, and found just prove as effective as would be the whistling of jigs to a milestone, is apparent from the solemn statements of every man and woman who has ever spoken *en connaissance de cause* of Russian prisons, whether as a servant or a prisoner of the Russian Government.

"The complaints of many provincial doctors (who visit the prisons in an official capacity), concerning the injury inflicted on the health of convicts by the mode in which they are confined, and the abnormal conditions of their existence, remain a voice crying out in the wilderness. Cases have come under my notice where this conscientious discharge of the duties imposed upon them by the law, was 'recorded against the doctor as a proof of his disloyalty.'" [2]

"I was present at one of the official visits of the Government procuror," says the same author, "and when the cabbage of which the prisoner complained was by his order brought before him, and he saw with his own eyes that it positively teemed with worms, I *heard him command the prisoner to eat them up*." [3]

The sensational element in all this, if it be found to possess one, must be admitted to be inherent in the facts themselves, which are certainly striking, even should it be proved that the miseries described are inflicted on abandoned wretches in whose souls the most approved purificatory processes, human or divine, would fail to leave the slightest residuum of truth, honesty, or humanity. This, however, is so far from being proved that the contrary is most frequently the case. It is perhaps needless to insist on the circumstance that the usual crimes and misdemeanors for which men are sent to Siberia or to prison are scarcely heinous enough to justify their being treated worse than destructive vermin. But even if they were, the justification of the Russian authorities would be as far off as before; for it is unfortunately a fact, and a lamentable one, that tens of thousands of inno-

---

[1] *Novoye Vremya*, 8th April, 1890.
[2] Cf. *Law Messenger*, No. ii., p. 335.
[3] *Ibid*.

cent men and women, known and *officially* acknowledged to be innocent, who were never charged with, nay, never suspected of crime, subjects of the Tsar supposed to be in the full and perfect enjoyment of those extensive civil rights of which we have heard so much of late, are subjected to the worst forms of the treatment described above.

Let me explain what must seem to English readers a riddle or a joke. There are many members of the *Mirs* (peasant societies who till and own land in common), who for no more serious misdemeanors than that which caused the Greeks to ostracise Aristides are expelled from their community, without trial or accusation, and sent to Siberia by the Government acting on the suggestion of the *Mir*. The judicious distribution of a cask of *vodka* by a rival is sometimes quite sufficient to ruin an unoffending man in this way; and even this is not always needed. The expelled peasant is then deported to Siberia along with cut-throats and highwaymen, shut up with them in the forwarding prisons for months, for years, starved, sent on for hundreds of miles, naked or nearly so, crushed down by the privations and restrictions for which the prison authorities are responsible, and tortured still more acutely by the inhuman ruffians into whose uncontrolled power the authorities hand him over. Whether he lives or dies under this treatment no man cares.

But it is not of the hard lot of these people that I speak. Nor yet of the thousands of innocent men and women who are kept languishing in the prisons described for long years, until at last the judgment day arrives and they are proved innocent. They are subjected, exactly like condemned felons, to the treatment just detailed, which were it practised in Africa or connived at in Armenia, would speedily call forth all the latent horror of which a correct English public is capable.[1]

---

[1] I trust it is needless to dwell on the circumstance that this paper is written from a humanitarian and therefore a purely objective point of view. It is certainly not meant as an indirect glorification of English humanitarianism. Englishmen, it must be admitted, are rarely in love with their own laws and customs; but those who happen to be, and who feel flattered by the contrast afforded by the present record of Russia's doings, should remember that in England there are occasionally abuses to reform even in the prison system. The following is doubtless an isolated instance and was speedily remedied, but this is no reason why it should be wholly lost sight of: "Shocking Treatment of Prisoners. — Mr. Justice Wills, at the Leicester Assizes, yesterday, called attention to the disgraceful treatment of prisoners at Leicester Castle. He said he was painfully surprised to learn that persons waiting for trial were confined in boxes which were 2 feet by

But, terrible as their lot is, it is not even of these people that I am speaking, but of a very numerous class of men and women, boys and girls, who are wanted by the authorities (not on account of crime, but for other reasons — to give evidence, for instance) — or sent for by their own relatives; or simply because they have accidentally mislaid their passports, or are kept a week or two without them by the greedy official (the village *pissar* or secretary), who is waiting for a larger bribe. All these people are imprisoned, starved, tortured, precisely in the manner described above; they become subjects of the oligarchs, are whipped, beaten, killed; their sufferings are nowhere recorded. The Russian law calls them "persons accompanying convict parties, not in the capacity of prisoners." This sounds incredible. It is grimly true.[1] The following is one of the innumerable ways in which it comes to pass.

A peasant leaves his home to seek for work as a field laborer wherever he can find work to do, and, like every Russian, male and female, he takes his passport with him, which is quite as much a part of him as his soul is. It is always a half-yearly passport, which he must renew at the end of the six months, sending it home in a registered letter to the *pissar* of his native place, and enclosing the legal fee and something over for the trouble. The time of renewal draws near; the workman gets a letter written to the *pissar* of his commune requesting a new passport. The *pissar*, like the god Baal in Elijah's days, is pursuing, or is on a journey, or, peradventure, he sleepeth, as most Russian officials do, and must be awaked. Whatever the cause, he does not send the passport in time. The honest working man, who is earning his bread in the sweat of his brow, and by the practice perhaps of exceptional sobriety is trying to earn a pittance for his family, is suddenly arrested and "sent home by *étape*" — that is, is flung into a forwarding prison, whence he emerges to join one of those convict parties just described which contain the cream of criminality, and is ground down and made to suffer hell's torments before he gets home. When he arrives he gets his passport, and is a free agent

---

1 foot 8 inches. It shocked his sense of justice that they should be rendered miserable in cupboards in which no lady would hang her dress. It must be done away with, as it was intolerable that human beings should be shut up in places which were unfit for the accommodation of dogs." *Daily Telegraph*, November 30, 1880.

[1] Cf. *Law Messenger*, 1890, ii., p. 336.

once more, a loyal subject of his little father the Tsar. M. Ptitsin informs the Government that when he visited the Markovsk prison in February, 1883, all the prisoners there were confined only for passport irregularities.

Take another case. The daughter of a Russian official wishes to study medicine and obtain a midwife's certificate. Her father discourages her in every way; but in vain. She leaves home without his permission, and goes to one of the university towns to study. Her father writes a letter to the police, asking that she be sent home at once, and she is sent as a convict; hungry, naked, insulted, deflowered, in time only her dead body reaches her native place — perhaps not even that.

Or take another case: A soldier is sent by the Government to serve at Ak Boolak or some such place, thousands of miles away from his native village. He is married and thinks that life with his wife near him would be more tolerable than it is without her, and he requests the authorities to forward her on. They accede to his prayer, arrest the soldier's wife forthwith, and put her in prison till a convict party is organized, which she is sent to join; she becomes one of this dreary family, travels several thousand miles by *étape*, sleeps under plank-beds, is maimed, insulted, violated; this goes on for months and perhaps years, during which she cannot take a step without her guards until she reaches her destination.

"Unfortunately she does not always reach her destination; many a soldier's and priest's wife arrives in such a pitiable condition that she has nothing for it but to lay violent hands upon herself. When we undertook to Russianize Central Asia thousands of soldiers' wives were thus forwarded by *étape* from all parts of Russia to their husbands. Hard by Orenburg there is a little bridge across the river Sakmar, and many a soldier's wife has cast herself from it headlong into the river below, in order not to show herself to her husband, in order to escape from consciousness of her miserable existence after passing the terrible nights that she has experienced on the *étape*."[1]

"A peasant woman named Avdotya was sent in the same way, by *étape*, through the prison of Yelets to her native village of Berezovki (Kozinski district). One day she was found hanging from a piece of ribbon behind the door in the cell of the Serghievsk volost board (Yelets district). The guard on duty, who a few moments previous was chatting with her, while he was lighting the stove, had only gone for a moment to another room and, returning almost immediately, found her hanging. Instead of cutting her down at once and giving her assistance, he ran off, terrified at the sense of his responsibility, to fetch a vil-

---

[1] Cf. *Law Messenger*, No. ii., p. 337.

lage policeman and then to inform the hospital doctor. By the time medical help came it was fruitless. The motive for the suicide was the following: — Towards the end of August the deceased, along with several inhabitants of her own village, set out on a pilgrimage to Voronesh — a distance of sixty to seventy versts. On arriving they all repaired to the monastery, except Avdotya, who, lingering in the rear, got separated from her companions, who had her passport for safe keeping. Not possessing this important document, although it was in the hands of her friends, who were only a few miles off, she was taken up and put in prison, and sent home by *étape*. At last the wretched woman, having marched from prison to prison for about a month, reached Serghievsk (distant only from sixty to seventy versts) with unmistakable indications of unsound mind."[1]

"In the autumn of 1882, in the city of Astrakhan, the police arrested three workmen on the landing-place because they had not their passports on their persons. They were all three of them Russian peasants from the district of Laisheff. One of them had been ill, and had thus allowed the term for renewing his passport to expire; the two others had done their duty by sending the old one to the volost board in due time for renewal, inclosing the legal taxes and fees. These assertions of theirs were not, and in such cases never are, believed (nor verified). They were sent by *étape* to Tsaritsin, where they were kept in prison one whole month, waiting for the formation of a convict gang, of which, when organized, they were sent to form part. The gang was detained at so many junction roads on the way, that they did not get to Moscow till January, 1883. Here they were confined for several months, till a Siberian party was organized, and with whom they were sent to Nischny Novgorod. In this city the breaking up of the roads in spring kept them and their convict gang back for a considerable time, and it was only in May that they reached Kazan, where they were again confined in the forwarding prison: after which they were sent on to Laisheff, and thence to their native volost. When they arrived there the *pissar* told them that their passports had been already sent to Astrakhan for them, and that he would give them no others. So they had no option but to wait here till their passports came back from Astrakhan, and it was only in June, 1883, that they were free to return to Astrakhan, where they found themselves exactly at the starting-point where they had been nine months previously."[2]

These men had been robbed by the convicts with whom they were forcibly associated; an unnamable crime had been committed upon one of them, a young fellow of seventeen. They complained to the authorities, but they might as well have poured forth their complaints to the icy wind that blows from the Arctic Ocean. "I saw these men," says our authority of the *Law Messenger*, "when they were on their way from the Kazan forwarding prison to Laisheff; they were mere shadows of human beings."[3]

---

[1] Cf. *Law Messenger*, No. ii., p. 337.   [2] *Ibid*.
[3] *Law Messenger*, No. ii., p. 338.

Another class of innocent men who have to pass through this infernal ordeal are the unfortunate soldiers who, being sent from one place to another for service, or returning home when it is over, are forced to herd together with convict gangs and march on by *étape*. And lastly, any one, whether he have his passport or not, may, if any member or members of the police like to make him feel what they can do, be sent to his native place in order to verify his identity. The following instance will leave no doubt as to what is meant by this curious operation, and as the names and places are given, it may serve as a test case:—

"A priest's son, Hyppolit Krassotsky by name, educated in the Ecclesiastical Seminary of Nischny Novgorod, had taken up his permanent residence in the government of Ufa, where he served at first in an office under the crown, and afterwards became a clerk and manager on the estates of Colonel Paschkoff, and the former minister of the interior, General Timashoff (both these gentlemen are still alive; the former is said to be now living in London). After this he was appointed secretary of the District Court of the Justices of the Peace, and was confirmed in this post by the *Governor of Ufa*. Every one in the entire government of Ufa knew him perfectly well. And yet the police Ispravnik in 1880 conceived the plan of verifying the identity of this man. M. Krassotsky handed in his passport, his photograph, the affidavits of many persons and institutions who knew him both in the government of Ufa and in Nischny Novgorod. But the Ispravnik declared it desirable to apply to him a measure at that time temporary, *but now the law of the land*, namely, to send him by *étape* to his native place, in order to verify his identity. Krassotsky was arrested and the day was fixed for his deportation to join the ruffian gang, when the governor to whom numerous and energetic representations had been made, graciously dispensed him from going."[1]

"I know of nothing more helpless and hopeless than the existence of these unfortunate persons who accompany convict gangs 'not in the guise of prisoners.' I know of nothing more horrible than the treatment which they receive at the hands of the authorities and from the ringleaders of the prisoners, both on the march and in the prisons; for they have to submit to imprisonment on their way like the rest. They are pariahs among the offscourings of the criminal world, who insult, degrade, rob them, and do them all manner of violence. At night they are cast out of the plank beds and forced to sleep under them, on the cold, slushy, or frozen ground. The old men among them are beaten, the old women scoffed at and insulted, the girls and boys are violated and abused by convicts and guards alike."[2]

These things are hard facts, which need no commentary. They cannot be denied or explained away and no pæans sung to Howard's memory at the Prison Congress should cause

---

[1] M. Krassotsky is still living in Ufa.
[2] *Law Messenger*, No. ii., p. 336.

them to be forgotten. If those English optimists who eulogize Russian prisoners are aware of them and continue as ecstatic as before, the matter passes naturally from the hands of the logician and moralist into those of the psychologist.

RUSSIA: AN ODE.

(Written after reading E. B. Lanin's account of "Russian Prisons.")

I.

OUT of hell a word comes hissing, dark as doom,
Fierce as fire, and foul as plague-polluted gloom;
Out of hell wherein the sinless damned endure
More than ever sin conceived of pains impure;
More than ever ground men's living souls to dust;
Worse than madness ever dreamed of murderous lust.
Since the world's wail first went up from lands and seas
Ears have heard not, tongues have told not things like these.
Dante, led by love's and hate's accordant spell
Down the deepest and the loathliest ways of hell,
Where beyond the brook of blood the rain was fire,
Where the scalps were masked with dung more deep than mire,
Saw not, where the filth was foulest, and the night
Darkest, depths whose fiends could match the Muscovite.
Set beside this truth, his deadliest vision seems
Pale and pure and painless as a virgin's dreams.
Maidens dead beneath the clasping lash, and wives
Rent with deadlier pangs than death — for shame survives,
Naked, mad, starved, scourged, spurned, frozen, fallen, deflowered,

Souls and bodies as by fangs of beasts devoured,
Sounds that hell would hear not, sights no thoughts
    could shape,
Limbs that feel as flame the ravenous grasp of rape,
Filth of raging crime and shame that crime enjoys,
Age made one with youth in torture, girls with boys,
These, and worse, if aught be worse than these things
    are,
Prove thee regent, Russia — praise thy mercy, Tsar.

II.

Sons of man, men born of women, may we dare
Say they sin who dare be slain and dare not spare?
They who take their lives in hand and smile on death,
Holding life as less than sleep's most fitful breath,
So their life perchance or death may serve and speed
Faith and hope, that die if dream become not deed?
Nought is death and nought is life and nought is fate
Save for souls that love has clothed with fire of hate.
These behold them, weigh them, prove them, find
    them nought,
Save by light of hope and fire of burning thought.
What though sun be less than storm where these
    aspire,
Dawn than lightning, song than thunder, light than
    fire?
Help is none in heaven: hope sees no gentler star:
Earth is hell, and hell bows down before the Tsar.
All its monstrous, murderous, lecherous births acclaim
Him whose empire lives to match its fiery fame.
Nay, perchance at sight or sense of deeds here done,
Here where men may lift up eyes to greet the sun,
Hell recoils heart-stricken: horror worse than hell

Darkens earth and sickens heaven; life knows the
    spell,
Shudders, quails, and sinks — or, filled with fierier
    breath,
Rises red in arms devised of darkling death.
Pity mad with passion, anguish mad with shame,
Call aloud on justice by her darker name;
Love grows hate for love's sake; life takes death for
    guide.
Night hath none but one red star — Tyrannicide.

III.

"God or man, be swift; hope sickens with delay:
Smite, and send him howling down his father's way!
Fall, O fire of heaven, and smite as fire from hell,
Halls wherein men's torturers, crowned and cowering,
    dwell!
These that crouch and shrink and shudder, girt with
    power —
These that reign, and dare not trust one trembling
    hour —
These omnipotent, whom terror curbs and drives —
These whose life reflects in fear their victims' lives —
These whose breath sheds poison worse than plague's
    thick breath —
These whose reign is ruin, these whose word is death,
These whose will turns heaven to hell, and day to
    night,
These, if God's hand smite not, how shall man's not
    smite?"
So from hearts by horror withered as by fire
Surge the strains of unappeasable desire;
Sounds that bid the darkness lighten, lit for death;

Bid the lips whose breath was doom yield up their
    breath ;
Down the way of Tsars, awhile in vain deferred,
Bid the Second Alexander light the Third.
How for shame shall men rebuke them ? how may we
Blame, whose fathers died, and slew, to leave us free ?
We, though all the world cry out upon them, know,
Were our strife as theirs, we could not strike but so ;
Could not cower, and could not kiss the hands that
    smite ;
Could not meet them armed in sunlit battle's light.
Dark as fear and red as hate though morning rise,
Life it is that conquers ; death it is that dies.

ALGERNON CHARLES SWINBURNE.

CHAPTER VI.

SEXUAL MORALITY IN RUSSIA.

THE most didactically moral of Russian novelists has just succeeded in shocking even his friends by completing his indictment of the civilized world in the *Kreutzer Sonata*, a work of almost repulsive pessimism.

He has, it is argued, taken as types exceptional instances of sensual barbarity, and founded a theory of humanity on a few of its foulest members. Were that so, there would be ground for complaint; but, in fact, Count Tolstoï speaks for the halves of two continents, and speaks from the profoundest knowledge; for though he sees the rest of the world through the air of his country, he scans everything within it with unflinching and unfailing exactness.

With his conclusions we have nothing to do; but for the proportions and accuracy of his premises this article, which was in type some months before Lev Nikolaïevitch (Count Tolstoï) read his tale to a Russian audience, will avouch; and if not always with sufficient distinctness, it must be remembered that the tenderness of English vision compels one to print cautiously from so dark a negative, and, besides, there is no aspect of civilization more difficult to discuss and analyze from an ethical point of view than that which deals with the relations of the sexes to each other; the delicate handling at all times required by this thorny subject becoming an almost impossible *tour de force* when it is a question of depicting a state of things for which the English expressions have grown somewhat obsolete, and the English imagination has become too rigid and unbending. For the most accurate judgment upon Russian society from this point of view would be Gibbon's summary sentence upon that of Gaul under the Merovingians: "It would be difficult to find anywhere more vice or less virtue."

At first sight this would seem to run counter to ordinary experience, which goes to show that chastity and the kindred virtues are encouraged and fostered by the adverse conditions inseparable from the lower forms of social life, such as prevail in Russia; by the joyless existence of men engaged in a hard and precarious struggle for bare necessities, rather than by the ease, refinement, and comfort of advanced civilization. But the contradiction is more apparent than real, for sexual immorality in Russia is not the outcome of the same psychological process, is not accompanied by the same misgivings, succeeded by the same pricks of remorse, nor socially punished with the same obloquy and ostracism as elsewhere. It is one of the ordinary incidents of an unchequered life, like marriage or the measles. Whenever the force of evidence compels us to abandon this explanation and seek for another, we can safely have recourse to the probable hypothesis of an abnormal psychical state—a plea to which many intelligent Russians proudly lay claim as to a sort of national birthright.[1]

Instead therefore of poring over the pages of Congreve and Wycherley, as Elia was wont to do when desirous of taking an airing beyond the diocese of strict conscience and of respiring the breath of imaginary freedom, one need only to come to Russia. In both worlds one essential element of morality is wanting, namely, consciousness on the part of the actors that they are breaking through religious restraints or moral laws.

The foreigner who visits Russia ignorant of the language and the people, as are most, has little difficulty in gleaning data enough during the first few days of his sojourn to enable him to gauge with tolerable accuracy the abyss that separates Russian notions of morality and decency from those which prevail in the West. He has only to glance at that ever-open book, the street, which exerts a much deeper and more abiding influence upon the education of the populations of towns and cities than pedagogues or moralists are given to believe. "It is the street that infects," said M. Zola once, speaking of his own country; "vice is rampant in the streets, and is there seen and touched, and its contact is corruption." However true this may be of French cities, we are forced to admit that it is a perfectly accurate

---

[1] In Russia, where obscure and imaginary mental ailments are, for all legal and most practical purposes, confounded with insanity of behavior, the word *psychopath*, meaning a person who enjoys all the rights of a sane man and many of the privileges of a lunatic, though coined but a few years ago, is most extensively used by all classes of society. So many persons now describe themselves as *psychopaths* that it no longer confers upon them the least distinction.

description of Russian streets, which reek with unnamable corruption and foulness.

Vice in its myriad guises, or in its repulsive nakedness, is forever before the wondering eyes of children, who wither away by touching it as from the poisonous shade of some strange upas-tree. Sins against the ten commandments, and even monstrous crimes specified in detail by the circumstantial law of Leviticus, are oftentimes committed in the squares, the parks, the streets, and even in the shadow of churches. Should the eye of a conscientious policeman descry the abomination he considers that he has done his duty if he shouts at the offenders to move on, accompanying his censure with a string of objurgatory phrases which the most reckless of French realists would not dare to cast before his readers. These sights touch and taint the imagination of the young: excite within them a prurient curiosity about things they should not know, and make them fancy all nature as depraved as man.

It would be exceedingly misleading, however, to gauge the moral standard of any people by the unbridled debauch and brutish sensuality that prevail in populous cities, which in the purest of kingdoms are often hotbeds of vice. Sodom might be the capital of a modern Arcadia, and Babylon the metropolis of an empire with the chaste Diana as protectress; the frightful excesses focussed together in the capitals being no more typical of the manners and morals of the nation as a whole than the leper settlement of Molokai is a trustworthy exponent of the health of the bulk of the Sandwich Islanders. In Russia it is otherwise. The specific difference between that and other countries consists in the universality of the phenomenon. It is confined to no age; restricted to no class; typical of no profession. It is as national as the language or the music, and characterizes the peasant and the merchant to the full as completely as the members of the aristocracy, who have ever been a law unto themselves. Nor is there anything very surprising in this. The upbringing of those classes which are subjected to educational processes is, in truth, as little conducive as the street training of the poor to those conceptions of duty and obligation, to that practice of discipline and self-mastery which alone render possible a high standard of sexual morality. It is conceived in the same narrow spirit without relation to family, society, country; consisting mainly of unconnected scraps of doubtful information upon a very wide range of topics patched together without any intelligible purpose. That careful gentle training of the tender soul in the practice of self-restraint, love of truth and justice : those painful prunings and clippings of the early desires branching forth in all directions, which give moral strength and elevation ; that ennobling of the affections and gradual widening of the sympathies of youths brought up as befits the heirs-apparent of the accumulated wealth of humanity, in fine all that loving care, those wise maxims, and the still more efficacious preaching of example which modern pedagogues understand by education, are still unknown in Russia. The Russian grammar-school is little more than a machinery for bringing to bear upon children, in smaller doses perhaps than the parish schools, the influences of the streets. A lady, who has devoted the greater part of her life to the work of education, as directress of a girls' gymnasy, or grammar-school of the Ministry of Public Instruction, lately published a book on female education in Russia, in which she deliberately affirms that the foul atmosphere of the street and the market-place has invaded the school-rooms of young ladies ; and after giving proof of the criminal precocity of these young ladies in walks which in this country would necessitate their immediate removal from a grammar-school to a penitentiary, she tells us that these future mothers oftentimes spend their evenings in low *cafés chantants*, where " they conduct themselves loosely — indecently." [1]

Now, when the keystone is thus unfitted for the important part it has to play, what can be expected of the other stones destined to compose the broad arch of morality? Still, in spite of the force of such evidence, it would be unfair to suggest that this is the uniform character of all such establishments in Russia, or that the effects of the pernicious influence to which girls are undoubtedly exposed are invariably as mischievous as they might be. There are exceptions, providential escapes, miraculous justifications of the Russian *avoss* (mayhap) in the annals of education as well as in those of railway disasters. The distance between potentialities and their realization is considerable even in the sphere of vice, and should be liberally allowed for by readers disposed to launch into generalization. Some of the best and noblest types of Russian women—and they are among the noblest and most charming to be met with in the civilized

---

[1] Cf. *Graschdanin*, 14th August, 1888.

world—have passed through such schools, which require to be removed from the baneful shadow of Government interference if they are to lose those characteristics which are positively pernicious; although it would require much more than this to enable them to satisfactorily discharge the objects for which they exist — to unfold and foster the noblest instincts of female nature.

With what criminal neglect must not the education of mere boys be conducted if one may judge by the demoralization introduced into that of tender girls, destined, if poets speak truly, to twine the fragrant roses of heaven round the prickly thorns of human life! As a matter of fact, many educational establishments, especially Government boarding-schools, were a few years ago hotbeds of the most disgusting forms of vice, many of whose youthful inmates could have learned nothing new from the most corrupt of Eastern debauchees. Those unnatural relations which Moses visited with death, are not rare in Government boarding-schools, military, naval, and other, in which the children of the highest dignitaries of State are brought up. It is right to say that individual members of the Government have lately taken measures to check the spread of this evil. But very vigorous efforts must still be made, and a considerable time must yet elapse before these establishments become completely harmless — a rather curious ideal for educational institutions. In 1887 I asked an official of the Ministry of Public Instruction whether his long and varied experience tended to confirm this view of Russian boarding-schools. He replied in the affirmative, and communicated many characteristic facts in support of this opinion, which I am debarred from repeating here. As he went on to speak with the warmth and emphasis of conviction, I thought it safe to put the question, "Where are your own children being educated?" "In these very establishments that I am so bitterly inveighing against," was the smiling answer. My features assuming the expression of interrogative surprise, he went on to explain: "I am too much attached to them to send them abroad; my means are not sufficient to allow me to suitably educate them at home. I have therefore no alternative. Fortunately I am somewhat of a Fatalist, and my apprehensions are allayed by the reflection that children, like nurses in fever hospitals, are so constituted as to belie the forecast of science. Some never take the infection; others catch it mysteriously, as if it were sent directly by some invisible Apollo. Some, nay many, children remain untainted in spite of constant bad example; in others vice seems inborn."

Home influence, it is true, can always be utilized as a corrective, and may frequently act as an antidote against the strong poison of schools and streets to which the children are so continuously exposed. That it is so employed, at times with almost miraculous results, is evident to those who know the country. But not nearly often enough. Fatalism, reinforced by the lessons of bitter experience, has stamped into current belief the mischievous idea that private enterprise and effort in any cause are always as superfluous as they are frequently dangerous. And where more hopeful views prevail the parents are often utterly disqualified to have hand or part in the education of their children; for the union of excellent intentions with erroneous ideas is as baleful as deliberate perversity. I knew a widely respected Russian gentleman who took his son — a boy of between fifteen and sixteen — to a disorderly house, introduced him to the inmates, and bade him return whenever his inclinations prompted him. When telling me, in his son's presence, of this feat of moral sanitation, as he thought it, he seemed to regard it as the conscientious fulfilment of a clearly defined duty, not perhaps calling for exceptional praise, but still a proof of considerable enlightenment. My disapproval, expressed in no measured terms, elicited from my host, among other unconventional remarks, the statement, which he afterwards enabled me to verify, that this is no uncommon practice in the country. This is very shocking, no doubt, from an English point of view, but is it wrong, judged by a Russian standard? "Quando enim hoc factum non est?" the Russians may truly ask with Cicero, "quando reprehensum? Quando non permissum?" Why, he may insist, should the considerations of time, place, traditions, public opinion, moral ideals that render these views and practices blameless in Cicero, Cato, and their contemporaries, lose their force when applied to modern Russians? And it is somewhat difficult to suggest a satisfactory answer.

"No one interested in the welfare of our young generation — and who that loves his country is not so interested? — can look without a feeling of profound melancholy upon its appalling moral condition," exclaims a Russian publicist. "And, worst of all, it is impossible to foresee the end of this miserable state of things or to hope for a speedy change for the better."[1] Who is it to come from? The parents? The family? "It is certain," we are assured by a publicist in the *Novoye Vremya*, "that the majority of families to whom higher education is accessible have not the dimmest notion what education is."[2] Another writer, who treats this subject in a Government organ, affirms that those families in which the children are morally and irremediably wrecked by the criminal conduct of the parents are to be counted by "hundreds of thousands."[3] There is very little then to be expected from home influences. We have seen the tendency of the schools. It only remains to be noted that most of the acts of the Government in connection with education, whatever their real objects, have tended to demoralize the young generation. During the past few years, for instance, the *personnel* of most of the gymnasies and high schools has been changed and "weeded" of men of science and principle who were suspected of harboring liberal notions. Their places have been taken by individuals who endeavor to make up for the intellectual and moral qualities of their predecessors by immoderate zeal for autocracy. The nature of the influence of the new men upon the youths confided to their care may be imagined from the value they set upon good example. The following sketch is taken from a Government organ, and cannot therefore be suspected of exaggeration. In the district of Starobelsk,

"The educators of youth walk about in broad daylight in the public places with their mistresses on their arms, although provided with lawful wives. And this in presence of their pupils. *We are nowise surprised that society should look with friendly eyes upon such doings;* but it is surely unseemly that the director of the Gymnasy and the parents of the children should show themselves so thoroughly indifferent to the public profligacy of the trainers of their children."

In this way, long before the youth is sent into the world to fight his own way, his soul is swept and garnished by parents and pedagogues, and made ready for the reception of a legion of unclean devils. This accounts for the remarkable precocity in vice characteristic of too many Russian chil-

---

[1] Cf. *Graschdanin*, 3rd April, 1889.
[2] *Novoye Vremya*, 22nd September, 1889.
[3] *Graschdanin*, 3rd April, 1889, in an article entitled "The Modern Family."

dren, to which no European country supplies a parallel. Thus criminal *liaisons* are often contracted between school children at an age when German boys and girls are still firm believers in the Klapperstorch theory of the perpetuation of the human race, and English youths and maidens too much absorbed by marbles, tops, dolls, and hoops, to need any theories, mythical or physiological, on the question. When, therefore, we read of the trial of a schoolboy of sixteen for cleaving another child's skull "over a love affair," inflicting wounds which the physicians described as incurable, we are no more surprised at the origin of the assault than at the outcome of the trial. The prisoner, having been *found guilty* of wounding with intent to inflict grievous bodily harm, and of having disabled his victim for life, the court thoughtfully adjourned the case for a fortnight, to give him time to accept or reject the terms offered by the prosecutor — a full pardon and legal impunity in consideration of a payment of twenty-five roubles (about £2 10s.).[1]

If, as an English philosopher laid it down, the greatest of faults is the consciousness of none, it would go hard with Russians, who are seldom troubled with misgivings.

But fortunately for them, circumstances which would intensify guilt in one stage of social progress annihilate it in another; and what is gross immorality in England or Germany would be mere blameless pleasure in Russia. A partial test of the truth of this thesis is afforded by whole categories of acts which are reprehensible from two different points of view: first, as clashing with certain precepts of honor generally recognized in other countries, and also as violating the indefeasible rights of others. In Russia these acts derive their ethical coloring exclusively from that one of their tendencies by which the rights of others are affected; and whenever the axiom *volenti non fit injuria* can be applied to this aspect, all more delicate criteria are brushed aside, and the misdemeanor becomes a perfectly legitimate transaction. The ceremony of public betrothal, for instance, still frequent in the middle and lower classes of Russian society, is clearly understood not only to confer certain rights upon the bridegroom, but likewise to impose upon him certain obligations, mainly of a negative character, in the interests not merely of an individual but also of society.

---

[1] *Graschdanin*, 16th September, 1889.

In Russia these duties are frequently shirked with the implied consent of the party in whose sole interest they are erroneously held to be imposed, and I know one case in which the consent was plainly expressed; the bride herself, the daughter of a wealthy merchant, being solicitous that her future husband should remain absolutely free from fetters until the marriage ceremony should solemnly deprive him of his liberty. In such cases no crime is perpetrated, no sin committed, no scandal given.

Although it would be too much to maintain that these grotesque conceptions of morality are the direct products of serfdom, it cannot be gainsaid that it did much to perpetuate them. And is still doing much. For, strange as it may sound, serfdom in many of its most repulsive aspects is not dead nor dying. In what, for example, is the condition of a young woman of the lower classes different from, or better than, that of a serf? When she takes service as field laborer, factory hand, chambermaid, apprentice, clerk, saleswoman, she is a mere chattel in the hands of her master, whose pay entitles him to dispose of her services — her virtue, her body, and her soul — and he insists upon the terms of the purchase with the pertinacity of a Shylock. Now, as in the days of serfdom, the price put upon the virtue of these white slaves by their masters and their masters' sons is positively prohibitive. The authenticated cases that might be brought forward in support of this assertion would fill a volume. Those who are desirous of forming an idea of the vast proportions which these practices have assumed, of the impunity of those who are responsible for them, and of the helplessness of the uncomplaining victims, who are taught to regard compliance with such unscrupulous demands as included in the list of services paid for by the paltry twelve or fourteen shillings monthly wages, should read two papers of Serghei Atava which appeared in the *St. Petersburg Gazette* several years ago.[1]

As to the upper classes, the so-called "good society," it should be judged, not by any of the received standards of morality, but by the maxims of La Rochefoucauld and the apophthegms of Arsène Houssaye. In no other country are the conversations and the interests and the aims of the men and women of gentle blood, high-sounding titles, large fortunes, and little brains so utterly frivolous, shallow, soul-

---

[1] Cf. *Petersburg Gazette*, 22nd and 23rd December, 1888.

less. There are indeed brilliant exceptions — small select *salons* in which the entire aristocracy of talent meets and mixes with a few gifted representatives of the aristocracy of blood; gatherings, admission to which is more eagerly sought than the ribbon of an order. But these exceptions scarcely weigh in the balance. French society under the Regency, with all its cynicism and blots and foulness, possessed certain redeeming traits which are lacking in that of St. Petersburg to-day. The pleasant little suppers, those feasts of reason and merriment at which human passion seemed to become etherealized, the idyllic amusements, brilliant masquerades, and other æsthetic aids to sin, are wholly wanting in Muscovy, which has no fringe of intellectuality or setting of elegant refinement to impart to glaring improprieties the appearance of eccentricities of genius. Compliments, small talk, and scandal constitute the daily bread of the mind; and the spiritual nature wastes away on such unwholesome nourishment. The gifts of God and of man are put to no better use than that of fuel for a sorry display of drawing-room fire-works that leave but smoke and ashes behind. Intrigues, underhand negotiations, treacherous plots, are also engaged in at times; but these are the nobler efforts, the loftier flights of men and women whose natural element is contented stagnation. These people never dream of the glorious potentialities of human nature; they have no fixed standard of right and wrong; the furniture of their souls contains nothing answering to the words duty, sacrifice, truth, love; they breathe an atmosphere of poisonous conventionality infinitely removed from the natural. "Spiritual interests do not exist there," we are told by a Russian journalist, "nor are they alluded to otherwise than as mental aberrations."[1]

I once interrogated one of these ladies — a person pure by temperament, richly gifted by nature, among other things, with the eye and talent of an artist, a ravishing voice, and uncommonly good looks, who, when she perceived the drift of my questions, fixed her liquid eyes upon me and said laughingly, "Those aspirations, ideals, and aims in life which you suggest, I have never set before myself. To the people with whom I consort they mean nothing. I know that I have, or rather had, talents; but why cultivate them? For what and for whom? I am also con-

---

[1] Cf. *Novoye Vremya*, 22nd September, 1889.

scious at times of a yearning for other and better things; but I suppress it. Why encourage selfish dissatisfaction with one's lot?" The ideal of such persons, if indeed they can be supposed to have any, is to raise the dignity and the comfort of being to a degree that would render superfluous the trouble of doing.

That the Imperial family should have escaped the breath of detraction in this poisonous atmosphere is as remarkable as it is gratifying to all friends of Russia. Hereditary authority is not always — nor often — consistent with intellectual superiority; it is nowhere so much in need of it as in Russia. It is edifying, therefore, to behold a powerful monarch sobered by the heavy responsibility of his position, striving in the order of grace to win triumphs denied him in the order of nature, especially if the task should require unusual force of character. It is much to be regretted that his Majesty is unable to breathe some of his own salutary spirit into the souls of his servants. Even the Court which has his excellent example before its eyes is as unlike the Emperor as it is possible to conceive. With the least respectable Court of modern times it would compare unfavorably. The anecdotes current at St. Petersburg and Moscow about its occasional sallies of shamelessness and perverse folly would not bear repetition in an English review. The stories, which without being current in either of the capitals are perfectly authentic, could not even be distinctly hinted at. It is an Augean stable that a radical revolution might wash clean, but not any ordinary half measures. A year has not yet passed away since one of the fashionable restaurants of St. Petersburg witnessed coarse, stormy, disgraceful scenes enacted by some of the highest, fairest, and most powerful in the empire, which if transferred to canvas by a realist like Verestchagin would seem a gross caricature of one of the least æsthetic paintings of Adriaen Brouwer.

Anna Karénina,[1] Helen,[2] Irene,[3] Natasha,[4] Katerina,[5] are some of the types one most frequently meets with to-day. In Russia they are appreciated, glorified, imitated; in this country they might be silently pitied, and would be

---

[1] The heroine of Count Tolstoï's novel of that name.
[2] One of the chief female characters in Count Tolstoï's *War and Peace*.
[3] The heroine of *Smoke*, one of Turghenieff's best novels.
[4] The chief actress in Dostoïeffsky's *Humiliated and Insulted*.
[5] The heroine of Ostroffsky's famous play *The Thunderstorm*, which lately proved a *fiasco* on the French stage.

inexorably ostracized. Their number and their vogue, however, should not blind us to the existence of other and far nobler types, as the zealous preacher in Vienna was blinded, who once said in holy haste that the chaste women of that gay but somewhat dissipated capital could be readily removed in a single carriage, were the city about to be consumed by fire from heaven; and, when called upon to make good this sweeping accusation, was constrained to shield himself behind the unworthy subterfuge that he had not specified the number of journeys the carriage would have to make. There are numbers of women in St. Petersburg and Moscow, in Kieff and Kazan, whom religion, education, or temperament have lifted up to the perpetual snow-line of purity, and who would have shed a lustre on Port Royal itself; women whom Cornelia and Lucretia would have been glad to know and might have called their friends. But having said this much, it must be admitted that, compared with the gay choir of their sinning sisters, they are but as small dust in the balance. The *dame du grand monde* is not one of this noble order. She is usually followed by a crowd of admirers whose number is never limited by usage or tradition, and seldom by fastidiousness. Young officers of the cavalry guards, students of the law school, pages of the Imperial corps, and other incipient Hercules in attractive uniforms, are kept for years in inglorious servitude by these Slavonic Omphales. The frankness, the absence of disguise or concealment, what Englishmen would call the shamelessness of the procedure, is such as to make one doubt of one's own principles of right conduct. A woman whose only attraction, like that of Mrs. Pinchbeck, is modesty, would be poor indeed among the graces of that brilliant circle. Every one knows, for instance, and no one is in any degree scandalized by the knowledge, that Countess X. or Princess Z., who is married and is blessed with almost as many children as Hecuba, is adored by five or six young scions of noble families, and two or three old generals or former ministers with one foot in the grave and one hand in the Treasury, who have no faith in Platonic love, all claiming a place in her affections, and each having his claim allowed, the husband looking philosophically on, mindful of society's precept, "Go thou and do likewise." Now these acts, which are done with the unreflecting impulsiveness of an Undine unconscious of impropriety, cannot possibly be termed crimes or sins.

"Sin," Jeremy Taylor assures us, "first startles a man, then becomes easy, then delightful, then frequent, then confirmed." It would take some extraordinary and as yet uninvented sin to startle a man in Russia; and as for the acts we are discussing, they seem there as natural as breathing — and almost as necessary.

This is bad enough. Still worse is their application as means to an end, whereby they derive whatever moral coloring they are held to possess from the character of the object in view. Thus the promotion of a Russian official, seldom the reward of merit or the recognition of honest effort, is not unfrequently the work of his wife's hands. I am personally acquainted with several families whose relative well-being has been obtained in this manner. A friend of mine, a mild, kind-hearted, well-educated man, who would not knowingly hurt a fly or hesitate to make a heavy sacrifice to save or help his sworn enemy, is a case in point. His promotion, which took place a few years ago, was the goal for which his young, handsome, easy-conscienced wife had been eagerly striving for two years before, constantly consorting with two profligate officials, through whom the nomination was at last made. All this was done without my friend's countenance or connivance, his wife being separated from him until the matter was ended. His qualifications for the post, which he now occupies, are about equal to those of a Red Indian fresh from the prairies for that of a Channel pilot, and he does more unintentional harm than a thoroughly dishonest man could effect of deliberate purpose. Another notorious case in point is that of a high official very well known to every Russian journalist and author from Warsaw to Vladivostok, from Archangel to Tiflis, whose wife lives openly with a Cabinet Minister, her husband's protector. From this coign of vantage she has watched for years over her husband's material interests to considerable purpose; and it is greatly to be regretted that the man whose official duties demand a degree of wisdom, knowledge, and kindliness far superior to that called for by any other post in the empire, should have no stronger point of resemblance to Marcus Aurelius, in whom all three qualities were so harmoniously blended.

Such combinations and compromises, in which love, or any sentiment remotely akin to it, is wholly out of the question, seem common or trivial enough to pass practically unnoticed. When the husband, not being an official, has

neither promotion to hope for nor neglect to fear, the petty
Zeus is constrained to have recourse to the golden shower,
and the problem resolves itself into a question of hire or
purchase. I was slightly acquainted with a Russian noble,
M. G., who, having convinced himself that a certain married
lady was essential to his happiness, had little difficulty in
persuading her husband to cede her to him, as Cato ceded
his wife to his friend Hortensius. The yearly payment of
1,200 roubles in advance constituted the business part of
the transaction. And this satisfactory arrangement lasted
without a break down to G.'s sudden death a few years ago,
when this dutiful lady returned to the arms of her husband.
What struck me as the strangest aspect of this strange drama
was the circumstance, established beyond reasonable doubt,
that this married couple loved, or rather liked, each other
with all the ardor of which their imperfect natures were
capable. Were these odd methods of correcting the errors
of inexperience or the neglect of fortune of rare occurrence
they would still deserve to be mentioned as characteristics
of those original beings who show their faith in their
efficacy by employing them. It is safer to rest their frequency upon the testimony of the Press than to endeavor to
prove it by heaping Pelion upon Ossa in the way of examples. "Do they love each other, this husband and wife?"
asks one journal which has devoted some serious articles
to the subject; "yes, they love and esteem each other as
far as such sentiments can take a hold upon people who are
free from the fetters of religion, the rules of honor, and
such-like prejudices. At all events, they tenaciously cling
to each other and stand back to back till the end. For
the sake of attaining their common objects it happens that
both husband and wife are guilty of conjugal infidelity;
this guilt they incur without a moment's hesitation, but with
such cool calculation, such well-poised sagacity as dispel
all fears as to the toughness of their matrimonial alliance:
the task performed, he will return to her and she will hasten
back to him; and, foreseeing this, they both feel quite
easy in mind."[1] A case of purchase once came under my
notice which attracted considerable attention at the time,
owing to the position of the parties, with all of whom I was
well acquainted. The husband ceded his rights for a lump
sum to a gentleman of noble family who occupied a high

---

[1] *Novosti*, 16th March, 1889.

administrative post. As soon as the legal difficulties were smoothed down, the lady, whose liberty was thus purchased, had her union with her new knight solemnized with all the formalities of the law, and all the rites of the Church. Another lady, whose acquaintance I made in the *salon* of a *grande dame*, was allowed by her husband — a most honest, benevolent, inconsistent gentleman, well known in official spheres — to spend a twelvemonth abroad with her lover, in his house, and at his expense. If coldness, indifference, or positive dislike had killed this gentleman's marital affection, his conduct would be intelligible without ceasing to be inexcusable, but I know that he idolizes his wife, that she in her own way is fond of him, and that the mystery is insoluble.

If irregular relations springing from mercenary calculations are not treated even as peccadilloes, it is not surprising that those that are founded upon mutual, or even one-sided, attachment should be invested with the aureole of virtue. A married lady, for instance, sets her heart upon a cold, selfish libertine, a Mr. Horner after Wycherley's own heart, and her whole duty forthwith consists in forgetting the claims of husband, home, children, and following her lover as a dog follows his master, in spite of his subsequent coldness and her disenchantment. It is not in Russia that Riccordi's young bride, meeting her Ferdinand on her wedding morn, would have left it open to the poet to impute to her the "unlit lamp." I know a lady who, meeting a gallant three weeks after her marriage and three years after his, separated from her young husband as speedily and as resolutely as if in obedience to a religious vocation, and spent two years *in the house and family* of her elected affinity, after which she returned to her husband, with whom she is at this moment living happily, esteemed by a large circle of friends.

Religion suggests no scruples to the minds of these apostles of free love, public opinion begets no shame; for "honor and duty," as Horner says in the *Country Wife*, "only depend upon the opinion of others," and neither priest nor neighbor thinks less highly of them, for making thus light of plighted troth, than those whose rights are most cruelly violated thereby. The entire category of such acts is put outside the pale of morality, neutralized, so to say, and deprived of all influence on the career of individuals, public or private. *Quidquid libet licet* is the universally recognized maxim in such matters. A man who covets and takes his neighbor's wife is trusted, esteemed, and loved as if he had remained faithful to his own, and he can have that erring lady received by his friends with the consideration due to his lawful wife, unless there are some very unusual circumstances to justify exceptional treatment. The wife of a celebrated Publicist is received, I am credibly informed, at all the houses at which her lover visits, although she is separated from the former and has a family by the latter.

"People look lightly upon marriage," says a Government organ which has ways and means of obtaining statistics inaccessible to other journals, "as an alliance entailing no obligation whatever... It costs them nothing to abandon each other; in fact this is so often the upshot of the union that it is practically the established custom. Whithersoever you turn, you meet with such shipwrecked families, the husband going one way, the wife going another. Their position in society is not one jot the worse on this account; no one dreams of censuring their conduct. On the contrary it is held to be perfectly natural and justifiable: their characters forsooth are not in harmony. Sometimes they live ten years in peace and friendship, and suddenly in the eleventh it is revealed to them that they were not created for each other and straightway they separate. Nor is it a rare occurrence for them to part the day after the wedding, just as though they could not have learned to know each other a little better on the eve of the marriage."[1]

Whether love is the word that best describes the short-lived affection, holy or unholy, of the impulsive Russian, depends entirely on the definition one accepts of this sentiment or passion. In the extreme north of Europe it is oftener a sentiment than a passion, and more frequently an appetite than a sentiment. The ancients relate that in the beginning men were created with four legs and four arms, as self-sufficing as the late Laurence Oliphant would have wished to see their degenerate successors. The original sin of pride, however, caused them to be split into halves, an arrangement which opened the door to sexual love and all the evils that come in its train. It was of these halcyon days of humanity that the two lovers were thinking who, asked by Vulcan to express the wish nearest their hearts with the certitude of seeing it fulfilled, replied: "Fuse us in thy fire, divine Artificer, and make us two but one." Now no Russian lovers in like circumstances would have preferred such a strange request; if they could brook

---

[1] *Graschdanin*, 3rd April, 1889.

divine interference at all in such matters, it would be to request a miracle in the very opposite direction, for love to the Russian, whether holy or unblest, is a law of man's nature which it would be as vain to kick against as to rise up against the law of gravitation.

The common people differ in no material respect from their betters. The essential points are identical in both, the varnish alone is lacking in the former. Nor could it well be otherwise, for no Ezekiel has ever yet prophesied to the dry bones of Christianity that were carried across the Black Sea in the tenth century from effete Byzance, and have ever since been slowly mouldering away in youthful Russia; and as there has been no moral or religious force to check the brutal coarseness or soften the savage rudeness of the Middle Ages, a description of the state of society of any epoch of Russian history will read as if drawn up in the present. One of the most accurate and trustworthy historians of his own times, Kotoshikhin, who has left us a description of the institutions rather than the people of the seventeenth century, describes his countrymen as coarse and ignorant, and generally sunk below the freezing point of civilization. Schtschapoff, one of the most impartial and philosophical of Russian historians, gives "coarse unbridled license in moral life and gross lewdness and slothfulness," as the chief characteristics of the Russian people of the seventeenth century;[1] "carried away by the torrent of his carnal passions, the common Russian man, restrained neither by shame nor by any moral law, gave his coarse material nature full sway, stopping short at nothing."[2] The Patriarch Philaret described his countrymen in a letter to Archbishop Cyprian as follows: "Many Russians . . . seize upon and take to themselves as wives their own sisters, and their cousins, while others commit incest with their own mothers and daughters and marry their mothers and their sisters."[3] All that happened many generations ago, but what takes place at the present day is quite as deplorable. "It would be difficult," writes a parish priest, "for Russians to become more immoral than they actually are. Children of thirteen stay away from home by night, spending their time in haunts

---

[1] *Russian Rasskol*, p. 177.
[2] *Russian Rasskol*, p. 178.
[3] *Collection of State Papers*, part iii. No. 60. Cf. also *Schtschapoff, l. c.* p. 180.

of unbridled profligacy.... When they marry they separate, after the first few days, for a year or more — often for ever.... All their social relations are permeated by coarse, cruel, brutal egoism. The husband robs his wife, the wife her husband, children their parents.... On holidays Russians are transformed into wild beasts, and even on working days they are unfitted for any social organization."[1] "'The district courts,' we are told by M. Pachmann, 'do not look upon adultery as a serious violation of conjugal rights.'"[2] "Such is the coarseness of manners," we are informed by a writer who has assiduously studied the conditions of this intricate and forbidding subject, "such is the coarseness of manners that frightful types of men are coming into being — men whose presence in a civilized community cannot possibly be tolerated."[3] But what more convincing proof of the stationariness of social life needs be offered than the marriage customs that still obtain in Southern Russia? To mention but one: It is well known to all who have sojourned in that part of the empire that when the rich symbolism and picturesque ceremonies with which the humblest wedding is celebrated, have been duly performed and the revelry is coming to a close, a number of the guests invariably assemble in a body outside the bridal chamber, often under the window in the street, howling and shouting, using most obscene expressions, and making disgusting demands which are literally complied with.

The Arcadian simplicity of manners which one is wont to associate with rural life in Old and New England is not one of the characteristics of the Russian peasantry, who rather resemble those pinched, crabbed, old-fashioned human mites who have never known the delightful thoughtlessness of childhood, have never dwelt in the paradise of youth and innocence, but seem to have been born into this life before sleeping off the ills and cares of a previous miserable existence. Like Ibsen's Oswald Alving, they are the ghosts of their sinning fathers born to expiate terrible sins. What to them are the barriers between the lawful and the unlawful, the proprieties, the amenities of civilized life? The social position of woman is admittedly the keynote of

---

[1] *Graschdanin*, 12th August, 1889.
[2] Cf. *Book about Women*, p. 59.
[3] Cf. *Northern Messenger*, January, 1889, No. 1, p. 54.

a nation's civilization, and all the parts that a woman plays all the world over are recapitulated in Russia, where she is an article of luxury, an instrument of pleasure, as in the harems of the Mohammedan East, a beast of burden as among most savage tribes, and a friend and companion as in New England. The great bulk of Russian women now as in the eleventh century are drudges first and mere females afterwards.[1] The Ustav of Yarosslav the Great puts women upon a level with the blind, the lame, the mendicant poor, the crippled, and deformed humanity. The Orthodox Church has shown itself to be as great a misogynist as the Koran. You could almost count on the fingers of one hand[2] the women whom it has admitted to the rank of saints.

The views thus authoritatively put forward by Church and State are scrupulously acted upon by the docile people whose proverbs on the subject are at least terse and expressive. "A hen is not a bird, nor is a woman a human being," is a doctrine seldom belied in practice. Wife-beating has often been looked upon as a sign of genuine attachment, though in Russian proverbial philosophy it figures mainly as a condition of the happiness of the husband. "He is not drunk who drinks not wine, nor is he happy who beats not his wife." "Beat your wife with the butt end of your axe; bend down over her and smell her, and if she lives and imposes upon you it's a sign that she wants more." There need be no fear in all this of her powers of endurance, for a "wife is not a pea — you cannot crush her," and she evidently needs to be constantly reminded of her duties, for "A girl's memory and her sense of shame last only to the threshold of the door." "Woman," says a religious manuscript of the Rasskolniks — who have preserved the habits, manners, and views of the sixteenth century unchanged — "woman is the weakest creature, the receptacle of all woes, the red-hot coal of dissensions, the baneful toy, the enemy of the angels, an insatiable animal, an abyss of credulity, a bunch of obstinacy, vanity of

---

[1] An honorable exception to one part at least of this statement should be made in favor of Little Russians, whose ecclesiastical union with Rome and political relations with Poland fostered nobler views of women. At the present day the liberty enjoyed by Little Russian women is one of the characteristic traits which distinguish Little from Great Russians.

[2] I think the exact number is six, the chief of whom possibly deserves a place in a Russian Walhalla, but has assuredly a very flimsy claim to a throne in the Christian heaven.

vanities, an attraction in the distance, an angel in the street, a devil at home, a magpie at the gate, and a she goat in the garden." Give a dog a bad name and hang it, is a true saying; and barbarous notions of women, their nature and their mission, however ludicrous they now may seem to English readers, have been and still continue to be productive of wide-reaching effects upon the social condition of the Russian people. What wonder that women brought up under the influence of such demoralizing maxims should, when they find field work or domestic service too trying, or are moved by the vague spirit of restlessness, deliberately lead a life of immorality *for the sole purpose of qualifying for the well-paid position of wet-nurse in populous cities?* What kind of wives can these wretched creatures prove, with their highly-developed animal instincts and imperviousness to all sense of shame?[1] The answer is writ large in the statistics of illegitimate children, in the charge-sheets of assize courts, the physical degeneration of the people, and the disintegration of society. Here are the kind of advertisements, for instance, that one reads in the *Village Messenger*, a newspaper edited for peasants by the Ministry of the Interior: "We respectfully request all persons in authority to seek for and arrest our wives, the peasant women Daria Vyssotina and Agrippina Tarassenkoff, who went away from us, their husbands, on the 23rd inst. without passports. Description: D. Vyssotina, eighteen years, middle sized, light hair, brown eyes, clean face. A. Tarassenkoff, nineteen years, of medium height, light-haired, clean face, *enceinte*. Signed," etc.[2] How can one expect the young girl's sense of shame to last beyond the threshold of the door, or even so far, when we are cognizant of the circumstances that in districts of Russia more extensive than the United Kingdom it is customary for married men and women, young men and girls, and children of both sexes, to take their vapor and water bath all together without a blush or a scruple?[3] With what sacramental forms or pious beliefs can the sanctity of the family be hedged round in a country where polyandry exists, not

---

[1] It is the virtues of these well-meaning but miserable beings that a recent English traveller in Russia exhorts his countrywomen to imitate. That sort of praise is more offensive to Russians, who wish to be rather than to seem, than the bitterest sarcasm. We feel like the soul of the damned sinner during the fulsome eulogium delivered over his tomb.

[2] Cf. *Novoye Vremya*, 16th November, 1889.

[3] In the governments of Nischny Novgorod, Tamboff, Baku, for instance.

the polyandry of Thibet, but the most loathsome form which this custom is capable of assuming — which uproots all respect for the most sacred ties of nature. In the country of the Dalai Llama the joint husbands are generally brothers; in Russia they are frequently father and son. This practice, confined to country districts, and fortunately not nearly universal even there, is yet widespread enough to have received a technical name and to be regarded as a permanent institution.[1] Equally strange and not less demoralizing is the custom, prevalent chiefly in Southern Russia, of allowing two young people who feel attracted towards each other to sleep together during the period of courtship. In its origin this usage was not intended to lead to gross immorality, and stories are told of some who availed themselves of this right, which remind one of the continence of St. Ammon or St. Melania; but mere barren intentions are powerless to modify the play of cause and effect in this rough realistic world, and one has no difficulty in accepting the statement of an accurate Russian writer, that it is the welcome occasion of systematic debauch. "We may possibly affirm," says M. Nekliudoff, "that if the law were to punish debauchery, concubinage, and adultery, *young boys would have to officiate as judges, all the rest would be prisoners.*"[2]

I had intended to insert here some evidence of the moral condition of the lower orders on the testimony of journals which are universally read in Russia, and which, judging from the reports of the Divorce Court published very fully in her daily papers, I thought might be tolerated in England. I am told that is not so. The point, however, of most consequence is not the frequency and barbarity of acts for which brutal is a misnomer and a libel on creatures with natural instincts, but the callousness with which they are regarded, and the price at which they are assessed. Crimes which in the eyes of Western law can only be atoned for by life-long incarceration are treated in Russia as peccadilloes which may be compounded for at the rate of a few shillings per case. We have it on the authority of a lawyer and public prosecutor that cases of criminal assault are very rarely brought to the official cognizance of the

---

[1] This custom partly attributable to economic causes, is called *snokha-tschestvo*, from the word *snokha*, meaning daughter-in-law.
[2] Cf. *Book about Women*, p. 57.

administrators of the law. "They are all settled at home, a sum of money being paid for the dishonor."[1]

To persons not entirely dead to all feelings of humanity, who can realize the savage brutality, the fiendish cruelty, that these things imply, comparisons between Russia and the West would be superfluous. They could add nothing to the effect produced by the recital of the bare facts. One is only astonished at the forgetfulness of them displayed by the Russian Government, which is capable of being shocked at "Bulgarian barbarities," horrified at Turkish excesses in Armenia, and fired to noble eloquence at the thought of Russia's civilizing mission in all these countries; and yet finds no more urgent measures of reform to be carried out at home than the closing up of the schools of the *Zemstvo* and the condemnation of the people to ignorance. No doubt this strange interpretation of the duties of governors is the result of conviction — not of a Satanic plan to rule by demoralization. The conviction has been expressed over and over again; recently, for instance, by a well-known publicist and supporter of the governmental system, who in a book which has just reached a second edition seriously says, "Whether there would be any advantage to the peasants from education, *at least from a moral point of view*, is extremely problematical."[2] This same writer, having established the fact that the number of children taught to read and write in Russia is very inconsiderable, piously exclaims, "And thanks be to God for this same!" But whether the cause be a mistaken sense of duty or the inexpiable crime of killing the soul in order the more effectually to keep the body enthralled, the result is the same.

Immorality never ruins a man in Russia, nor even disqualifies him from "honorably serving his country," in whatever capacity he may thus be engaged. I once met an employee in Warsaw, the efficient discharge of whose duties implied a degree of honesty, truthfulness, and noble-mindedness by no means common in more advanced countries than Russia. His "friends" believed him to be either a heartless scoundrel or an idiotic egoist. Although he was married and possessed a large family, no one was at all surprised to learn one day that he was being sued by a lady

---

[1] Cf. *Northern Messenger*, 1889, No. i., p. 51.
[2] *Modern Russia*, 2nd edition, St. Petersburg, 1889.

with whom he had lived for many years, and by whom he had a numerous offspring whom he refused any longer to support. The case was taken before several courts and he was finally condemned to pay a monthly sum which the Ministry undertook to deduct from his salary and make over to the injured lady. A few weeks later another lady took proceedings against him on similar grounds. Then day after day fair ladies with pale faces, eyes red from tears, and cheeks hollow from want, would come to the Department, sometimes with their children, at other times alone, and ask the heads of the Department to take pity on them, and compel that heartless man to contribute to their support. To which the officials made answer that they must appeal to the courts, and that in any case more than one-third of his salary could not legally be held back for the use of his creditors, were they legion. And meanwhile this Don Juan continued regularly to perform his duties in the Ministry, successfully to cater for his pleasure, and comfortably to keep himself afloat on the troubled waters of life; and he is still "honorably serving his country" at the present moment. Another official, M. Lebedenko of Vassilkoff (Government of Kieff), seems to have been treated by his wife as the wife of the above-mentioned gentleman was treated by her husband. She considered her marriage with Lebedenko an error, and having separated from him, she made repeated efforts to repair it. After some years had thus elapsed, last year Lebedenko forwarded a formal petition to the police of Odessa, in which city his wife was staying, requesting them to find out with whom she had been living since she left him, and to compel these persons to pay him the sum of five roubles a day, or at all events to amicably settle with him the money question, without causing it to be brought to court.[1] This petition has been published throughout the length and breadth of Russia, and Lebedenko's practical turn of mind commented upon, criticism touching all the extremes of opinion, and yet he continues to discharge his duties as usual; his extraordinary readiness to turn his wife's infidelity into a source of pecuniary profit not having unfavorably impressed his superiors, who seem to thoroughly understand and sympathize with human nature as it is in Holy Russia.

If immorality were uniformly taxed in Russia, as certain

---

[1] Cf. v. g. the *Odessa News*, 21st July, 1888.

forms of it actually are, the revenue would on the most moderate calculations immediately be doubled. But what no government could possibly attempt has long since been accomplished by private enterprise, and it would be difficult to point out any, the most degrading, aspect of vice that is not already transformed into a hen laying golden eggs for some trade or calling. Thus several fashionable restaurants in the two capitals are well known to be the rendezvous of a number of men cursed by the worst vices and unredeemed by the graces of Oriental civilizations. And these restaurants, fitted up for their reception, do in consequence a very profitable business. Then there is not a public bath in all Russia which is not a thinly disguised house of ill-fame, intended to cleanse the body and begrime the soul. Again there is a shop in a frequented quarter of St. Petersburg — not by any means the only one of its kind, I am assured — in which positively no business is done in the wares exposed for sale from the 1st January to the 31st December; but an immense trade is carried on in what may be appropriately termed the sale of souls — white slavery. Taken by itself this fact may not seem very startling or exclusively Russian, nor does it become so until we take into account the notoriety of the thing combined with its perfect impunity.

In the comedy called *The Troglodyte*, printed in Moscow (1884), and lately given for the first time in the Abramoff Theatre of that city, one of the *dramatis personæ* warmly recommends to his colleague two *cocottes* from the circus of Herr Soloman, and a local place of amusement known as the Salon. He gives the detailed addresses of these members of the frail sisterhood, the hotels at which they are staying, and the very number of their rooms.

"At first," says the *Moscow Gazette*, commenting on this curious style of advertising, "we refused to believe our ears when we heard these addresses given from the stage. What! a circus, and a famous circus to boot, is pointed out as an asylum for such persons! This is tactless, improper, impossible."[1]

But the force of these and similar instances lies less in their immense number than in the view held of them by the Areopagus of the people. Who takes cognizance of them day by day in the press, in the courts, in the bazaars

---

[1] Cf. *Novoye Vremya*, 30th October, 1889.

and public places? Are they censured as crimes, connived at as peccadilloes, or passed over as indifferent actions? This is really the all-important question for the moralist. For there is always an immense gulf between a nation's ethical ideal and its every-day performance; with communities as with individuals it is always a case of exclaiming,

> " Video meliora proboque;
> Deteriora sequor " ;

but in an age of progress the meliora of one generation prove the deteriora of a succeeding one, as the truths of one epoch become the prejudices of the next. Enough has already been said to show that to sins of sexual immorality the public conscience in Russia is perfectly insensible; that they are looked upon as questions of taste, of feeling, of comfort, and hygiene, but not as matters calling for attention, censure, or reprobation on ethical grounds. Juries refuse to convict even when the most cruel and abiding wrong accompanies the gratification of bestial lusts, and would suffice elsewhere to send the criminal to penal servitude; the Government accepts infamy as the price of promotion, and appoints to positions of influence over thousands individuals fit only to serve as drunkards served the ancient Spartans, namely, as object lessons inspiring disgust; the Church complacently administers her sacraments to the married lover and his mistress, asking for no sign of repentance, no pledge of amendment; and even the press, when not positively contributing to perpetuate this insensibility to sin and shame, adopts the equivocal expedient of damning it with faintest blame. The disgusting articles that appeared in scores of Russian newspapers a year or two ago, describing the slips of the *grandes dames* of the two capitals grown oblivious of their plighted troth in the seductive company of Tartar peasants in the Crimean summer resorts, were in all respects worthy of their classic models in the *Gil Blas* of Paris. They could not be literally translated here. The following extract from an article that was reproduced in many provincial journals breathes an infinitely healthier spirit: —

"For many a long day, it has been known to each and every one of us that there are less females in St. Petersburg than males, although to the eye they seem in the majority, because the females are continually strolling about the streets while the males sit in closed premises making domestic and foreign history. The enormous numerical irregularity of the sexes has always shown itself in the almost hereditary propensity of the males to seduce other men's wives and the habit of the females to gradually mix up the husbands as if they were cards. These matrimonial deviations from the fixed standard, however, were explained as effects of the rigor of the climate, of the laxness of morals and the exorbitant cost of ladies' necessaries. It occurred to no one to glance at statistics and take the opinion of science upon this delicate question." [1]

And then it goes on to show, in the same bantering tone, that as there are 403,830 men to 277,397 women, every husband can have only a 675th part of a wife, the natural consequence of which is a combination of polyandry and polygamy. The following extract from the Russian *New Review*,[2] while characteristic of the tone of a large section of the press when dealing with such questions, has the additional advantage of throwing a side light upon the manners of the people: —

"Throughout the world the duty of bathers to don some kind of underclothing while in the water, is imperative. In our country it is completely lost sight of. If you pay a visit to the seaside your mind is involuntarily carried back to those happy days when our mother Eve had not yet tasted the fruit of the tree of knowledge. At first such simplicity shocks you; but once grown used to it you yourself think nothing of plunging about in the blue waves side by side with a pretty naïad who is endeavoring, not without a touch of coquetry, to show you her skill in swimming deftly in various postures. Hard by you descry a kind-hearted paterfamilias leisurely making his preparations on the open beach, together with all the members of his family, not excluding the pretty maid-servant or nurse." [3]

And yachtmen in the Bosphorus, who may have innocently anchored by some Russian man-of-war, are startled the next morning to see almost the entire crew ranged naked round the bulwarks, waiting, regardless of their proximity to other shipping, to plunge into the sea by word of command.

This is not the place to discuss the influence of the Russian clergy for good or for evil upon their docile flocks, and the remark I am about to make has no bearing whatever upon that question; my sole object in making it is to bring out in stronger relief the inability of the Russian mind, as at present constituted by manifold influences that have been brought to bear upon it, to seize the relation between unclean living and moral wrong. If it be true that

---

[1] The article from which this extract is taken was reprinted in most of the provincial organs during the first half of September, 1888.
[2] *Novoye Obozrenie* is the Russian name of the journal.
[3] Cf. also *St. Peterburgskia Vedomosti*, 13th July, 1888.

> "'Tis not what man
> Does that exalts him, but what man
> Would do,"

it is equally certain that the place a man occupies in the esteem of his fellow-men, and his consequent power of doing good, depend far less upon his real merits than upon the good or bad qualities for which, rightly or wrongly, they give him credit. This being so, what conclusion are we warranted to draw from the fact that the popularity of a well-known parish priest was not in any perceptible degree lessened by the rumors circulated, and firmly believed by his parishioners, to the effect that he was addicted to a terrible vice, a vice for which no name can be given which could stand in these pages. His real guilt or innocence is beside the question. Charges of that grave nature should never be believed, still less repeated, in the absence of overwhelming evidence; and, in my own honest opinion, the rumor in question was a diabolical calumny. But that is not the point; what astounds and perplexes the foreigner is, that a firm belief in the truth of this terrible accusation did not, and even were it supported by unanswerable evidence would not, materially affect the relations between priest and people.

Public opinion as represented by a parish is not a whit more easy-going in the matter of clean living than public opinion embodied in the machinery of the law, whether we consider the popular jury or the cool-headed judges of the Senate. Latitudinarian views resulting from the habits and customs of the country, and from a course of education in harmony with them, rather than criminal connivance, constitute the true explanation of this strange fact. A law framed in accordance with abstract principles may commend itself to the reason of intelligent individuals; it may create new crimes and inflict Draconian punishments, but if it runs counter to the popular feeling on the subject it can never inspire disgust of the prohibited action, nor bring about that permanent moral improvement which it was the legislator's object to secure. A jurisconsult lately brought to my notice a case which throws considerable light on many of the dark corners of Russian life, and on none more than this question of morality. A gentleman who moved in the best society was popularly believed, nay, known to be engaged in committing acts which only in ancient Greece or modern Orient could be indulged in with impunity. But the shocking barbarity with which they were accompanied would have insured his condemnation even there. The axiom *volenti non fit injuria* would have been powerless to save him. Moreover the diabolical way in which he went to work to first introduce the subtle disintegrating poison into the very souls of his victims threw in the shade the worst charges that Anytus or Lycon ever ventured to insinuate against Socrates. In England he would have been condemned to what would practically amount to penal servitude for life. On the initiative of a private individual this gentleman was indicted for the offence. A cloud of witnesses proved the charge, bringing details to light that would have caused him to be lynched by the most apathetic and lax-minded community in Christendom. The defence set up was that the alleged acts were sins, not crimes; that they entailed and merited, no doubt, divine punishment hereafter, but were merely foibles in the eyes of enlightened men of the world, weaknesses shared by kings and emperors. This defence greatly irritated the jury. "Listen to him," they said of the defendant's counsel; "he is merely making use of this case to throw dirt at our beloved Emperor; let us show him how we treat such conduct," and they promptly brought in a verdict of guilty. The condemned man moved for a new trial on a writ of error based upon a puerile quibble. The point was referred to the Senate, the Supreme Court of Appeal, composed of men of the world well stricken in years, but in touch with the best society of the empire. The Senate quashed the verdict on that formal ground, and ordered a new trial, which was a repetition of the old one in all respects but one; the defence was less defiant and the verdict was an acquittal. I am assured by persons whose testimony is worthy of belief, that before his formal accusation, during his two trials, and after his curious acquittal, this gentleman continued to move in the best society; a privilege not nearly so extraordinary as it seems, if we remember that many of the gentlemen who compose it are well known to be continually rendering themselves liable to be acquitted in like manner of this identical charge.

But the Government, it may be urged, should not be held in any degree responsible for such glaring miscarriage of justice; it is incapable of dictating to juries and powerless to influence the decision of the Senate. The reply to this is obvious: if a poor student, a feather-brained, gencrous imitator of Schiller's *Don Carlos*, is found in possession of a book of Hertzen's, a photograph of Mazzini's, a pamphlet of Professor Dragomanoff's, no degree of respect for juries or senates is allowed to stand between him and irremediable life-long ruin. And if a ruffian, whose soul hellfire could scarcely cleanse of its foulness, is tried and found guilty, if he have friends in the Government, a powerful hand that reaches even to the bleak deserts of Siberia, is stretched out towards him, strikes off his fetters, and sets him free. Some five or six years ago there lived and flourished in St. Petersburg a director of a very fashionable grammar school, to which the Ministry of Public Instruction accorded extensive privileges. His name was Bytschkoff; were it Seneca or Epictetus his unparalleled depravity would have made it a Nessus' shirt of infamy. His school was an Eastern *parc aux cerfs*, and it might be so still, had he not presumed upon prolonged impunity and gone beyond Hercules' Pillars of depravity. He was brought to trial, found guilty, and sentenced to deportation to Siberia. The sentence was carried out, and he set out for Siberia, leaving behind him a beloved brother, whom his ruin did not disgrace, and who remained in high favor at court, a personal friend of the Tsar. And in course of time it came to pass that the exile received money enough to enable him to undertake a long journey; and his jailers were warned against excess of zeal, and while they were busy thinking of other things, he escaped to Switzerland. There he was seen and spoken to two years and a half ago by astonished Russians, who sent the news to St. Petersburg, where it was published as sensational without delay. The next day the Government ordered the newspapers to publish a categorical denial of the statement, and to assure their readers that he was in Siberia, not in Switzerland. And the journals obeyed and lied.

This is a sample of the action of the Government. As for the people, enough has been said of their past and present to justify despair of their future. But a more robust faith in humanity and a more intimate acquaintance with Russians make one hope rather than believe that their truly rich nature may be endowed with some irrepressibly recuperative force, to enable it to assume its original form under more auspicious circumstances, to impel their many latent qualities to work their way onwards and upwards through the hard crust of ages, till they burst into the light of day and fertilize the field of European civilization. The genuine Russian gentleman and the ideal Russian lady — both exist, and are to be found among sectarian peasants as well as in certain exclusive salons of St. Petersburg — are among the noblest specimens of civilized humanity; the refreshing unconventionality of thought and expression, the graceful simplicity of manner, the wonderful delicacy of feeling, the generous aspirations and noble yearnings — might, if they grew to be the characteristics of the nation, effect great things. But is there any serious hope of this? Let the Archbishop of Kherson and Odessa reply, who, himself sprung from the people, has spent a long life in their midst working for their weal, like a solitary swallow hopelessly coming to make spring before the sap stirs within the trees, the frail blossoms are hung out on the branches, or even the snow-drop has looked up at the sun. "On the whole," he said last year, on a very solemn occasion, "the state of things in Russia is sad. The people's minds are wofully dark, and *there is no sign of the coming dawn.*" Nor is it likely that day will break for many generations yet to come. Under a Government that systematically refuses to allow the people intellectual or moral instruction, that closes up elementary schools, appoints profligates to teach in higher educational establishments, banishes forever devoted apostles who, like Colonel Pashkoff, of the Horse Guards, were vigorously and successfully cleansing the Augean stables of moral filth — under such a Government there can be but faint hope of better things. English readers cannot realize the profound bitterness of heart with which a Russian who loves his country discusses these things with his fellow-countrymen. It is gall and wormwood to him to have to write of them to foreigners. But there is no other way of influencing rulers who are impervious to shame. The Government is responsible for a state of things which every honest Russian admits to be a scandalous disgrace to the civilized world. The side on which man comes into contact with the fathomless depths of spiritual nature is closed up in the Russian, made inaccessible to the waves and surges of the spiritual ocean. There is no ideal. The *video meliora proboque,* productive in most men of a salutary dissatisfaction with themselves and nerving them to the performance of higher things, is here completely lacking. The ordinary Russian knows no better than he does, and it is forbidden to teach him. His falls are not, like that of

Antæus, a source of increased strength. There is no honest effort to make the dead of to-day the rung of a Jacob's ladder, by which to ascend to a higher level to-morrow, and so onwards to perfection. No matter how deep he may sink in the well of vice he descries no loadstar in the artificial night above him, no faintest glimmer or twinkle to suggest that high over his head arches an infinite starry heaven, and not a mere amalgam of clouds, mist, and fog. His eyes are not lighted up by even a stray gleam of that transcendental reason which is of all ages and most men. They are murky, sad, blinded, as it were, by the smoke of extinguished spiritual fire. In a word, the life of a Russian is not a progress; it is a station, a filthy hovel, magnified into an abiding mansion by vision as distorted as that of Titania when she mistook Bottom the joiner for Adonis.

CHAPTER VII.

THE JEWS IN RUSSIA.

> "Something is wrong, there needeth change.
> But what or where?"
> *Song of Rabbi Ben Ezra.*

IT has often been a matter of wonder to me that in these days of rapid communications, "private wires," special correspondents and international journalism, so very little should be known and so very much rashly written in this country about Russia. France, Germany, and England are perhaps equally guilty of this crime of *lèse-majesté* against reason — their writers and politicians forming and expressing confident opinions about important questions, without the slightest foundation in fact, — and Englishmen have not quite so much reason to blush as their neighbors, seeing that they are but a little less familiar with the economical, intellectual, and moral condition of a foreign and not over friendly people than with that of their own kith and kin in the colonies. A more serious excuse might perhaps be found in the circumstance that the press of the country rather than its readers should bear the blame of ignorance which is, in many cases, equalled only by conceit; as it is the press that furnishes the so-called facts, solemnly pledging itself to their accuracy, while the public can no more be condemned for not sifting them critically than a bookkeeper can be blamed for not spending his time in verifying the statements of his ready-reckoner. Thus a few months ago *The Times*, through its correspondent, informed its readers that Madam Tsebrikoff had been exiled to Pensa in the Caucasus, whither she had been driven in a *kibitka*, thus giving circulation to a statement containing about as much truth and meaning as if a Russian journal of the same day had announced that Mr. Davitt had been imprisoned by the Irish Secretary in the frightful prison of Sing Sing, in Tipperary.

Two months ago a "well-informed" and "widely circulated" paper assured its readers that a new and barbarous law had just been passed in Russia, the practical effect of which was to doom the unfortunate Jews of that country to exile or death; and this caterer for political information for the million was so well informed of what was passing in "higher spheres" in Russia, that he was able to quote textually several clauses of the new law, the mere perusal of which reminded Englishmen — who had begun to grow as tired of Stanley as of the fasting man — of the halcyon days of Bulgarian horrors. And it needed several weeks of the most solemn assurances of the Russian Government to allay an excitement that ought never to have been roused or to have made itself felt to some good purpose some years ago.[1]

As a matter of fact, no project of law ever passes the Imperial Council in June, July, or August, because there are no sittings of that body all through the summer months, and consequently the statement of the correspondent could not have deceived any one who had any real knowledge of Russia. Moreover, it has never been a serious question, with those who govern the Russian Empire, of banishing the Jews *en masse*, as they were expelled from Spain in 1492. A portion of the Russian press has, it is true, often advocated this drastic method of dealing with them, but the press has less effect on the Government than the scarcely audible buzz of the tiny fly struggling in the web on the callous spider that eyes it coldly from on high.

On the other hand, it would be a grave mistake to suppose that because the Russian Government goes methodically to work, judiciously blending cunning with cruelty, patience with hatred, the lot of the Jews is an enviable one; just as it would be wrong to conclude that, because prisoners in Russia are often treated with more revolting cruelty than African slaves, the movement now on foot to put an end to the slave-trade in Africa has therefore lost its *raison d'être*. How far the lot of the Russian Jews will enlist the sympathies of Englishmen is in truth of very scant importance to and one; to what extent it deserves those sympathies may perhaps appear from a simple statement of the case.

---

[1] It is only fair to say that the *Daily Telegraph* published a few serious papers on Russian Jews at the time, denying the promulgation of new laws, and giving a fairly complete and very candid statement of the whole question,

In the olden times of the Grand Duchy of Moscow there
was no Jewish question to disturb the peace of mind of
Russian statesmen: the peaceful Jews were then kept out of
the country more successfully than the martial Tartars,
more resolutely than the plague. Every Jew found there
was seized and expelled,[1] no reason, however weighty,
being accepted as sufficient to justify the pollution of the
land by the presence of a member of the race that crucified
the Saviour. And thus the native population were left to
their own devices — the stream of Russian civilization kept
exceptionally pure from Jewish admixture — until the policy
of annexation was first fairly inaugurated, when Russia ravenously swallowed, along with the luscious morsels that
belonged to her neighbors, the trichines that found such
a congenial soil in her body politic and are now bidding
fair to bring about a collapse of the entire system. The
struggles of Russia now to throw off, now to assimilate and
neutralize this dangerous element, are instructive if not
edifying.

Little Russia was the first territory annexed, and with it
were taken over the Jews who for generations had been
wont to look upon that country as their fatherland. But
if the Little Russians, who had been induced to unite by
tempting promises, were treated with scant ceremony, the
Jews could scarcely complain of receiving still less, and in
1727 the High Privy Council promulgated an order signed
by the Empress Catherine I., to expel the "scurvy Jews,[2]
male and female, who are living in Ukraine (Little Russia)
and in Russian cities generally, and never again to allow
them under any pretext to re-enter the country, and to take
due care that in future the land be vigilantly guarded and
kept free from them." But as the frontier, even in those
days, was extensive, its guardians venal, and the Jews
persevering and ingenious, many of the latter succeeded
in maintaining their foothold without sacrificing their
religion. Peter II., the gentleness of whose character
reflected itself in the irresolution of his policy, relaxed

---

[1] Cf. Complete Code of Laws, No. 662, year 1676. In a treaty concluded
with Poland in 1678 it was expressly stipulated that "the merchants and
tradesmen of both sides will be free to travel without hindrance into each
other's country 'except the Jews.'" — *Ibid.*, No. F30.

[2] There is no adjective in the original, but the word for Jews is an oppro-
brious one implying still more than is expressed by the epithet I have added.
The same word is still employed by such conservative organs of the Russian
press as the semi-official *Novoye Vremya* and *Graschdanin*.

the severity of this law to the extent of allowing Jews to visit South Russia for the purpose of attending the fairs there; a privilege which he thoughtfully saddled with the condition "that they should not take out of the country gold or silver money, nor even copper coins." "As to living in Little Russia," this curious ukase concludes, "it is strictly forbidden, nor shall any one dare to harbor scurvy Jews; in all these respects it is decreed that the ukase of the year 1727 shall remain in force."[1]

The Empress Anna, in the beginning of her reign, gave permission to Jews to visit Russia for purposes of commerce, but shortly before her death, repenting of that and other sins, reverted to the old policy of exclusion, which, however, was again for a time suspended during the Russo-Turkish war. In 1742, the Empress Elizabeth framed still more stringent laws against the Jews than any of her predecessors, and piously appealed to heaven for her warrant. "Except irremediable harm to our faithful subjects nothing can ever come of the presence in the land of such inveterate haters of the name of Christ the Saviour."[2]

Catherine II., whose policy was as little guided by her philosophy as were the metaphysics of many venturesome old schoolmen by their religious faith, began by following in the steps of her predecessors, and in the manifesto she issued during the earlier part of her reign inviting foreigners to come and settle in Russia, in consideration of special privileges offered them, Jews were expressly mentioned as disqualified. But the annexation of certain Polish governments, inhabited by large numbers of Jews, which she soon afterwards effected, compelled her to modify a policy that was based upon changing interest rather than fixed principle; and in the year 1769 she permitted the Jews to make Russia their home, on condition that they settled exclusively in the south, in the government of New Russia. This decree,[3] was the foundation-stone of the famous *Pale of Settlement*, which remains to the present day the main grievance of the Jews — the fruitful source of all their sufferings. All followers of the Mosaic law who inhabited the Polish provinces at the time of their annexation were allowed to remain where they were, and to enjoy

---

[1] Complete Code of Laws, No. 5324.
[2] *Ibid.*, No. 8673.
[3] Complete Coll. of Laws, No. 13383.

the same rights as Russians; but it was not open to them to circulate in Russia proper, and towards the close of the Empress's reign they were condemned to pay double taxes.[1]

But all these attempts of Russia to kick against the pricks proved ineffectual. The Jews obeyed the laws of nature rather than those of shortsighted men, with results that alarmed the statesmen who were responsible for having made the two incompatible. An Imperial Commission was then created (1802), by the Emperor Alexander surnamed the Blessed, to study the question, and two years later a law was passed which appears to have been an honest endeavor to carry out two opposite lines of policy, on the principle of doing incompatible things by halves. One half of the measures are intended to protect the Christians against the heartless exploitation of the Jews, who are thus treated as born enemies of their Orthodox fellow subjects, while the other half is meant to bring about the brotherly union and ultimate amalgamation of the two avowedly hostile races. Very sordid motives were put before them to induce them to become Christians, care being meanwhile taken to keep them well within their Pale of Settlement, which was considerably narrowed, no Jew being allowed to live within fifty versts of the frontiers. It was obviously legislation of the half-hearted kind — an attempt (to use a popular Russian expression) to give the wolves a feed and keep the sheep whole, and like all such efforts it deservedly failed.

The Emperor Nicholas began his reign by issuing various ukases in the same spirit — forbidding the Jews to circulate in Russia, narrowing the Pale still more by excluding from it the cities of Kieff, Nicolaïeff, Sebastopol, and even certain of the streets of Vilna, and generally carrying out a policy of mild repression. On its becoming obvious in 1835 that most of these measures were but mere waste paper, the whole structure of previous legislation was pulled down and a bill passed "to enable Jews to live comfortably as tillers of the soil or artisans, and to keep them from idleness and illegal occupations." They are permitted by this law to attend fairs in the great centres of Russia — Nischny Novgorod, Irbitsk, Kharkoff, etc. — and special privileges are promised to those who turn their

---

[1] *Ibid.*, No. 17224.

attention to the cultivation of the soil, an occupation which had proved so fatal to Russian Christians. The legislator was evidently desirous on the one hand of removing all distinctions between Jews and Christians, and on the other of localizing the religion of the former as he would an infectious disease. Evidence of the former disposition is to be found in the clauses which throw open schools, gymnasies, universities, and other educational establishments to the members of the proscribed faith, and proof of the latter in the express declaration that in country districts the Jews were, as theretofore, to remain aloof from their Christian fellow-subjects, their communes to be separated from those of orthodox Christians; and even in the cities the same barriers and distinctions to be rigorously maintained. Worse than all, as soon as it became evident that the proscribed people thoroughly appreciated the offer of education, by sending their children to Christian schools, where they became the most successful pupils and students, the Emperor issued another ukase (in 1844) to the Minister of Public Instruction, declaring it necessary to open Jewish schools for Jewish children, and ordering him to appoint a commission of rabbis to draft a scheme and to see that a special tax be levied on the Jews for the support of these denominational establishments.

The late Tsar Alexander II. was desirous of contributing as far as was possible, by means of legislation, to the assimilation of the Jewish element by the Christian population, but before taking any steps towards the accomplishment of this desire, he ordered the Minister of the Interior to have detailed reports drawn up by the governors and governors-general of the districts inhabited by Jews concerning the working of the laws already in force and the defects remarked in their conception or administration. The Governors of the provinces of Vitebak, Mohileff, and Minsk gave it as their opinion that the Jews of their districts were suffering incalculable harm from the action of the law depriving them of the rights of ordinary Russian subjects without relieving them of any of the corresponding obligations. Moreover, the towns, they added, in which Jews were authorized to live were so congested that they could get but little work to do; and "when they do receive orders for work, they are compelled to have recourse to fraud. This explains why they so often become noxious members of society, instead of conferring upon the community and upon themselves those benefits which, under more favorable conditions, one would naturally expect from them." The Governor of Poltava informed the Minister that the Jews of the south of Russia differed to a very considerable extent in language, dress, and mode of life from their co-religionists in other parts of the empire, and that the difference was entirely to their advantage. As a result of this, "they have almost wholly assimilated themselves with the native population; wherefore I would respectfully suggest that all the restrictions now in force against them be forthwith abolished." The remaining governors were of the same opinion, and the Minister of the Interior came to the conclusion that the accumulation of skilled Jewish artisans and workmen in the cities of the Pale of Settlement, and the competition resulting between themselves on the one hand and between them and the Christians on the other, "have an exceedingly injurious effect on both sides."

Nothing could be more candid than this avowal, nothing more well meaning than the intentions it called into being; but between intentions and their realization lies an abyss — at times an impassable one. "Before the sun rises," says a Little Russian proverb, "the dew may eat one's eyes out." Half-hearted measures of relief were gradually doled out, certain restrictions abolished wholly or in part, and the administration of the existing laws became less severe, a difference which was, in itself, as long as it lasted, almost as welcome as a repeal of the exclusive legislation complained of. For men, not measures, really rule or ruin the nation; no other country possessing such a ponderous, voluminous collection of laws as the Empire of the Tsars, no other people so utterly lacking the conception of law, as of established rules to be respected and obeyed; and what can be more demoralizing to a nation than the possession of laws, the transgression of which is the rule, the observance the rare exception?

Had the Emperor Alexander II. lived a year or two longer, it is highly probable that there would now no longer be a Jewish question in Russia; for the emancipation of that people was one of the points of the constitution which he had consented to grant. His son and successor is credited with a strong personal dislike to all followers of the Mosaic law, and is resolved, men say, to grind them down to the intellectual (they are already far below the economic) level of his orthodox subjects. As this would be a heinous crime, it may possibly be a foul-mouthed calumny; but it is not a dispassionate survey of the main acts of his reign that would bring one to doubt the truth of the assertion. The chief measure now in force against the Jews is — and has been since the days of Catherine II. — the prohibition to leave the Pale of Settlement. No doubt this district is immense in extent, comprising the governments of Vilna, Volhynia, Grodno, Kovno, Minsk, Podolsk, Yekaterinoslav, Poltava, Tshernigoff and, under certain restrictions, portions of Kieff, Vitebsk, and Mohileff.[1] But for the Jews, who are not tillers of the soil, who are compelled to belong to merchant guilds or trade corporations that exist only in cities and towns, and are debarred from engaging in many pursuits open to Christians, the immensity of this territory shrinks to an incredible extent. And lest the Pale, even thus narrowly circumscribed, should seem too vast a hunting-ground for the "scurvy Jew," his Majesty enacted, three years ago, that "until further orders," no Jew will be permitted to leave the villages or hamlets in which they were living up to the 15th May, 1882. And as during those six years hundreds, nay thousands, of families changed their place of residence to other villages and towns, the execution of this law has reduced a large number of Jews to misery and ruin; for not only do those suffer who are compelled to leave villages where they have their houses and their capital, but the community to which they are compelled to return, and in which competition has already reduced wages to the starvation line. So that the arena is in reality very circumscribed in which Jew meets Jew in the bitter struggle for life, and defeating his adversary inflicts incurable wounds upon himself.

There are one or two narrow and winding paths that lead out of this human penfold, but those who take them have often cause bitterly to regret their enterprise or unrest. Jews who have traded for not less than five years as members of the first merchant guild[2] within the Pale have the

---

[1] Cf. Law concerning Passports and Runaways, vol. xiv., div. i., chap. i., art. 16.

[2] In Russia there are two merchant guilds (there were three till a few years ago) : the members of the first pay much higher fees than those of the second, and both pay larger fees and taxes than the petty traders. One must be a man of considerable means to belong to the first merchant guild in St. Petersburg or Moscow. In the latter city there are but four hundred members of the first guild all told, many of whom are foreigners.

right to apply for admission to the same guild outside of
it. But the exercise of this right bristles with difficulties.
Thus, to say nothing of the petitions which he must send
to the guilds, the police, the governors, and others, the
merchant's first real embarrassment is caused by the law
which prohibits him from hiring Christian servants, coupled
with the circumstance that he has no hope of finding any
in Russia proper, where Jews are few and belong exclusively
to the privileged classes from which the ranks of domestic
servants are never recruited. The law[1] which obtained
under former Emperors allowed the merchant in this case
to petition the Prefect of the Police of St. Petersburg or
the Governor-general of Moscow — if his destination were
either of these cities — for permission to take with him
from the Pale a certain number of clerks and domestic
servants, setting forth in the petition the reasons that
determined him to fix the particular number asked for. It
then depended on the decision of these dignitaries how
many might accompany him, and from their decision
there was no appeal. If he chose some other city for his
abode, he was allowed but one clerk and four domestic
servants, all of whom must be of irreproachable character
and free, not only from the accusations, but even from the
suspicion of crime. It is as easy to imagine the innumerable and serious embarrassments that this law is calculated
to raise up in the everyday life of the Jewish merchant —
the loss of time, of money, of health — as it is difficult
to divine the good purpose which the legislator had in
view in framing it. That law is still in force; but, apprehensive that the permission it accords is far too extensive,
his present Majesty's advisers have decreed that in case the
merchant should dismiss or otherwise lose his servants, it
shall not be open to him to send to the Pale for others to
replace them but he must shift as best he can.[2] Moreover,
if from any cause whatever he cease to belong to the first
guild before the lapse of ten years, he forfeits his right to
reside in Russia and must return to the Pale. The circumstance that he availed himself during his stay of his
legal right to purchase house property, or land in Russia proper, is not deemed sufficiently grave to cause

---

[1] Vol. xiv., div. i., chap. i., art. 16.
[2] Decision of Minister of Interior and Minister of Finances, given on 17
-29 April, 1885.

an exception to be made in his favor. Landlord or householder, it matters not, the law compels him to leave everything and return to the Pale, and logic and humanity are utterly powerless to help him.[1]

In Russia every Jew is compelled to belong to one of the established classes into which the tax-paying community is divided, and unless he has been received into one of the learned professions, he must be at all times ready to prove by documents, that require to be renewed every year, that he is a skilled artisan, a merchant of one of the two guilds, a petty trader, or an agriculturist. This means, besides endless worry and frequent insults from secretaries and petty puffed-up officials, the payment of considerable annual fees and — what is sometimes more irksome and oppressive — permanent residence in the city or town in which his guild or corporation has its headquarters.[2] If sheer want and the evident hopelessness of relieving it in a given town compel a Jew to disregard this law and wander about from place to place, as many have done and still are forced to do, he is arrested and treated or mal-treated as that most miserable of human wretches, a Russian *brodyag*.[3]

But, independently of those general taxes paid by Jews for the support of institutions from the benefits of which they are in most cases expressly excluded, they are also subjected to a special system of taxation, from which Christians are exempt, and which, though destined in theory for the special needs of the Jewish community, are nevertheless employed in part to replenish the imperial coffers.[4] Thus the so-called "Box tax"[5] is one of the most comprehensive tributes ever levied upon a community, its oppressiveness being intensified by the odious method practised of farming it out to greedy speculators. For every animal, fowl, and bird killed for food according to Jewish rites

---

[1] Cf. Complete Collection of Laws, No. 41779 and 48175.
[2] Complete Collection of Laws, vol. xiv., div. i., chap. i., arts. 1 and 2.
[3] This terrible word *brodyag* does not convey much to the ordinary English reader. Some facts relating to the subject of the indescribable tortures inflicted on this army of unpitied wretches have already been given in the chapter on "Russian Prisons." Cf. Complete Collection of Laws, vol. ix., art. 953.
[4] Complete Collection of Laws, vol. v., art. 281; Supplement, chap. i., art. 1.
[5] So called because the proceeds were kept in a box employed solely for this purpose.

(Kosher) a fixed sum has to be paid. And on every pound of that same meat, and on every one of those identical fowls, an additional sum is levied when they are sold. Jews who have taken their degrees in universities, or have succeeded in gaining admission to a learned profession, may, on satisfying their butcher that they are doctors or masters, purchase a certain quantity of animal food free of this duty: viz., two pounds and a half of meat a day, if the privileged person is single, and four pounds and a half if married; he may also, if a bachelor, purchase on the same advantageous conditions one fowl or bird daily, and two if he be a family man.[1] In addition to this there is a candle tax, the proceeds of which are employed to support those denominational schools with which the Jews would most gladly dispense, if they were allowed to avail themselves of the ordinary educational establishments, to which they have quite as much right as their Christian fellow-subjects. Over and above these oppressive tributes, all Jews have to pay a certain percentage — from which Christians are, of course, exempt — on the rent they receive for their houses, shops, stores, granaries; on the gross income they receive from the sale of wine in public-houses and inns; they are likewise subject to a special annual tax on distilleries and breweries, glass works, copper and iron works, tar, pitch, and tallow works, and for the permission to set up as cattle-breeders. In addition to this, all money left by deceased Jews pays a fixed percentage to the same common fund; and finally a fine is paid for the authorization to wear Hebrew apparel. "All Jews who desire to wear a skull cap" (I am quoting textually from the statute book), "are hereby subjected to a permanent tax of neither more nor less (*sic!*) than five silver roubles a year each."[2] This is not an extract from obsolete laws framed during the Middle Ages, but a clause of a law drawn up in the last quarter of the sober nineteenth century, and strictly enforced to-day. That the legislator was in grim earnest about the matter is evident from the following provision concerning the wearing of other articles of Jewish dress: "In fixing the amount of taxes to be levied for the right of wearing Hebrew dress, male and female, the governor of the district is hereby enjoined to take heed that

---

[1] Supplement to article 281 of fifth vol. of Laws.
[2] *Ibid.*, art. 10, observ. 4.

it be considerably augmented in comparison with the other objects subject to the Box Tax."[1]

It is difficult to convey anything like an adequate idea of the vexation, disputes, and bad blood caused by the spirit in which this law is administered. But it is scarcely needful to descant upon the spirit, when the letter itself contains so much to bear out the charge of deliberate injustice which has been frequently advanced against it. Take, for instance, the provision made for the not uncommon case in which the animal or fowl is slaughtered in one place and sold in another. "Whereas the Box Tax is levied according to weight on the sale of the objects liable to it, be it ordained that if a Jew, having slaughtered an animal within the boundaries of one tax farm, desire to carry it to another for the purpose of selling it, he is liable to pay the tax in the first tax-farming district for the slaughter alone; but the tax farmer of the second district possesses the right to exact payment both of the tax for slaughter and also of the tax for sale."[2] This is but a sample. The voluminousness and minuteness — to say nothing of the vexatiousness — of the laws against the Jewish millions who have appreciably contributed economically and intellectually to the prosperity of the empire, would drive any one but a Talmudist or a Benedictine to despair.

But besides merchants of the first guild, university graduates of the highest standard, and doctors and masters, are also privileged to pass beyond the Pale of Settlement. Skilled artisans can likewise seek admission to the corporations, or "Tsekhs," of their respective calling in any part of the empire. This clause enfranchises, to all appearance, a numerous class of men, which might perhaps be made to include the best portion of the Hebrew people. These appearances, which would probably be trustworthy enough if observed in any other part of Europe, are rightly deceptive in Russia, and Englishmen who come in contact with the wan, worn, wizen-faced Russian Jews — like so many Lazaruses risen too late from the dead to live longer than a few short hours — who played such a tragic part in the sweating scandals that came to light in London some time ago, will readily understand that the children of creatures of this stamp — and the majority of Russian Jews are such

---

[1] Supplement, chap. iii., art. 14.
[2] Ibid., Supplement, art. 45.

—have as much chance of becoming astronomers as of qualifying for what the law in Russia understands by "skilled artisans." It is less difficult, however, for the daughters of the classes who possess a fairly sufficient income to become midwives—a profession which also confers upon those who practise it the right of passing beyond the Pale.[1] But his present Majesty's Government, noticing that many young Jewesses succeeded in passing the examinations required for the certificate of midwife, instead of withdrawing the privilege accorded by law to this profession, as would be natural under the circumstances, acted somewhat like the scrupulous Quaker of apocryphal celebrity who, when the pirate caught hold of one of the ship's ropes in order to board the vessel, exclaimed: "Thou wantest this rope, friend?" (and speedily cutting it) "take it; may it stand thee in good stead"; they confirmed the privilege, but explained that from December, 1885, it would not extend from midwives to the children of such Jewesses, who would be compelled to live in the Pale.[2] Another instructive instance of the way in which laws favorable to the Jews can be made oppressive without being formally abolished occurred two years ago in Kieff. A certain M. Goldenberg, who had obtained his degree at the University, and is therefore qualified to live in Russia proper, own houses, and land, etc., resolved to hand over to his wife a house that belonged to him in the Sophia Street. The deed of transfer was duly drawn up, but the authorities refused to register it. M. Goldenberg appealed to the law courts, relying upon the express terms of the law (Art. 100, vol. x., parts 1 and 5), which enacts that the husband communicates all his civil rights and privileges to his wife. But the law courts decided that every statute concerning the Jews must be interpreted in a restrictive sense, and consequently they upheld the refusal of the authorities to validate the act of transfer, dismissing the suit with costs, on the ground that, though M. Goldenberg himself possesses civil rights, he does not communicate them to his wife.

The most arduous way of obtaining the right of free circulation throughout the empire would naturally seem that which leads through the universities, or one of the higher

---

[1] Coll. of Laws, vol. xiv., sect. i., chap. iii.
[2] Decision of the Department of the Police on the 30th December, 1885.

educational establishments, for the children of men who can never tell in the morning whether they and their families may not have to go to bed supperless at night. And yet so painfully vivid was the consciousness of the horrors from which they would thus escape, so powerful the aversion to go back to vegetate and rot in the hateful Pale, that hundreds of young men entered the universities, valorously battled for years with want, sickness, and discouragement, many of them like Heyne, the German classical scholar who first raised philology to the dignity of a science, often exchanging their dinner for tallow-candles, which burned during whole nights in their garrets and cellars, lighting them on to knowledge and to fame. And the Government, seeing that knowledge is power, and that it is not good that power should be placed in the hand of "vile Jews," resolved to close up this issue out of misery, ignorance, and the Pale. When the present Tsar succeeded to the throne the educational law, in so far as it affected the rights of Jews to have their children taught in the ordinary schools of the empire, was formulated as follows: "Jewish children may be admitted into and educated in the State educational establishments, private schools, and boarding schools of the district in which they reside, no difference whatever being made between them and other children."[1] This law was in force down to the 19th June, 1885, when his Majesty ordered the admission of Jews to the Technological Institute[2] of Kharkoff to be limited to 10 per cent. of the total number of students. Nine months later his Majesty was "graciously pleased," says the official document, "to forbid absolutely the admission of any Jew to the Veterinary Institute of Kharkoff." On the 17th December, 1886, the present Minister of Public Instruction — an Armenian by birth — promulgated a law the preamble of which declared that whereas very many young Jews, eager to partake of the benefits of higher classical, technical, and professional education, were annually presenting themselves for admission to the universities, etc., passing the examinations and prosecuting their studies in the various establishments of the empire, it was found desirable to put a stop to such an unsatisfactory state of things, to which end it was enacted that in future the number of Jewish students in

---

[1] Coll. of Laws, vol. ix., book i., chap. iv., art. 966.
[2] There are but two Technological Institutes in all Russia.

Russian universities should not exceed 10 per cent. of the entire number of students in the universities within the Pale, 5 per cent. in other provincial universities, and 3 per cent. in those of Moscow and St. Petersburg; and on the 8th July, 1887, the same measure was applied to all gymnasies or grammar schools without exception.

The immediate results of this curious legislation were painful in the extreme; thousands of young men who, by dint of years of hard, steady work and stoic self-denial on their part and on the part of their parents, had at last come within sight of the promised land, were rudely awakened from their day-dreams and jeeringly told to return to their "vile" people to live and die, pariahs among helots. I shall never forget the harrowing scenes I witnessed, the tears, the entreaties, the wailing and despair immediately after the passing of that drastic law; parents begging their Christian friends — ay, and entreating their Christian enemies — to intercede with the minister to except their only child from the operation of the Act; young boys putting on the ill-fitting masks of dissimulation and endeavoring by flattery administered to the sons of high officials — their own schoolfellows — to obtain permission to finish the studies already brilliantly begun or well-nigh ended; orthodox priests, grave Russian officials, and even well-known statesmen gibing and jeering at the checkmated Jew. One of the bitterest and possibly best deserved reproaches which Christian writers administer to Julian the Emperor was the insidiousness of his persecution of the Christians, as manifested in the order he issued prohibiting them from attending lectures in the schools. Julian couched that order in language as elegant and brilliant as that of Lucian, and defended it with arguments worthy of Aristotle — invulnerable to anything more logical than an appeal to a highly-developed sentiment of humanity. The legislators of Holy Russia succeeded in closely copying Julian's insidiousness without imitating his wit or appreciating his logic. My readers do not, I feel confident, need to be told whether the grave legislators of a vast empire engaged in the practical solution of a most delicate question — fate of millions of their subjects — are justified in giving to laws adverse to these millions the odious form of a sneer at their religious tenets. It had been usual in Russia at all times to profess and occasionally to practise respect for the Jewish observance of the Sabbath. Jewish boys were not compelled to attend school on Saturdays, nor witnesses — if they objected — to take an oath in courts of justice on that day. But since the present Tzar ascended the throne all that has been changed. Thus, among the laws concerning the education of Jews we read: "The learned Committee of the Ministry of Public Instruction, having deliberated upon the question whether Jewish pupils of grammar schools should be excused from written examinations on Saturdays, . . . decided that once they enter public educational establishments Jews are bound to submit to the rules thereof, and the *very act of entrance into these schools is of itself a proof that they and their parents have outgrown that exclusiveness which stickles for the strict observance of the Sabbath.*"[1] This jest is the deliberate work of the most learned body of men in the most enlightened department of the Government of Russia — work for which they are paid out of the hard-earned wages of the Jew, at whose religious convictions and moral courage they thus poke fun!

The circumstance that Jewish children seek for education in schools founded for children belonging to all religious persuasions being thus authoritatively construed as a proof that they and their parents laugh in their sleeves at one of the fundamental tenets of their faith, the only course open to parents who objected to the practical consequences of this interpretation was to found schools of their own — a costly solution, it is true, but the only feasible one. Several communities unhesitatingly adopted it and set about availing themselves of the law which conferred this right upon them.[2] But the Government, informed of their intention, forthwith repealed that law, and declared by a decree of the Minister of Public Instruction that it was no longer advisable to authorize the opening of such schools, inasmuch as the ordinary educational establishments that exist for children of all religious persuasions outside the Pale would also satisfactorily meet the requirements of the Jews.[3] The logical outcome of these two legislative acts is therefore that, on the one hand, Jewish parents desirous of having their children instructed must send them to Christian schools, if there happen to be a

---

[1] Circular of the Ministry of Public Instruction. No. 15038.
[2] Collection of Laws, vol. ix., sect. i., art. 969, and observations.
[3] Ministerial Circular, No. 7, of the year 1888.

vacancy there; and on the other hand, their doing so is regarded by the Government as a sort of mild apostasy, in consequence of which they will be no longer treated as strictly orthodox Jews.

Thus foiled and checkmated on every side, small wonder that some of the most ambitious or least steadfast among them brought themselves to purchase such instruction as grammar schools could give them by the formal rejection of all the specially Talmudic doctrines, and the adoption of the faith of the sect of Karaim, who in Russia enjoy privileges that are denied the Talmudists. Thus a number of young men in the Crimea, after much inner struggling and hesitation, resolved to stifle their scruples and take this doubtful course; but they had first to petition the Minister of the Interior (an Atheist, as it chanced) for permission to take the fateful step. They were soon made aware, however, that they were asking for the moon; the heavens and the earth may pass away, but no Russian Jew can ever abjure his faith in order to become a member of the Karaim sect—for a law of Catherine II. forbids it. There was now only one other way to obtain the coveted boon, namely by stealth, and this case has also been thoughtfully provided for by the wise legislators, who decreed that those Jewish parents who, on sending their children to school, neglect to make declaration that they are Jews, will be subjected to exactly the same punishment as if they were convicted of—forgery.[1] This sounds somewhat harsh to Englishmen; it may also seem strange to logicians and legislators of every nation: but the Jews feel that they have reason to be thankful for the leniency that refrained in such cases from treating them as incendiaries or regicides.

The Hebrew people in Russia are characterized by an insatiable thirst for such education as can be had in that country; it would seem to partake of the nature of a passion that grows with their growth, gaining strength from the very opposition it encounters.[2] The Government, on the other hand, is firmly resolved to starve it out and to thrust

---

[1] Collection of Laws, vol. ix., art. 968.
[2] According to the statistics collected by the Ministry of Public Instruction before the introduction of the measures forbidding Jews to educate their children (1885-6), the percentage of Russian children in the higher educational establishments of the empire was twenty-two in ten thousand, whereas the percentage of Jewish children amounted to forty-eight in ten thousand.

the Jews back to ignorance, blind obedience, and the Pale. And this is perfectly natural; if it seems immoral, it is only to those English Russophiles with whom fanaticism is the sole substitute for knowledge, and who damage the cause they would further by judging such acts by a European standard of morality — a mistake which no Russian statesman will ever commit. The reasons that make a dispassionate observer look upon the present persecution of five or six million Jews as natural are not far to seek: they are all comprised in the one principle of self-preservation applied by a people which is standing on a much lower moral and intellectual level than the bulk of Europeans.

An autocracy may at times be quite as good and wise a government as a republic or a constitutional monarchy, and no honest student of history, whatever political opinions he may profess, can withhold his admiration from men like Oliver Cromwell, or even Dr. Francia. But the autocracy of Russia, in which tens of thousands of irresponsible starlets devour, like human locusts, all the material and moral resources of the people, is a foul stain on modern Europe, which only crime can perpetuate and human blood wash away. The logical correlative of such rulers is an ignorant, broken-spirited, shiftless people; and the rulers are resolved to keep the bulk of Russians ignorant, broken-spirited, and shiftless, on the principle that he who wishes for eggs must put up with the cackling of hens — *qui vult finem vult media*. This is the key to that series of oppressive laws enacted during the past five years, the undisguised object of which is to deprive the masses not only of what is usually termed education, but of all kind of instruction whatever. The results obtained up to the present moment are magnificent or disastrous, according to the angle of vision from which we view them; the bulk of the Russian people are disgustingly servile, incredibly superstitious, hopelessly shiftless and improvident, the natural prey of every passing quack or impostor, and the power of the Tsar is proportionately strengthened.[1] The semi-official jour-

---

[1] To give a case in point, the *Novoye Vremya*, describing how the Jews of the district of Starokonstantinovsk return to hamlets and villages in which they are forbidden to reside, almost as fast as they are driven out, adds: "The Russian peasantry, instead of assisting the police to expel them, do just the reverse — harbor and screen them from justice, and when interrogated deny that the Jews in question live there, and assert that they

nal of the capital describes the Russians as "a people run wild, savage, supine. The judges and crown lawyers of the empire," it adds, "can testify that *the number of words in use among the Russian peasantry does not exceed from one to two hundred. Even the Kirghecz nomads,* with their wonderful memory, foresight, imagination, and shiftiness, *stand on a far higher level than our Russian peasantry.*"[1] Over against these "country louts" stand the Jews with wits sharpened by necessity and appetites whetted by gnawing hunger — "like ravenous wolves beside appetizing sheep," as an official organ once described them. And the Russian Government is engaged in solving the problem how to keep them together in a state of semi-starvation without a catastrophe. Blinding the wolves is the latest solution that seems to have suggested itself, and, on the principle of self-preservation, why, it may be asked, should Russian statesmen not give it a trial?

Naturally, much more is hereby implied than deprivation

---

have only come on a visit. *A Jew has only to buy a glass of vodka and promise a trifle besides, and for this Russian peasants will, almost without exception, lie when questioned in a court of justice — ay, lie in the most affronting way conceivable, even though, as is often the case, they are giving evidence upon oath.*" — *Novoye Vremya,* 4th April, 1890. None of the conflicting conclusions which can be drawn from this unanswerable and lamentable fact are of good omen for the speedy settlement of the Jewish question in Russia.

[1] *Graschdanin,* 19th January, 1890. Cf. also *Novosti,* 20th January, 1890. An English Russophile organ which might possibly render some services to its Tsar by courageous honesty which it can never effect by mere coarse flattery, *à tort et à travers,* recently alluding to a former paper of this series, the statements of which it completely garbles, seriously puts forward the following argument: If the Russian people are such ignorant, shiftless loons as they are represented to be, they are solely in need of an autocratic government that will protect them against their own instincts; if they are enlightened, moral, well-behaved, autocracy is likewise the best government for them, for they would otherwise have long ago cried out against its existence. "If the books are in accordance with the teachings of the Koran," said the fanatic Caliph, of the Alexandrian library, " they are needless, and must be burned; if opposed to the Koran, they are heretical, and must be destroyed forthwith." The accusation brought against the Russian Government, and demonstrated by unanswerable facts, is that they are *deliberately demoralizing* the wretched people in order to perpetuate the chaotic misrule on which they are thriving. What would any honest, unprejudiced Englishman say to the following candid avowal of the Government's programme, made by the aristocratic organ subsidized by the Government: "The Russian peasant possesses *great powers of endurance and remarkable patience. And these, in sum, are the qualities of the Russian which should form the basis of the relations of persons in authority to the peasants;* and it must be admitted that the authorities have to deal with a soil very favorable if it is *only ploughed and harrowed intelligently.*" — *Graschdanin,* 2nd January, 1890. If this be not Macchiavellism, its defence in an English periodical is disinterested love of the good, the beautiful, and the true.

of mere lay instruction. The Talmudic religion, whatever else may be said about it, is in itself a course of mental training capable of rendering the mental powers as supple and sharp as would a course of mathematics or of German metaphysics. And as long as a Jew is allowed to remain a Jew he will continue to be infinitely better equipped for the battle of life than the best of his Russian competitors. Hence the natural desire of the more far-seeing among the Russian politicians to extirpate Judaism, root and branch; hence the feverish efforts now being made to realize that scheme by employing every known form of injustice and violence that stops short of death.

Every sordid motive that a legislator well versed in this lower branch of his profession could suggest is put before the Jew to induce him to abandon the faith of his forefathers, without replacing it by anything better. Privileges denied his brethren, money and its various equivalents, even the hope of unlawful plunder, have been deliberately relied upon by these champions of Christianity to tempt the Hebrew to please his Emperor by denying his God. Imagine one of those lean, cadaverous caricatures of humanity who crowd the cities of the Pale, and whose existence under the actual circumstances is a stronger argument against Russian Christianity than any that could be drawn from the writings of Strauss or Huxley; and suppose that accident or design puts it in his power to defraud a wealthy co-religionist, by abuse of confidence, fraud, or downright robbery. He succumbs to the temptation, beggars his brother, and immediately becomes a member of the orthodox Church, as a sort of corollary. His victim prosecutes him and summons a cloud of credible, respectable witnesses who can prove the charge to the satisfaction of the most sceptical. He, on his side, suborns two or three abandoned Christian wretches, whose life is one coarse libel on Christianity. The case comes on for trial, and the Russian courts, guided by Article 330 of the Tenth Volume of Laws, will refuse to allow the Jewish witnesses to depose against the defendant, because they are naturally supposed to bear a grudge against an apostate; and the light-hearted perjury of the orthodox Christians (which costs, as we have seen, but a small measure of *vodka*) sets the seal of legality on crimes that would send their author into penal servitude in England. Of course, there is one way out of the difficulty: the plaintiff may go to work and bribe his witnesses to commit perjury too, *i.e.*, to embrace Christianity, which they hate, and then their testimony will be received with credence and respect. For when a Jew finds the truth, supposing that truth to be the "orthodox" faith, he is caressed and made much of for the time being; the law requires "that he be baptised only in a city church, and on a Sunday or festival, and with all possible pomp and ceremony."[1] If he be married he must either divorce his wife or compel her too to subordinate her religious convictions to her conjugal affection; and if she refuses to become a Christian, neither herself *nor* her Christian husband will be permitted to leave the Pale.[2] Finally, in order to contribute to the sacredness of the family, which, Russians complain, is lacking among the Jews, the new laws give a Jewish boy or girl the right and the encouragement to abandon the faith of his fathers without consulting his parents.[3] The difficulties thrown in the way of opening synagogues and prayer-houses are as numerous and as prohibitive as those which have been so effectually opposed to opening of schools, and the Rabbis of those that already exist are harassed and persecuted till they resign or go over to the enemy. In one place the ministry refuses to confirm the election of a respected Rabbi, conducted in strict accordance with all the laws and regulations, simply because, penetrated with a deep sense of his moral responsibility, he refuses to prostitute a religious office to the desires of political Chauvinists, and they unceremoniously put in his place an upstart who was not disliked only by those who did not know him. The Jews of Yekaterinburg, who had lived there for generations, summoned up courage once to ask permission to have, not a synagogue, but merely a house of prayer.[4] The Govern-

---

[1] Supplement to art. 76 (section 5).
[2] Complete Coll. of Laws, vol. x., part i., art. 81.
[3] *Ibid.*, section 3.
[4] The abject fear which the Jews have of displeasing the authorities exceeds belief. Take, for instance, a man in the position of Baron Ginsburg, of St. Petersburg, a millionnaire and a baron of the Russian empire, who might well venture to undertake much that is forbidden to his poorer brethren; and yet he is mortally afraid of saying, or doing, or leaving unsaid and undone anything that might possibly offend even a petty Russian official. He dares even not speak even in favor of the Russian Government, lest that should seem an attempt on his part to patronize; and he would as soon cut his tongue out as say a word against it. A few years ago he caused all the Russian laws concerning the Jews to be printed in one volume at his expense; but when the work was done he reflected that his motives might be misinterpreted, so he withdrew it from circulation; and no en-

ment, in reply, very quickly discovered a long forgotten
ukase, which absolutely forbids Jews to reside in that city,
or in any part of the Ural, and they are now about to be
dragged thousands of miles to the Pale, which many of
them have never seen before. In the village of Kakhovka
the Hebrew community was lately summoned to appear
before the new police superintendent, who at once informed
them that he had orders to close up and seal their prayer-
house, and to bring them up to trial for having four years
ago opened one, "and for having frequently prayed therein,"
without being authorized to do so by the Government.

These are some of the measures which have driven
thousands of Jews to apostatize; and one reads very frequently in the Russian newspapers of "sixty young Jews
who, desirous of entering the university, have abjured the
Law of Moses"; of forty others who became Christians
because their business called them outside of the Pale, and
scores of others who for equally valid reasons are introduced every month into the true fold, where they are as
much in their place as eagles in a barnyard. Any one of
the measures employed against the Jews would be enough
to "convert" three-fourths of the Christians of Russia to
Shamanism or Buddhism in a week; and the circumstances
that about six million persecuted and miserable wretches
remain steadfastly faithful to a religion that causes their
life to be changed into a fiery furnace without the angel to
keep it cool, is the nearest approach to a grandiose miracle
that has been vouchsafed to this unbelieving generation.
The Orthodox Church cannot be congratulated on these
wedding guests whom it is daily picking up in the highways and byways, and bidding, or rather driving, into the
spiritual banqueting hall. Not only is one prepared for
the discovery that they are not provided with the indispensable wedding garment, but one cannot affect surprise
to learn that such raiment as they have is swarming with
disease germs which will do dire execution on the assembled
guests. I have conversed with numbers of "converted"
Jews of all classes of society, and I can affirm that, with
few exceptions, not only have they not the faintest glimmer of faith in Christianity, but they hate the very name,

---

treaties on the part of his own intimate friends could persuade him to
give away one of the thousands of copies that were lying on the shelves of
his library. In Odessa, where the governor is Judophobe and more, a Jew
will soon be afraid to sneeze in the street.

despise its priests, sneer at its ceremonies, and loathe themselves for perjuring their souls by receiving its sacraments and praising the name of its founder. And they bring up their sons and daughters in the same sentiments. I know a respectable family in Moscow, the father of which was "converted" like thousands of his co-religionists, and I can answer for it that not one of his sons or daughters had a shred of belief in God or devil, their religious faith being summed up in the one conviction that the Orthodox Church is deserving of the intense hatred of every honest man and woman, and that no opportunity should ever be missed of contributing to its ruin.

Some of these "converts" repent of what they have done, secretly do penance for their sins, and return to the synagogue. But their sighs and tears are as unavailing as those of their forefathers who, sitting down by the waters of Babylon, wept as they remembered Sion; no Rabbi would dare give them help or advice, much less admission to the community; he would forfeit his position if he did. One of these poor wretches, Fichtenstein by name, a venerable old man of sixty, was induced in a moment of weakness to "embrace Christianity," for which he afterwards did penance, literally in sackcloth and ashes. He visited the synagogue as often as he could, where his fervent, tearful prayers attracted the attention of the congregation. The authorities set a watch on his movements, acquired the conviction that he did really pray in the Jewish place of worship, and had him straightway arrested and sent for trial. The example of these men, it is complained, does not tend to raise the moral level of the Russian Church; "they scatter the seeds of infidelity and insubordination — religious, political, and social — broadcast throughout the country," say the astonished spiritual and civil authorities, "and the harm thus done is incalculable." Harm it may be; incalculable, however, it certainly is not. The Jews may all of them in time be brought to "embrace Russian Christianity," as the Moorish chieftain Almanzor embraced his Christian enemies; and in both cases the embrace is pestilential, deadly.

But the written laws against the Jews, severe as they undoubtedly are, can give no idea of the actual amount and kind of suffering inflicted on this unfortunate people by those who administer them, and from whose interpretation and conduct there lies no appeal. Not only must one take into consideration the kind of whip with which they are beaten, but likewise the arm that wields it; and in this case it is the sinewy, bloody arm that knouted so many Christians to death. For some officials the Jews exist as a fertile source of revenue — a godsend to be grateful for — the bribes they are compelled annually to pay exceeding by a large amount the total of their double annual taxes. This state of things reminds one of our own Henry III. pledging all the Jews of his kingdom to his brother for the loan of a considerable sum of money, authorizing him in return to keep them in his power until they paid the debt to the last farthing. Russia's solution of the Jewish problem has not advanced beyond that stage yet. Here is what one of the most trustworthy and impartial newspapers of Russia has to say on the subject: —

"The restrictions laid upon the Jews serve in reality as an unfailing and inexhaustible source of income to the authorities charged with their execution; all those Jews whose rights are more or less doubtful manage to get them changed into undoubted rights by the payment of uninterrupted blackmail; *battues* and domiciliary visits, which assume the most improbable forms, also wind up with a money tribute. Thus on a dark night, when profound silence reigns everywhere—usually a Friday night is chosen, when every Jew is at home—suddenly the Jewish quarter of the city is surrounded by a cordon, and a great multitude of people, men, women, and children, old men—nay, often even the sick—are arrested and packed off to the police station; here, for lack of room, they are kept all night in the courtyard in the open air, no matter how severe the cold may be, no matter how inclement the weather. These are facts."[1]

And facts, I may add, that are related not of last century, nor last year, but last winter.

This hunting of Jews who are living where they have no right to reside, whose passports have expired, who have transacted some business which their faith disqualifies them from transacting, or who are working hard to keep body and soul together in a position which they are not allowed to occupy, has now become an everyday occurrence, that no longer excites surprise and seldom even evokes compassion. The newspapers chronicle these things with as perfect indifference as a huxter's change of residence. "The authorities have ordered the assistant notaries who belong to the Hebrew persuasion to be immediately dismissed from their situations in Kovno," says the *Warsaw Courier*, and

---

[1] *The Week*, 7th September, 1890.

people read and pass on phlegmatically to the next item of intelligence. "M. Akimoff, the President of the Divisional Court," says another paper, "has informed all notaries that they must dismiss their clerks who are members of the Jewish communion, and fill up their places with Russians."[1] And people yawn and read on.

The suffering inflicted by this wholesale proscription of the Jews is intensified a hundred-fold by the wantonly savage manner in which it is carried out, the victims being treated in many cases exactly as if, instead of human beings, they were brute beasts, who might be chased without impropriety in the fields and highways, and tied up in an outhouse, when caught, till they could be conveniently whipped or physicked. The following incident will illustrate my meaning: A considerable number of Jews repair every year from various parts of Russia to the Liman in Odessa, to test the medicinal virtue of the waters, which are strongly recommended by Russian doctors in cases of rheumatism, gout, scrofula, skin diseases, paralysis, etc. Numerous petitions, stamped with revenue stamps, certificates, and documents of all kinds have to be drawn up, presented, and verified before a Jew can receive his double passport and permission to pass a few weeks at the waters of the Liman. And when he has passed through this wearisome and expensive ordeal and has begun the cure, he is not even then free from persecution. He or she may, at any time of the day or night, be pounced upon by the police, snatched up, ladies as well as men, and ignominiously subjected to a medical examination and pronounced impostors who are at the waters under false pretences, having none of the disorders which the latter are supposed to cure. No farther back than the month of July, the Jewish ladies and gentlemen who were using the waters of the Andreieff Liman in Odessa, were thus unceremoniously arrested one day — night is usually the favorite time for arrests, domiciliary visits, etc., in Russia — and marched off to the city doctor, who was commanded to examine them thoroughly, and to find out whether they were really suffering from the diseases for which they were being treated, or had merely come for their pleasure! It is no easy matter even for a physician to decide in the twinkling of an eye, so to say, whether a man has or has not rheumatism, gout,

---

[1] *Odessa News*, October, 1886.

tic, scrofula, etc., etc. The Odessa doctor, however, knew exactly what was required of him, and justified the confidence with which he was honored: he declared that two-thirds of the entire number of Jews were in good health and had no need of the Liman waters. Even if this were demonstrably true, the services of these persons might be desirable or even indispensable to their invalid relatives, and on this ground their presence might have been tolerated; but the authorities sent them home at once.[1]

It is no light matter for the Jews, who, after all, are mere human beings, to make a stand against a powerful government which is mobilizing its numerous army of officials, employing all its pecuniary resources, and all the ingenuity of human hate to crush them out of existence. Still they cannot — on the whole — be accused of not doing their best to dispute every inch of ground, of not struggling for some few of the rights of men, when possible, on a strictly legal basis. No losing game — with stakes so high — was ever yet played with such unfaltering spirit. No fox hotly pursued by eager hounds and joyful huntsmen ever employed more profound cunning, more suppleness, more talent for adapting, on the spur of the moment, all the rapidly changing circumstances of time, place, and persons to the main end in view, than the Jews. The tragic-comic element that results from this pitting of intellect against brute force, the adventures, curious escapes, the plots and counterplots, would, if properly treated, make a most entertaining volume — but entertaining as were the jokes and puns and witty remarks made at the gladiator fights in Rome, and which drew their point from their contrast to the human being grimly fighting on the threshold of eternity, to prolong for a few minutes the brutal pleasure of a jaded rabble.

The laws that regulate the military service of the Jews are characterized by their Draconian severity. Most of the alleviations and privileges accorded to Christians, and which tend so visibly to promote good feeling between the men and their superiors, are inexorably denied them, and the hardships inseparable from life in the barracks, with its long winter night-watches and exhausting summer manœuvres, are needlessly made unendurable to the soldier who keeps holy the Sabbath. A Jew can never become an officer as a Christian can — nay, as even a Mohammedan

---

[1] *Novoye Vremya*, 23rd July, 1890.

can, who is not disqualified from the highest position in the military hierarchy, filling offices of trust and responsibility. This is a remarkable — it seems an unjust — restriction; but the Jew, hardened by use and want, is prepared for it. But why go still further and allow every soldier who calls himself a Christian, a Mohammedan, or a Buddhist to lord it over him, and not only hector and bully, but assault him with absolute impunity, sometimes with direct approbation? The paralyzing fear of encountering these untold miseries of soldier life, from which the only escape is suicide, accounts for the deep-rooted aversion which many Jews manifest to don the livery of the Tsar, and the desperate attempts they make to escape from serving in the army. Hundreds of mothers secretly leave their native places before the birth of their children, which, when the children are boys, they refuse to register, thus placing their innocent offspring, almost from the moment of its birth, in a position bristling with still greater difficulties, with more terrible hardships than the one they so greatly dread.[1]

It is impossible for a Jew to do anything in a simple, straightforward manner. He could not even if he would: he sets to work to carry out the most commonplace and lawful business transaction just as if his negotiations were but a blind to mask some hidden design, the nature of which you have no means of guessing — it may be to rob you, it may be to murder you. All his dealings are fenced and hedged round with so many provisos and conditions, and contingent obligations, that a very experienced lawyer would have no light task if he were set to unravel the web. The following is a very typical instance of the trouble taken by Jews to wrest to their own benefit one of the laws framed for their ruin. Intending to conclude a business arrangement, whatever its nature may be, the validity of which may hereafter be called in question by the other party to the contract, a Jew first makes a pretence of lending him some costly furniture or delivering valuable goods — which he himself never had to give or lend — and then sues him

---

[1] "My attention was drawn to the strange fact of the virtual cessation of male births among the Jews, as if by common accord all Jewish women had resolved to put an end to the tribe of Israel. From private sources, however, I learned that things were pretty much as they had always been, . . . but that the far-seeing, provident parents refused to register their births, in order to free them from the necessity, many years thence, of serving in the army." — *The Vilna Messenger*, 11th December, 1887.

for the value. The case comes on for trial (the Russian law courts are literally clogged with such fictitious lawsuits, which prevent the hearing of really important actions); both parties are heard with all the conscious seriousness and dignified leisure which beseems a Russian judge. The defendant seems to make a determined stand, but loses his case and is condemned to pay the sum demanded. Now this is exactly the sum that would represent the plaintiff's loss, *if* at any future time the defendant should call in question the validity of the contract which they *have not yet concluded*. He would then claim a writ of execution to recover the sum adjudged him by the court.[1]

Formerly a Jew could lend money on landed securities. Now this is absolutely forbidden; so, before advancing the sum demanded, he requires the borrower to give him a note of hand for the capital and the interest combined, he next sues him for the amount, and when judgment is given in his favor, advances the sum of money required. Or, suppose a merchant or petty trader has business in some town or city which his quality of Jew precludes him from visiting. If he petitions the authorities to allow him to go there and spend a week or a fortnight, he is insulted for his pains. Instead of this, however, two of his friends or dependents quarrel and summon him to give evidence before the local magistrate, which he does; but one of the parties appeals to the higher court, which sits in the city he is so desirous of visiting, and he is again called upon to give evidence, this time on oath. This also he does, if it is a criminal prosecution, as it probably would be, at the cost of the crown. One of the litigants is perhaps condemned, but the prosecutor thereupon generously forgives him, and all parties are satisfied. The law courts of the west of Russia are positively brought to a standstill by the overwhelming number of fictitious actions of this kind entered by Jews, who thus compel the imperial judges to spend their time and labor and the resources of the State in assisting the Jewish community to evade the very laws which they are sworn to administer.[2] A more ludicrous sight was never witnessed in the law courts of modern times. "Lately the local authorities," a Kieff journal announces,.

---

[1] *Novoye Vremya*, 24th December, 1889. These artifices are rendered possible by the important circumstance that in Russia law is not costly, and a man can and generally does conduct his own case, even if he is unable to read or write.

[2] *Novoye Vremya*, 24th December, 1890.

"set about verifying the right of the Jews in Shmerinka to reside there. Many of them were living in little huts of their own. Before the verification took place, however, many of the resident Hebrews deemed it advisable to flee. There are several hundred Jewish houses there, the majority of which were erected, like the palaces of the fairy tales, by night. The work was done in the daytime in bits and scraps, at some distance from the city, and when ready the complete house would be drawn by twenty or thirty pairs of oxen, and set up in the place destined for it. For convenience' sake these houses were made to move about on wheels."[1]

The poverty of the greater part of the six million Jews who are caged up in the few plague-stricken towns and villages of the Pale surpasses that which excited such a cry of horror in London when the sweating system and its results were dragged into the light of day. The late Minister of Finances, Reutern, declared candidly in a memoir to the Emperor, that "the poverty in which the Jews live is extreme, and the extraordinary demoralization of the Hebrew race in Russia is mainly the outcome of the extremely unfavorable conditions in which they are placed for gaining a livelihood."[2] The amount of taxes which they owe is enormous.[3] It was shown by the census that whereas the average proportion of Christians to the total number of houses owned by Christians in the governments of the Pale, is between 410 and 510 persons to one house, the average number of Jews is 1,229.[4] In most parts of the Pale, they are cooped up like insects or animals rather than men. In Berditscheff, the official statistician tells us

"the Jews are huddled together more like salted herrings than human beings; tens of thousands of them are devoid of any constant means of subsistence, living from hand to mouth; several families are often crowded into one or two rooms of a dilapidated hut, so that at night there is absolutely no space whatever between the sleepers. . . . The lodgers turn these rooms into workshops in the daytime, refining wax therein, making tallow candles, tanning leather, etc.; here whole families live, work, sleep, and eat together, in that fetid atmosphere, with their tools and materials lying around on all sides."[5]

The *Moscow Gazette*, describing the state of the Jews in Berditscheff, says:—

"The streets of the Jewish quarter of the town are not more than four feet wide; on either side of them the tumble-down old houses

---

[1] Cf. also *Novoye Vremya*, 10th January, 1890.
[2] Cf. Complete Collection of Laws, vol. xl., 42264.
[3] *Novoye Vremya*, 10th January, 1890.
[4] Shooravski Statist., *Description of the Government of Kieff*, vol. i., p. 247.
[5] *Ibid.*

seem ready to fall to pieces; children are lying before the houses on the street in a state of almost complete nudity, wallowing in the slough, and among them numbers of slovenly women — the mothers of the children — also stretched out sideways and lengthways on the street, sleeping under the rays of the burning sun."

The statistician, M. Bobrovski, writing on the condition of the Jews in the government of Grodno, says: —

"By far the greater part of the Jewish population are poor and are always engrossed by the one care: how to get their daily bread. Burdened with numerous families, the crowded state in which they live surpasses anything one can conceive as possible. Frequently one hut consisting of three or at most four rooms lodges as many as *twelve* families, whose lives are an unbroken series of privations and pains. Whole families sometimes live on three-quarters of a pound of bread, one salt herring, and a few onions."[1]

"In the Government of Kovno," — and in every government inhabited by the Jews — "there are families who never break their fast till night, and then only if the father and bread-winner had found work to do and has received his wage."[2]

This, no doubt, is very unsavory reading, and I inflict as little of it upon my readers as will barely suffice to enable them to form an opinion upon the Jewish question in Russia. Russian Judophobes — many members of the Government included — positively take a pleasure in these disgusting things. And yet what the object of all this persecution is — beyond the one I have already suggested — no man can tell. It is not the Jewish religion that is so unrelentingly pursued, for it is admitted even by the Orthodox Church to be superior to Mohammedanism, which enjoys toleration in Russia. Neither is it the Jewish race, for once a Jew adopts Christianity as his "faith," he is placed on a level with born Christians. It cannot be the supposed economical influence for evil exerted by the Jews, for the same evils complained of, only in much larger dimensions, are to be found in those parts of the Empire in which a Jew never sets foot. And yet, objectless as this persecution evidently is from any reasonable point of view, not only is it warmly advocated by a portion of the press, but a fiendish delight is taken in contemplating the results. The following is a short extract from a description of Vilna,

---

[1] *Description of the Government of Grodno*, vol. i., p. 858 and fol.
[2] Afanassieff, *Description of the Government of Kovno*, pp. 582, 583.

published in the *Vilna Messenger*, a Government organ, and quoted with relish by the *Novoye Vremya*: —

"All the narratives of travellers about Asiatic and African cities dwindle down to the level of the commonplace in comparison with the sights that meet your eye here; even the glorious city of Berditscheff, the very name of which is become proverbial as a synonym for dirt and rottenness, is as nothing when confronted with this pearl. . . . Glance at the Jewish Synagogue. The dirt in the courtyard is indescribable, the noise and tumult like unto that which accompanied the confusion of tongues. But the atmosphere? You should breathe it, to be able to conceive what it is like. Beside the women's wing of the synagogue are the baths in which the sons and daughters of Israel cleanse their sinful flesh. You can judge of the internal tidiness and cleanliness of these baths by the high dunghill carefully heaped up beside the steps of the entrance." [1]

But the rest of this foul essay is, at least in parts, too filthy to be given in English. Imagine the Nawab of Bengal sneering at Mr. Holwell and his twenty-two companions for the mephitic atmosphere of the Black Hole of Calcutta, and you have a parallel to the good taste and the humanity of Russian Judophobes.

It would be asking for a miracle to expect that men condemned, as are the Russian Jews, to rot away in forced idleness, in Augean filth, breathing air poisoned by the smell of untanned leather, and charged with the noisome exhalations of the dead and dying, to be clean, or even to be merely dirty in the ordinary acceptation of the word. What a harrowing picture of their life does not the following scene conjure up — one of the most pathetic of the tragi-comic incidents to which I allude above? In the middle of the town of Berditscheff there is a large channel or sink in which is thrown all kinds of foul unnamable filth. One day it occurred to a police superintendent that he might have it cleaned out gratis, and he hit upon the following happy expedient: Strolling along the edge of this putrid cesspool, he suddenly stood still and then bent anxiously over the brink, stirring up the filth with his stick. A crowd of Jews soon gathered round him, and inquired what was wrong. He replied that he had dropped a valuable ring worth £25 into the *cloaca*, and he promised a reward to the finder. "In about fifteen minutes," says the journal, "all this putrescent garbage was taken out in handkerchiefs, buckets, pots, rags, etc., and brought *home* by the

---

[1] *Novoye Vremya*, 29th August, 1888.

Jews, who scrutinized it in their courtyards, each one hopeful of finding the ring. And in this way," it concludes, "the superintendent succeeded in *cleansing that canal.*" What extraordinary notions the Russian police must have of the meaning of the word sanitation!

The majority of the other charges brought against the Jews are in equal good taste. In fairness to both parties, however, it must be admitted that from one fault — or perhaps the word crime would more accurately connote it — it would be difficult to exculpate them; and this partly explains, if it does not justify, the indignation of the Russian Government. I allude to a lack of ardor, amounting at times to a positive aversion on their part, to risk their lives in the service of the Tsar, in return for the rights and protection which they enjoy in Russia. And this, in spite of the solemn oath which they all have to take, "in all things to serve and obey his Imperial Majesty, not sparing in his service my life-blood, but shedding it, ay, to the last drop,"[1] in defence of throne and beloved fatherland. This may be perjury and high treason combined, but, whatever its name and degree, many Jews[2] are guilty of it. And if that be a satisfactory answer to the charge of undue harshness brought against the Russian Government, there is an end to the matter. At the same time one fails to understand why the Government, which taunts the Jews with being cowards, takes more pains to draw or drive them into the Russian army than if they were so many Hectors and Achilles. Lest a Jew follow what is supposed to be the bent of his inclination and shirk his "sacred duty to his Little Father the Tsar and his dear Fatherland," his personal appearance must be minutely described in his passport in much greater detail than if he were a Christian. Thus every pimple, mole, malformation, and other mark by which he may be identified is to be clearly mentioned![3] If the medical commission declare him unfit for service, and the authorities entertain a well-founded or absurd suspicion that he himself deliberately contributed to bring about this unfitness, he is received into the army in spite of his physical defects, and told off for special service.[4] If, when called

---

[1] Supplement to Article 1061 (1886).
[2] The percentage of Jews who neglect to present themselves for military service, or afterwards desert, is larger than that of the Christians; but the difference is not considerable.
[3] Military Law of 1886. Explanation of Article 8.
[4] Explanation of Article 40.

upon, a Jew fails to present himself to the military commission whose business it is to accept or reject him, he is not imprisoned, for this would be no punishment to a man whose life is a crownless martyrdom, but heavily fined. This may be a just and certain method of engrafting that love of Fatherland and Little Father which neither their feelings nor their reason have been able to evoke, but it seems needlessly harsh to inflict upon the hard-working old parents of the defaulter a fine of £50 besides; and this is exactly what the law does.[1] But many young men are orphans at this age, or their parents are literally beggars, so that, not possessing a copper coin, they have no fear of the penalties. Such youths ingeniously turn the law to account, and compel it to yield them and their relations a slight profit. They run away from the parish or city in which the commission holds its sittings, and are declared fugitives. For all such deserters — if only they be Jews — a reward of fifty roubles is always liberally paid. A friend of the runaway is informed by the delinquent himself of his whereabouts, he communicates the information to the authorities and receives the reward, which he gives in part or in its entirety to the offender.

In this manner many of the Russian laws against the Jewish population either defeat their own purpose or inflict considerable loss upon the Christian subjects of the Tsar. Thus there are numerous districts in Russia — fertile stretches of land which are in sore need of workmen to till the soil or reap its fruits. It often happens that the corn rots on the ground for want of hands to cut it. The landowners have been for years crying out for some measure calculated to restore what the emancipation of the serfs deprived them of — cheap labor; and the Government did enact a law a few years ago, which has created a class of agricultural laborers who sell themselves for several years, and even descend to the heirs of their master, should he die before the expiration of their term. But this measure has not brought the looked-for relief to Russian landowners, who are often driven to despair at the sight of their riches melting away like snow for want of laborers, while the miserable Jews are perishing of sheer starvation, almost devouring each other, like Ugolino's offspring in the tower of the Gualandi, because there is no work for them to do in

---

[2] Article 350 of the Military Law.

the Pale. These hungry wretches are then accused by sleek, over-fed ministers in their warm drawing-rooms, of a disposition to outreach the Russian peasant whenever they have a chance. The accusation, it is to be feared, is not wholly groundless, for Jews belong to the genus animal no less than to the species man, and the instinct of self-preservation is as strongly developed within them when their rival is a Russian as if he were only a vile Jew, like themselves. Men of mild, amiable disposition, tossed about in an open boat on the ocean for a week or ten days, and tortured by the pangs of hunger and thirst, have even been known to harbor wicked thoughts of cannibalism, which the children of Israel in Russia have not yet been known to entertain.

I am personally acquainted with a rich Jew in a flourishing provincial city who is compelled to pay in bribes to the authorities a sum that would support half the Jews of Berditscheff. He raises the necessary amount by imposing an illegal supplementary tax on all *kosher* food sold by him to his co-religionists. His arrangements with the police enable him not only to do this with impunity, but likewise to have all his competitors removed from the city "administratively," that is, by an order issued by the police, without rhyme or reason. These "administrative" orders are much more demoralizing than the *lettres de cachet* of the French monarchy, because much more easily obtained. If a Christian have an obliging friend in the police administration, he can treat many Jews of the lower classes just as if they were serfs. I knew a respectable young girl of very honest parents privileged to live in one of the capital cities. A Christian "fell in love" with her, and under pretext of giving her lessons and preparing her for admission to one of the high schools, seduced her, solemnly promising marriage. I heard her once ask him to marry her, and I also heard him reply that he would have her sent out of the city in twenty-four hours for her presumption. And he did. A cousin of his is serving in the police department, and he had no difficulty to obtain an order for her banishment "as a disorderly Jewess." "But how could you bring yourself to do such a damnable act?" I asked. "Oh, she is only a Jewess," he answered. "What else is she good for. Besides, everybody does the same."[1]

---

[1] At present a Jew can be sent out of the city on the ground that he has been *impolite* in the street or in a crowd. And this law has been made by

Yes, everybody does the same, and the lives of six million people whose instincts, aptitudes, and moral sense place them on a much higher level than their Christian fellow subjects, are thus made literally unendurable. Scoffed at, terrorized, and robbed by every petty official with that certain impunity which invites to crime; insulted, beaten, and kept in constant fear of violence by a vile rabble whom they dare not irritate by even a slight success in business or trade ; held up to the scorn and indignation of all Russia by the Governmental press as the authors of every calamity avoidable and unavoidable;[1] education and instruction denied them, the learned professions and higher branch of the profession of arms closed to them; trade and commerce rendered very difficult by intolerable taxes and endless restrictions, and *wholly impossible without bribery and fraud;* their personal liberty now at last completely taken away from them; their religion proscribed, and their very souls killed by the perjury with which they are forced to blacken it, Russian Jews may well defy their persecutors to frame any further laws calculated to make their position worse than it is.

Surely English journalists and politicians carried distrust too far when they doubted the solemn assurances of the Russian Government that no more stringent laws were in contemplation at present, just as the American coroner's jury, finding a paper with the words, "I have killed myself," on the corpse of an inveterate liar, brought in a verdict that he was not dead at all. Still, it is to be regretted that the monster meeting which the Lord Mayor of London was to have convened was not held, as it might have led to some beneficial results; not, of course, by passing impotent resolutions of indignation, which would have had as much effect on the Russian Government as dewdrops on a goose's back, but by respectfully petitioning his Imperial Majesty — as a daily paper lately suggested — to commute in his

---

a governor whose politeness is shown by kicks and cuffs and blasphemous oaths, as the whole south of Russia is well aware.

[1] Cf. *Novoye Vremya*, which published a long article at the time of the accident to the Tsar's train at Borki to show that the danger of sudden death had been brought about by the Jews, while his escape was miraculous and actually foretold by one of the minor Hebrew prophets, who, when read aright, mentions him by name. This same enlightened organ, the most extensively circulated in Russia, also countenanced the fable that the Jews periodically murder a Christian child, whose blood they require for their ceremonies.

clemency the present unbearable sufferings to which the law condemns six millions of men and women for worshipping God as Christ did — for painless death by electricity or poison.

CHAPTER VIII.

RUSSIAN FINANCE: THE RACKING OF THE PEASANTRY.

SINCE the halcyon days of Controller Calonne, the miraculous transformer of bland smiles and promises into ready money, that, like Cinderella's finery, had a nasty way of reverting after a brief period to its original forms, no country would seem to have made such marvellous financial progress in so short a time as Russia, under the guidance of her present Minister of Finances, M. Vyshnegradsky. A cursory survey of the chief items of this improvement would probably silence the majority of those prejudiced politicians who are ever contemptuously inquiring—as the Jews of old about Nazareth—"Can any good thing come out of Russia?" The wilful pessimism of these professional Russophobes is less excusable than the childish optimism of Slavonian patriots who, with Oriental hyperbole, complacently dwell on the unparalleled prosperity and magnanimity of their fatherland, whose gold, they allege, pulled England through the late financial crisis.[1] The means by which M. Vyshnegradsky raised his country's credit in the eyes of the world were neither few nor simple. He naturally began by cutting down the expenses of the administration as low as was consistent with his own tenure of office; he diligently tapped such new sources of revenue as suggested themselves to a mind ambitious of distinction and fertile in resources; he raised loans; effected conversions; collected debts that seemed hopeless: and literally "scraped together" every available rouble in the country. In all this human ingenuity was admirably seconded by chance, and favorable circumstance improved in turn by clear insight and ready resolve. Two abundant harvests changed

---

[1] In the semi-official *Novoye Vremya*, for instance, we read:—"In bygone times the Russian Government was occasionally subsidized by England, but now the London Exchange is saved from a crisis by the money of the Russian Government. Our conduct is in this case extremely magnanimous when one takes into consideration the nasty tricks played by the English Exchange in 1876-7, in order to undermine our credit." — *Novoye Vremya*, 20th November, 1890.

his gloomy if prudent anticipation of a small deficit into a welcome little surplus, and his own skilful manipulation and extreme munificence towards certain bankers struck off the golden fetters that had previously bound Russia to Berlin, thus establishing identity of French and Russian interests, if not in politics, at least in finance. Some idea of the extent to which Russia is beholden to French sympathy in all these financial achievements may be gathered from a few eloquent figures. The Russian loan of 500 million francs (22nd December, 1888) was covered two and a half times over and issued at 448¾; that of 700 millions (10th April, 1889) was responded to by an offer of eight times that amount, although it was issued at 448¾; that of 1,242 millions (5th June, 1889) likewise elicited an offer of eight times more than was called for, and was issued at 457½; while the last loan of 360 millions (March, 1890) was, to use the expression employed by Russian papers, "gulped down" by the French with an enthusiasm scarcely surpassed by that with which they invested their hard-earned savings in the equally promising venture of the Panama Canal.[1] Some of these loans were quoted at 96 a month after issue, and it is not impossible that they should yet reach par, while at present Russian stock stands 2 per cent. higher than Austrian, and about 12 per cent. above Hungarian.

Then, again, if we glance hastily at the rapid development of industrial manufactures in the empire, we are lost in astonishment at the seemingly miraculous results effected by Protection. Thus the chemical works in the country have a yearly output of 2½ millions sterling, as against £450,000 in 1867; Russian tanneries have an output valued at 4½ millions sterling, instead of the 1¼ million of twenty-three years ago; the value of woollen manufactures has increased during the same time from half a million to 3 millions; in a word, most of the advantages that could be reasonably expected to accrue to the country from the policy of encircling Russia with the Chinese wall of a commercial tariff have already been realized. The manufacturers have wonderfully prospered under the system, and Russia can now significantly point to a class of merchant princes

---

[1] When the last Russian loan was floated, 772 bonds satisfied the wants of all British capitalists combined, while Frenchmen demanded over 5¼ millions of them, and received 123,000.

created by Protection; men who equal, possibly surpass, the historic Childs of London, the Coutts of Edinburgh, the Blundells of Liverpool, in riches, if not in refinement; millionnaires who can afford to give themselves the exquisite pleasure of employing choice champagnes to wash their hands, too seldom cleansed with vulgar soap and water; who can pay £300 for a seat in the theatre,[1] and preside at entertainments that combine the luxury of a Lucullus or an Apicius with the taste of Bruegel's boors.

But these considerations, to which it cannot be denied that Frenchmen gave all the weight they deserved, can scarcely be said to exhaust the question. There are other important points of view from which the economic position of a country may and should be studied besides that of the reputation of a finance minister or the enrichment of a score of manufacturers, many of whom are foreigners. The chief of these in the present case is the state of agriculture, which, in a country like Russia, bears the same relation to all those outward appearances of prosperity which a clever minister can conjure up at a pinch, that a noumenon is supposed to bear to phenomena or gold to the paper currency based upon it. But before touching upon this important question, it may not be amiss to analyze very briefly the series of brilliant financial operations effected by M. Vyshnegradsky and belauded as a stroke of genius by the patriotic press of Russia. The first impression they leave upon the minds of those who run as they read is that of some wonderful improvement in Russia's solvency and credit, the gourdlike growth of which is explicable by no known cause. Why, one involuntarily asks, should a nation's creditors consent to receive 4 instead of the stipulated 5 per cent. on an immense debt of 531 millions of roubles, unless they had good reason to believe that the nation's prospects and solvency had considerably improved? And on what facts unknown to the most diligent students of contemporary Russian history can this flattering belief be based?

In the days when science was still to a great extent mere guess work, a certain monarch is reported to have asked a number of scientists to explain why it is that a live eel dropped into a vessel brimful of pure cold water swims

---

[1] The last instance of this extravagance occurred in St. Petersburg in February, 1890.

about without causing the liquid to overflow, whereas a dead eel, in exactly the same conditions, causes it to overflow at once. Many and ingenious were the explanations offered and rejected before a matter-of-fact individual, who believed in taking nothing on trust, declared that no explanation whatever was needed, seeing that the so-called phenomenon did not exist. Now this is exactly the case with the late financial operations. There has been no conversion. Russia in reality, instead of converting a 5 per cent. loan into a 4 per cent. one, has taken a very decided plunge in the opposite direction. She continues to pay practically 5 per cent. (mathematically 4.7), but on a much larger capital sum than before, and has bound herself to do so for a very much longer time.

What is a conversion? It is an alleviation of the relations of a debtor to his creditor, consisting in the substitution of a lower rate of interest on the debt, the capital sum of the latter and the term remaining unchanged. This being so, it is evident that the word conversion, as applied to the financial operations of M. Vyshnegradsky, is a misnomer, for both the capital sum and the term during which the payments are to be continued have both been very considerably increased. Suppose a person borrows a sum of £320, promising to refund it in monthly payments of £30 during twelve months; but finding it difficult to meet his obligations, has an interview with his creditor, who consents to lighten his burden to the extent of accepting £20 a month on condition that the payments continue for two years and a half; would that constitute a real alleviation of that individual's financial obligations? And yet such is, roughly speaking, the character of the recent Russian "conversions."

Let us take the loan of 1877 ($81\frac{1}{3}$ million roubles bearing interest at 5 per cent.) which was converted in November, 1888. The annual charges on that debt, including repayment of the capital, amounted to about $5\frac{2}{3}$ millions,[1] and would have ceased in twenty-five years had no conversion intervened. The effect of the conversion, however, was to increase the capital sum from $81\frac{1}{3}$ millions to $97\frac{1}{6}$ millions and to lessen the yearly payments from $5\frac{2}{3}$ millions to $4\frac{1}{2\frac{1}{6}}$ millions, but instead of continuing them only for twenty-five years to cause them to be persevered in for

---

[1] The exact amount was 5,688,000 millions of roubles.

$81\frac{1}{2}$ years. The dead loss to the country from this curious operation, which can be calculated by a simple sum of multiplication, is enormous: the "gain" consists in the shifting of a portion of the burden from the present to the future. If this was a wise move, there seems no reason why the minister did not improve upon it and astonish the natives — of Russia, at least — by issuing bonds bearing as little as 3 per cent. interest, a feat that could easily have been accomplished by increasing the capital sum by 83 per cent. One may form a pretty fair estimate of the nature of the above operation from the following consideration: At the time of the conversion only twenty-five yearly payments of $5\frac{2}{3}$ millions were needed to wipe out the debt completely. Now, suppose the Government, in a fit of mad benevolence, suddenly agreed to make its creditors not twenty-five but fifty-nine such yearly payments, the loss to the country, it is clear, would be enormous. And yet, strange to say, even that would be a more profitable operation than the actual conversion, inasmuch as the country would pay less than it now must pay by £1,100!

The remaining operations are of a piece with this. A government must indeed be sorely pressed for ready money if it consents to issue 4 per cent. bonds for 28 millions[1] redeemable only in eighty-one years, in return for a sum of $23\frac{1}{4}$ millions; for the bonds represent 19 per cent. more than the Government received.

One is sorely embarrassed to reconcile the exorbitant premium paid on these conversions with the alleged prosperity of the country and the solidity of its credit at the time the operations were effected. Many years ago, when avowedly in great distress and sadly in need of funds to construct strategic railways, and to enter the field against the Turks, the premium paid by Russia on a loan of $87\frac{1}{2}$ millions amounted to $8\frac{3}{10}$ per cent. of the sum realized, whereas last year, when the country's credit was alleged to be unimpeachable, and no need of funds felt, it amounted to $19\frac{1}{2}$ per cent. of the sum realized.[2] Between the years 1870 and 1889 Russia realized from seven loans a sum of $463\frac{1}{7}$ millions, on which she paid her creditors the enormous premium of $170\frac{1}{10}$ millions. During these nineteen years only $22\frac{3}{4}$ millions have been wiped out, and it will

---

[1] The exact sum is 27,834,000 roubles.
[2] 7,584,000 roubles.
[3] Viz., 15,834,056 roubles.

require fully *forty-nine years* more merely to pay up *the remainder of the premium*, so that it is only in the year 1939 that the posterity of the present generation will have got at the debt itself, viz., 463½ millions, which they will have to cancel in the relatively short period of 32 years, *i.e.*, by the year 1970.

Another aspect of these conversions which throws considerable light upon the solvency of the Government that negotiated them, is the percentage paid to bankers for their services. To find the rate of the commission paid to bankers, it is only necessary to subtract from the amount subscribed the cost of realization. Now, for the first loan of 125 millions a little over 1½ per cent. was charged.[1] If it be true, as has been alleged, that the circumstances in which this loan was floated constitute an irrefragable proof of a wonderful improvement in Russia's credit, one would naturally expect that the commission charged for the next loan, negotiated shortly afterwards, would be considerably less, especially if the amount of the loan were much greater. And yet it is the unexpected that occurs: for although the sum raised amounted to 175 millions, the bankers refused to have hand or part in it for less than 2.85 per cent., and the third loan, which was nearly twice as large,[2] could not be floated for less than 2.779 per cent. If the conversion lately negotiated by Mr. Goschen had been effected on the lines of the Russian conversion, this country would have had to pay away 83 millions sterling, of which about 17 millions would go to the bankers and the remainder find its way to the pockets of the creditors.

Taking the entire conversion scheme as applied to the various loans redeemable at various terms, and amounting in all to 508½ millions at 5 per cent. interest, we find that its chief effect has been to increase the capital sum by nearly 15 per cent., viz. 582⅔ millions.[3] The annual charge on this extra sum alone calculated for eighty-one years amount to 24⅓ millions.[4] Owing, however, to the lower rate of interest, the reduction of the yearly expenses during the first twenty-five years is appreciable, although it is but as dust in the balance when compared with the increased expenditure during the remaining fifty-six years. The

---

[1] 1.573.
[2] 310,498,000 roubles.
[3] Viz.: 582,664,000 roubles.
[4] 24,288,716 roubles.

effect, therefore, of the conversions has been, not to alleviate the burden of the taxpayers, but to shift it from the first twenty-five years to the ensuing fifty-six, whereby the augmentation of the expenditure during the latter period is out of all proportion to the gain during the former. Expressed in figures the alleviation afforded during the first twenty-five years amounts to $3\frac{1}{2}$ millions [1] yearly, or $90\frac{3}{4}$ [2] millions in all, while the loss during the following fifty-six years reaches the colossal sum of 448,689,169 roubles!

It seems scarcely necessary to point out that the explanation of this suicidal policy is not to be sought for in any real or alleged shortcomings of the minister. Nature has not made M. Vyshnegradsky shortsighted or dull-witted, but imperious necessity compels him to take very short views of his country's interests. *Après nous le déluge* is the natural device of a government convinced that a crash is inevitable, and anxious to stave it off even for a short time at the certain risk of extending its sphere of ruin. The minister accepted office with the avowed object of mobilizing the finances of the country, and he is now working out a problem in finances the data for which were supplied to him by his imperial master. When the present Emperor came to the throne he made known to his then Minister of Finances his intention of signalizing the beginning of his reign by a measure rendering the paper rouble equal to the gold rouble, and was deeply pained to find that laudable ambition treated as a mere *pium desiderium* which there was no specific way of realizing. The first man to promise to grapple with this task was M. Vyshnegradsky; and if he was well advised in undertaking it, he is certainly worthy of high praise for the successful way in which he seems to have begun to accomplish it. He has taken a leaf from the book of the historic commander of the beleaguered city who had all the victuals that he could collect from the hungry inhabitants placed conspicuously on the walls in order that the soldiers should feast and make merry and lead the besiegers to infer that, whatever else was scarce, food was plenty enough; half the garrison and nearly all of the inhabitants meanwhile dying of hunger.

A government that borrows on such conditions as those analyzed above must indeed be sorely pressed for money;

---

[1] More exactly, 3,630,477 roubles.
[2] More accurately, 90,761,925 roubles.

as the proverb says, He must be very badly in want of a bird that will give a groat for an owl. I have it on the authority of two Russian specialists, one of whom was recently an adviser of the Tsar, that the Government was extremely embarrassed to effect the yearly payments in gold that fall due on the metallic bonds. And what further proof of this is needed than the acts of the Administration: — the ruinous haste with which, in 1889, in spite of the alleged surplus of $34\frac{1}{5}$ millions, they gave bonds for 28 millions in order to raise the paltry and — on their own showing — unnecessary sum of $23\frac{1}{3}$ millions; the reckless way in which they imperil the country's good name — for Russia's reputation as a punctual payer of the stipulated rate of interest was heretofore above reproach — by nipping and filing[1] the coins they are too timid to confiscate;[2] the imposition of a tax upon movable property changing hands by gift, in flagrant violation of the acknowledged rights of Russia's creditors;[3] the establishment of a tax upon interest-bearing coupons, which was likewise a serious infraction of the rights of her foreign creditors as defined by Russian law; the statutes touching the conversions; the augmentation of various taxes; the issue of prize lottery bonds — a confessedly immoral way of raising money — more than 100 millions of which were silently appropriated

---

[1] The Government effected the conversion on the very eve of the drawing of the old bonds, and managed to adjourn the first drawing of the new ones for a considerable time in order to put off paying a paltry sum of 514,500 roubles. The drawing should have taken place within six months, but it was adroitly deferred for nine, and as the amortization of drawn bonds does not take place until three months after the drawing, one whole term was passed without any amortization. This means the addition of six months to the eighty-one years before which the bonds are not redeemable.

[2] It is only fair to say that M. Vyshnegradsky is not responsible for this law, which was enacted on the 27th June, 1882. I refer to it because it shows that the need of ready money felt by the Russian Government existed before the present Minister's nomination.

[3] Russia's progress in the direction of Protection during the past two decades may be briefly described as follows: — In 1868 only machines and linen goods were taxed higher than before, while the duties on all other foreign imports were lessened. In 1876 all duties were made payable in gold, a change which at that time was tantamount to a rise of 40 per cent. In 1880 the free importation of metals for the purpose of constructing machines, ships, and railroads was abolished, and in 1881 all customs duties were increased by 10 per cent. In 1882 the duty on metals and metal goods was again augmented; in 1885 there was a general rise of from 10 to 20 per cent. on all foreign imports. In 1890 the imperial receipts were found to be falling off so rapidly that all duties were with unprecedented suddenness increased by from 20 to 40 per cent., and as this seems still too little, a new tariff with still higher duties — a sort of Russian McKinley Bill — is being drawn up.

to the pressing needs of the Government; the sudden increase, a few months ago, of all customs duties by from 20 to 40 per cent., the object of which was admitted to be purely fiscal; the further increase of that tariff which was promulgated a few days later, and bears no closer relation to Protection than bankruptcy does to philanthropy; and, lastly, the cruel measures now being resorted to in order to compel ruined peasants to pay exorbitant taxes. Things have gone so far that there has more than once been question of withdrawing the sums of money which, as an obtrusive proof of solvency, Russia usually keeps in England, and I should not be at all surprised if that shewbread, at present in the keeping of the Rothschilds, were speedily withdrawn and ravenously devoured.

It is generally believed by political economists of this and other countries that the Russian Government has acquired the conviction that the development of native manufacturing industries is the one thing needful to a purely agricultural country, and that the most effective way to foster them is to have recourse to a rigorous policy of Protection; for this reason it has gone on year after year augmenting the tariff until at last Protection seems to be merging into prohibition pure and simple. If this were the true explanation of Russia's commercial policy of the past ten years we should find that articles that cannot be produced in the country would scarcely be taxed at all, and certainly not to the same extent as those which seriously compete with goods of Russian manufacture, while the duties levied on foreign goods would in no case be allowed to pass the line where they become, on the one hand, a premium upon the sluggishness of producers, and on the other a galling burden on the taxpayers. But the truth is, that the Government is in such pressing need of ready money that it snatches at all the miserable cheese-parings that can be scraped together by increase of duties, even at the risk of ultimately undermining the very manufactures it would gladly protect and develop. Hence the fiscal character of most of the items of the tariff. Those who hope therefore by dint of detailed discussion of the respective merits of Protection and Free Trade to persuade the Russian Government to strike out a different line of policy have as much chance of success as the nervous old lady had who screamed out to the man who had slipped and was rolling precipitously down a steep flight of stairs, "Go back! go back!" in the vain hope of compelling him to retrace or arrest his course.

Except in official documents, in which the observance of certain traditional forms is a matter of necessity, it never occurs even to the most extreme advocate of the Government's present commercial policy to make a pretence of believing that this enormous augmentation of customs duties is productive of the slightest benefit to the country or the industries.[1] It is perfectly understood that the gain is unequally divided between the Government and the manufacturers. "The Government is awfully good to us manufacturers," exclaimed a German settled in Russia to several Russians and foreigners in a Moscow hotel very lately. "We have *carte blanche* to tax the natives to our hearts' content. I raised a howl myself a year ago, and was immediately appeased by the imposition of a tax the amount of which I had myself fixed." "Is it likely to do any real good to native industry?" I inquired. "Well," he replied with a knowing smile, "I am the chief 'native' that profits by it. Half-a-dozen others engaged in the same trade will also make a good thing of it, but the people will have to pay more for the same goods; that's about all."[2]

No merchants or manufacturers in the world are so impatient to enrich themselves as the Russians. Ten per cent. on their capital — nay, 20 per cent. is not nearly enough to satisfy their cravings. Many of them look upon trade and industry as legalized robbery, and harmonize their actions with their theory. Hence their rooted aversion to every kind of enterprise that requires continued application to business and yields modest, though certain, profits; hence the contempt with which they allude to the markets of Persia, China, Bulgaria, Servia, which might be theirs by a thousand rights, but are now being gradually closed to them. As soon as they discovered that the Russian Govern-

---

[1] In the beginning of this paper I enumerated some of the apparent benefits of Russian "Protection," among which is the increase of industrial manufactures. As a matter of fact the greater number belong to foreigners who opened them on the very borders of Russia and Germany: "so that in this way all the sacrifices made by the nation are fruitless," remarks Professor Anstivol, a Russian authority on such matters. Even the trade balance is an eloquent protest against high duties. In 1882 Russian exports were valued at 667½ millions, and imports at 527¼ millions; in 1886 the exports had fallen to 450½ millions, and the imports to 379¾ millions.

[2] There are two Englishmen of note in the commercial world who were present at that conversation. They were amused at the curious revelation, and alluded sorrowfully to the 5 per cent. they receive on their own capital.

ment was willing to enable them to double and triple their profits without insisting upon their spending an extra copeck, petitions for increased duties were showered upon the minister like snowflakes in early winter. So eager has the Government been to avail itself of every possible pretext to raise the tariff, that it seldom discriminated between foreigners in Russia and genuine Russians. In the first merchant guild of Moscow there are four hundred merchants inscribed, and less than the half of them are Russians. Out of one hundred and thirty-two industrial export and commission offices in that city only forty are Russian; in the remainder the business is carried on, the books are kept, in foreign languages, and there is scarcely 10 per cent. of their *personnel* who are Russians, and the greater part of these are employed as servants, messengers, and watchmen. It is a very significant fact that the undignified whining and lamenting on the part of the manufacturers which usually precedes a new rise in the customs duties is termed *Goujoning* from the name of a foreigner, Goujon, resident in Moscow, who has raised the practice to an art.[1] This year the French opened an exhibition in Moscow, subject, of course, to all the lets and hindrances that handicap foreigners generally. These, however, seemed insufficient to the Moscow Goujons, who requested the minister to increase the duties on the goods destined to be exhibited; the same pillars of Russian industry, as soon as they learned that Captain Wiggins had arrived safe in Siberia, raised once more their plaintive cry, in response to which the sympathetic minister immediately drew up a Bill imposing considerable duties on all foreign goods imported into Siberia by the new route.[2]

M. Vyshnegradsky cannot, as some suppose, plead ignorance of the effects of his commercial policy. He perceives as clearly as any member of the Cobden Club that high duties alter the normal conditions of exchange between

---

[1] Cf. *West Slavonic News*, St. Petersburg, 14th August, 1890.
[2] Cf. *Svett*, 22nd November, 1888. The steamers and trading vessels that formerly used to come to Russia with cargo have now only ballast, which they unceremoniously fling into the sea near the ports, of the Azov Sea, for instance. They make up for the loss of the profit which a cargo would bring in by raising their freights and compelling Russian exporters to pay the difference. In the Azov Sea alone 12 million poods (a pood is 36 lbs.) of ballast is annually thrown into the sea. In 1888 the number of trading vessels that came into Russian ports with ballast and without cargo was 8,680, whereas those that carried cargo of any kind and quantity numbered only 6,291.

the tiller of the soil and the manufacturer, whose reciprocal relations are such that an abnormal profit given to the one can only be realized by a corresponding loss inflicted upon the other, so that the tariff which enables the manufacturer to sell his goods at a very high rate compels the farmer to part with his for a proportionately smaller sum. It is obvious, therefore, that the State has its eyes wide open when, in the person of the minister, it compels the unfortunate peasant to give up a portion of his income to be divided between the manufacturers and the Treasury. Can it be seriously advanced that what may be termed Prohibitive Protection is calculated to benefit, directly or indirectly, Russian manufacturers? The *Novoye Vremya*, an extreme Protectionist journal, replies in the negative, and calls this hope an idle dream utterly incapable of realization.[1] Some of the most honest manufacturers have solemnly made the same assertion.[2] Moreover the merchants themselves declare that industry was never so depressed as it is at this moment. Last autumn the Finance Minister, when on his inspecting tour in Eastern Russia, was deeply touched by the tears and lamentations of provincial Goujons, who complained that they were being ruined by the competition of foreigners, by the immigrant Germans, the wandering Jews, the intolerable taxes, the treacherous climate, the devastating hail, the unsparing lightning, the drying up of rivers in summer, the inundations of spring and autumn, etc., etc. In Nischny Novgorod they besought the minister to reduce their taxes, though for their sakes the peasants' taxes had been doubled, and the Mayor of Kazan assured the minister that — "Our trade and agriculture are being ruined, not daily, but hourly."[3] Figures, however, are more eloquent than words, and they tell us that after ten years of paternal protection of the iron and metal industries a plough (10-inch) can be made in Germany for 2 roubles 72 copecks, while in Russia the cost of production is 5 roubles 60 copecks; a 14-inch plough can be made in England and Germany for 2 roubles 53 copecks, whereas no Russian manufacturer can turn it out for less than 5 roubles 27 copecks, although labor is far cheaper in Russia; and an 8-inch plough costs its maker 2 roubles 94 copecks in Germany and 5 roubles 50 copecks in Russia.

---

[1] *Novoye Vremya*, 29th October, 1890.   [2] *Ibid.*
[3] *Northern Messenger*, October, 1890.

A few years ago when English coal coming to ports of the Black Sea was shut out by a protective, or rather, prohibitive, duty, the Russian coal-mines merely raised their prices without taking any means to provide for the increased demand. The result was a coal famine in the south of Russia; mineral fuel was sold at fancy prices, the cost of wood rose proportionately, while the last forests of the south were hewn down; many manufactories had to be closed for want of fuel (for instance, the works of Bellino-Fenderich, in Odessa): the poor inhabitants stood for hours in long rows waiting for their turn to receive a little coal gratis from the city; attacks were made upon the coal-stores in Kharkoff, and with considerable difficulty a rising was prevented.[1] In 1888, when the duty on agricultural implements was raised to 76 copecks (gold) a *pood*,[2] Russian manufacturers, although foreseeing the increased demand, conceived that they had done their duty by merely raising the price on all these productions without improving the quality, enlarging their own works, or providing an increased supply. The result was that hundreds of farmers had to be told that their orders could not be executed, as the articles in question were all sold.[3] In that same year there was also a large demand for threshing-machines, but there were practically none in stock, and the Russian manufacturers could not undertake to make them quickly enough, so that Russian firms were compelled to order them from abroad *by the mail trains*.[4] In the south of Russia alone, out of 400 threshing-machines ordered, Russian manufacturers could only supply 40, and the remainder had to be ordered *by telegraph* from abroad, whereby the farmers had to pay £80,000 duty.[5]

The only class benefited by these duties are the manufacturers, whose profits attract the ordinary Russian with the irresistible force of a newly-discovered gold-mine. Hundreds rush eagerly in, investing borrowed money and trailing a miserable existence crippled by the exorbitant interest which they have to pay on the initial debt. Those who

---

[1] Cf., for instance, the *St. Petersburg Journal* (*Vedomoste*), 4th March, 1888; the *Messenger of Europe*, December, 1890, p. 819. It seems very absurd that the owners of coal-mines, for whose benefit the duty was raised, were themselves obliged to order English coals by telegraph and deliver them to their customers in fulfilment of contracts for Russian coal (*loc. cit.*).

[2] 36 lbs.   [3] Cf. *Novoye Vremya*.
[4] *Agricultural Journal*, 1889, No. 4, p. 74.   [5] *Ibid.*

work with their own capital grow rapidly rich without spending a copeck to improve the machinery, extend operations, or otherwise indirectly contribute to establish native industry on a solid footing. We have it on the authority of the official journal of the Ministry of Finances that the ordinary rate of interest on the capital invested in Russian manufactures is seldom less than 20 per cent., and usually from 30 to 40.[1] As a matter of fact it is a good deal more. No industry has been so perfected, so cheapened, or rendered such a success as sugar-boiling; and yet, if we analyze it carefully, we discover a state of things that would seem utterly incredible were it not an acknowledged and incontrovertible fact. In Russia the prices of sugar are exorbitant, the manufacturers' profits are enormous, but they are most frequently eaten up by interest on their debts; the existence of many of the works is so precarious that a slight fluctuation in prices would suffice to give them their deathblow.[2] To obviate competition the producers agreed a couple of years ago to offer only a certain fixed quantity of sugar for sale in the home markets, and to export all the surplus production, selling it, if needful, under cost price. This is rendered possible by the premium offered by the Government for every pound of sugar exported, the excise duty being at once refunded. The effect of this on the export trade has been to increase the export of sugar to sixty-eight times what it was a few years before. On the other hand, it has to be sold so cheap that English and Persian consumers pay 350 per cent. less for Russian sugar than do the Russians themselves.[3] Consequently sugar in Russia is

---

[1] *The Messenger of Finances*, 1887. The woollen manufacturers, Thornton & Co., receive 45 per cent. on their capital; the Krenholm Works, 44⅗ per cent.; the Nevsky Cotton Works, 38 per cent.; the Nikolsky Works of Morozoff, 28 per cent.; the Tzmailovsky Cotton Works, 26 per cent.; those of Rabeneck, 25½ per cent.; the Katherinhof Cotton Works, 23 per cent., etc. As a matter of fact the interest is much greater than is here shown; "for in all such official reports the expenses are deliberately exaggerated in the first place in order that the profit should not give rise to new taxes on manufactured goods; in the second place, in order to lessen the amount payable to the Treasury in accordance with the law levying 3 per cent. on all net profits; and thirdly, that the manufacturers should preserve the right of bemoaning the hard times and robbing further the public." Cf. petition of the Imperial Economical Society for modifications in the Russian Customs Tariff, St. Petersburg, 1890.

[2] Cf. *Novoye Vremya*, 20th October, 1890.

[3] The quantity of raw sugar that is sold for from 1 rouble 41 copecks to 2 roubles 55 copecks in London, costs from 4 roubles 70 copecks to 4 roubles 85 copecks in St. Petersburg, while refined sugar that fetches from 5 roubles 80 copecks to 6 roubles 15 copecks in the Russian capital, is sold

an article of luxury which only a very limited number of persons can indulge in, the average Englishman consuming twelve times more sugar in a year than the Russian. In the latter country there are tens of thousands of people who anxiously keep one small piece of lump sugar in their mouths while they drink two or even three glasses of tea, which is allowed to wet without dissolving the sweet morsel. This is termed taking sugar *v preekooskoo*. There is another less wasteful method in vogue in many country places of entertainment for man and beast, where one large lump of sugar is suspended in a fine small net from the ceiling. I need not describe in greater detail how very gradually it is consumed, or by how many tea drinkers; it is also perhaps superfluous to remark that in no other country has the principle of communism or the absence of squeamishness been carried to greater lengths[1] than in Russia, whose inhabitants allow themselves to be thus tantalized while enormous quantities of sugar are being practically given away every year to foreigners. Another curious result of this abnormal state of things is the existence of a large contraband trade between Persia and Russia, Persian and Armenian merchants smuggling *Russian sugar into Russia*, and underselling Russian merchants who deal in the orthodox article which has not been exported.[2]

But whoever else gains by the high tariff, the tiller of the soil stands to lose, and the extent of his loss is incalculable. The limits of his resources can be as accurately gauged as were those of Tom Brown's box of marbles by his inquisitive schoolfellow. Questioned lately by the Government, merely for form's sake, as to the advisability of again raising the duty on implements of field labor, all the agricultural societies of the empire gave it as their conviction that Russian agriculture is at its last gasp. But perhaps the aim and object of these societies precluded them from giving any different reply? If so, the opinion of the Committees of Trade and Manufactures of Odessa, Kharkoff, Riga, Reval — *i.e.*, of bodies directly interested in the growth of Russian industry — comes with so much greater force, and

---

in London for from 1 rouble 81 copecks to 2 roubles 45 copecks. And this in spite of the circumstance that in Russia rents are much lower, labor far cheaper, and the price of land considerably less than elsewhere. (Cf. *Novoye Vremya*, 26th November, 1890.)

[1] The technical name for this extraordinary economical way of consuming sugar is *v preclizkoo*, which means literally, "sugar for licking."

[2] Cf. *Novoye Vremya*, 27th October, 1890.

they declared themselves opposed to the increase of those duties on the intelligible principle that it would be folly to kill the hen that lays the golden eggs.[1] The Agricultural Society of Poltava quoted figures [2] to show that the proposed duties on agricultural machines amounted to *three-fourths* of the taxes on land, and the Economical Society of St. Petersburg has made it clear that this statement is well within the truth. To take but one article — scythes — we find that according to the new tariff, if the most moderate of the different projects becomes law, it will impose a yearly tax of 311,000 roubles, exclusive of the rise in the price over and above the duties. That this is not being done in the interests of Protection is self-evident; scythes are not manufactured in Russia, and were the duties increased as much as 1,000 per cent., the peasants to whom they are now indispensable would still have to invest in foreign scythes. "Let us not mask this duty," exclaims the Protectionist organ, "with the fig-leaf of Protection, for we cannot possibly protect a branch of industry that does not exist."[3]

But it is not only in the guise of a heavy tax that these customs react upon the peasantry at large. In many cases they act as effective preventives of that gradual progress the absence of which is stagnation and ruin. Ploughs are so scarce among petty farmers that the Moscow *Zemstvo* lends a number of them gratis every year in the hope of inducing the peasants to buy them;[4] and as for scythes — a primitive implement enough in these days of mowing machines — the peasants of large districts of some of the finest meadowland in all Russia have not yet begun to see their utility. In the rich meadows of the Dvina Valley, the peasants mow the grass with an implement called a "hump" — a large reaping-hook, two feet in diameter, which, though too heavy for one hand, has but one short handle for both. "In order to mow with this, the laborer must double himself up, holding the short handle in both hands and turn the 'hump' round, after each stroke, from right to left and from left to right, so that its edge may be turned towards the grass to be cut down by the next stroke." It is a species of torture to

---

[1] Cf. *Novoye Vremya*, 14th November, 1890; *Russian News* (Moscow), 12th November, 1890.
[2] *Novoye Vremya, loc. cit.*
[3] *Novoye Vremya*, 14th November, 1890.
[4] *Novoye Vremya*, 30th November, 1890,

mow thus: "it is hard to breathe, the blood rises to your head, and on a hot day you have not the faintest shade around."[1] For agricultural machines and implements the Finns, among whom the Imperial Government intends to introduce Russian ways, pay 4.98 per cent. *less* than the Russians! During the last six years the average consumption of bread and corn by the individual has decreased by one per cent.

The agricultural class in Russia has been carrying on a desperate struggle during the past few years of the Protectionist era against adverse conditions that bid fair in a short time to reduce it to rack and ruin. Corn-growing has been found less and less profitable, while some kinds of it are positively ruinous. Among other misfortunes, the land has been rapidly losing its productiveness, and for want of artificial fertilizers is now, in many places, thoroughly exhausted. Yet in proportion as the profits diminished, or gave place to positive losses, the taxes — to pay for sentimental wars and barren conquests — have been steadily increasing. Unable to meet his obligations, the peasant at first found an easy way, by means of private credit, of transforming the taxes into debts which, augmenting from season to season, have at last reached such overwhelming dimensions that neither the fear of distraint nor the ignominy of the lash any longer suffices to sharpen his wits to the degree of inventiveness sufficient to raise the money, so the land is being sold and its whilom owners turned adrift in thousands to swell the militia of vice and crime. In many large districts the price of land, though greatly fallen, is still out of all proportion to the money value of its produce, and in few cases can the tillers of the soil realize by agricultural labor alone sufficient profits to support the stoical life of the Russian peasant. In the twelve governments drained by the Volga there are peasants to the number of one million and a quarter, whose land could not possibly maintain them, even if they were entirely exempted from rates, rents, and taxes. They struggle hard by means of domestic trades, or work in factories or shops in distant cities far away from their families, to eke out a miserable livelihood. Comparative success smiles on a few individual units, but grim want devours many thousands and tens of thousands.[2]

---

[1] Cf. *Moscow Gazette*, 14th November, 1890.
[2] Cf., *inter alia*, *Novoye Vremya*, 10th January, 1890; 15th March, 1890; *Nedelya*, 12th October, 1890.

The soil in Russia is tilled by two distinct classes of agriculturists, the nobles and the peasants, both of whom are hopelessly ruined. The latter possess much too little land to support life, wherever the soil is fertile, and far too much to pay rates and taxes for in districts where it is barren. The former have to cope with the difficulty of hired labor, which in Russia is such an insurmountable obstacle to success that it has become an economical axiom that the soil, to yield a profit, must be owned by those who till it and tilled by those who own it. The dismal tale of the nobles is soon told. Improvidence and the difficulties of hired labor soon brought them to the verge of ruin, to rescue them from which the Bank of the Nobility was founded. From 1886 to 1888 this institution advanced 24 millions sterling at a comparatively low rate of interest, with the following startling results: — the arrears in October, 1886, amounted to £6,000; in April, 1887, to £39,717; in October, 1887, to £109,104; in April, 1888, to £169,714. In 1889 a considerable number of estates belonging to noblemen were advertised to be sold for debts. But the Government which had turned the peasants into tax-paying machines, resolved to stretch out a helping hand to the nobles, and with this object in view, did not hesitate to demoralize the people by issuing a lottery loan. All arrears were thereupon wiped out with the proceeds and added to the capital sum of the debt, and even the interest on that for the six ensuing months was in great part wiped out, so that all the nobles were required to do was to pay a portion of the charges[1] that fell due during the six months that followed the issue of the loan. The result is far from encouraging; the loan in question is not yet fully paid up, and we already hear of over three thousand estates advertised for sale by the Bank of the Nobility.[2] Taking the average estate of a Russian noble to possess a money value of £4,000, it would follow that land to the value of 12 millions sterling is being put up for sale by the auctioneer. And yet the Bank of the Nobility was and is a benevolent rather than a business institution, and advanced money to its clients at a lower rate of interest than it paid itself.

The peasants are still far worse off than the nobles, who can generally manage to lead a parasitic life when an inde-

---

[1] The annual charges amount only to 5¼ per cent. yearly, including amortization and interest.
[2] Cf. *Nedelya*, p. 23, November, 1890.

pendent existence is no longer possible. The necessity of paying heavy taxes, made painfully clear by the unsparing application of the rod and the lash,[1] compels the peasant to mobilize his finances as quickly as may be, and if, as is generally the case, he have none, to borrow at a high rate of interest. The various species of mushroom which in England are eaten with relish and impunity, in Russia are usually poisonous; and in like manner the system of credit which in other countries materially assists the tiller of the soil to tide over hard times, in Russia not only gnaws the debtor to the bones, but, to use Tertullian's forcible simile, sucks out all his blood and marrow. Lest the expression, "high rate of interest," prove misleading, it may be as well to state at once that it should not be taken to mean 8, 10, or even 12 per cent. Indeed, "the Russian peasant thinks of terms like these as of a boon too precious to be obtained outside the realm of dreams."[2] "If you lend a peasant money at the rate of 18 per cent. interest, you have proved yourself a benefactor whom he will gratefully remember to the end of his days. The very notion of a bank that would be satisfied with 12 per cent. a year appears to him in the light of an idle dream."[3] In some districts of the government of Koorsk it has become a regular custom for whole communities to borrow money for the payment of the taxes at 60 per cent. interest. But this is rather exceptional. 100 *per cent. is the usual rate of interest; it often, however, amounts to* 300, *sometimes to* 800 *per cent.*[4] Among the usurers whom the peasants honestly look upon, or think they look upon, as benefactors, there is one well-known individual named Lebedeff, in the government of Pskoff, who is quite satisfied, when he lends money, to receive 100 per cent. interest. "What a wretched existence must be led by peasants who, in very truth, see reason to bless such a man as their benefactor!" exclaims the official investigator.[5] The money borrowed on such conditions is needed and employed mainly to pay the taxes, "which are always collected with inexorable severity."[6]

The pressure brought to bear upon the necessitous husbandmen must indeed be great, when we find them "quite

---
[1] Cf. *Law Messenger*, November, 1890, p. 377, foll.
[2] The (Russian) *Observer*, 1884, No. 11, and 1885, No. 2.
[3] *Messenger of Europe*, October, 1890, p. 763.
[4] *Ibid.* p. 765. [5] *Ibid., loc. cit.* [6] *Ibid.* p. 763.

ready in extreme cases to pay 1,200 *per cent a year.*"[1] Nor is this by any means the maximum; those who are curious to read cases of money being advanced to peasants *at* 2,500 *per cent.* interest will find them described in the most widely circulated newspaper of Russia.[2] These exorbitant rates of interest are rendered doubly ruinous by the dishonesty of the usurer and the ignorance of the borrower. A peasant borrows, say, £10, signs a receipt for £50, pays the high annual or monthly charges regularly, never receiving any written acknowledgment; and after having paid £50 or £60 finds to his amazement that he still owes more than before. A whole commune of the government of Moscow borrowed £14 in this manner at 33 per cent. interest, and in the course of twelve years fully paid up the capital sum and £160 interest besides, and yet, at the end of that time, strange to say, not only was the debt not wiped out, but it had increased threefold.[3]

Such is part of the curious mechanism by which Russia's finances are being mobilized. These things take place not in any one district or government, but throughout the length and breadth of the Empire. In the government of Tver, for example, we have it on the authority of the official statistician, that two-thirds of the taxes are yearly borrowed thus of private usurers by the needy peasants. Is not this in sober truth a burning of the dwelling-house by its inmates who warm themselves at the fire, to their intense comfort at first, but to their irremediable ruin in the end?

The usurer, when not a blessed benefactor like Lebedeff of Pskoff, constitutes a type apart in the Chamber of Horrors of the Russian Empire. It is needless to state that he is not a Jew; he is as Orthodox as the Metropolitan Isidore, as loyal as an official of the secret police. The very worst Jewish usurer in Russia is to the ordinary Russian *koolak*[4] as Antonio is to Shylock. In winter when food is lacking and work cannot be had, the peasant sells to this man for a mere song the harvest still hidden in the womb of the earth, and buys it back in a few months at a much

---

[1] *Messenger of Europe*, October, 1890, p. 763.
[2] Cf., for instance, the *Novoye Vremya*, 3rd November, 1890. I have no doubt that these are very exceptional cases; it would be much more satisfactory, however, if they were not facts.
[3] *Messenger of Europe*, October, 1890, p. 764.
[4] The technical name for peasant usurers who are members of the Orthodox Church. The etymological meaning of the word is *fist*.

higher price, to feed his own family, the transactions being carried on mainly by means of ruinous promissory notes. The usurer, however, deals in force as well as matter, and purchases with the same readiness the peasant's future labor, and the present produce of his farm. Many wretches who borrowed £5 or £6 and repaid it several times over, are often forced to sell their labor for the ensuing harvest and end by toiling and moiling for a number of years in the service of their "benefactor." One of the curious trades that has sprung into existence owing to these strange economic conditions is currently called the "soul trade." "In numerous districts," we are informed by the most serious of all Russian organs, "a new right of possessing serfs has come to be established. The slave-owners are no longer the landlords, as before; they are now the owners of public-houses, usurers, coarse half-civilized grabbers who ruin the people with relentless logic."[1] This curious phenomenon is observable in all parts of Russia, north, south, east, and west.[2]

In all Russia there are over seven hundred districts and in one district alone, though I cannot venture to say it is a typical one,[3] the *registered* debts of the peasants amount to two millions and a half (roubles), of which over one and a half are owing to money-lenders. The interest paid on this debt is equal to three times the sum of the imperial taxes. These debtors are compelled to work for their creditors, and they are deprived of the right to sell to any but to them, and dare not complain of the oppression to which they are subjected, of false weights and measures, extortion, etc. And this same phenomenon is observable in the most widely distant parts of Russia. The lenders profit by the ignorance of the peasants, who as a rule can neither read or write; they do not return them their promissory notes and frequently sue them several times for one and the same sum, on the same notes of hand.[4]

German physicians tell us that the disease known in Russia as scrofula is in reality malignant syphilis. In like manner, the transactions usually called credit in Russia are for the most part, in sober truth, a masked buying and selling under conditions that render the purchaser, to all

---

[1] *Messenger of Europe*, November, 1890, p. 762.
[2] Cf. *The Day*, 6th March, 1888.
[3] The Opotschetski district of the government of Pskoff.
[4] *Messenger of Europe*, October, 1890, p. 765.

intents and purposes, a criminal, and the vendor a victim.
For, suppose the average income of a peasant-farmer to
amount to 6 or even 10 per cent. on the capital invested
(that it is usually far less will be made clear enough later
on); nay, let us, for the sake of argument, put it down as
20 per cent.: — how can that individual borrow money at
100, 400, or 800 per cent. with the serious intention of
paying capital and interest out of his income? It is not
evident that he intends — or must be taken to intend — to
refund it out of his property, so that he is really the vendor
of his property, and his creditor the purchaser? In many
cases, however, the borrower's property is insufficient to
wipe out the debt, or, if not really insufficient, is temporarily depreciated until it becomes so. In such cases the
borrower must make good by labor the sum which the sale
of his property has left unpaid. The official representative
of the Imperial Economical Society, who very lately investigated this and kindred questions and presented his report
to the Minister of the Interior and the Finance Minister,
makes several statements concerning the condition of the
peasantry that are characterised by that wild improbability
which so often distinguishes facts from fiction. "In one
village[1] the whole commune begged me, some on their
bended knees, many in tears, to request the Imperial Society to rescue them from utter ruin. And when I drove
away I could see for miles, until the village itself was lost
to view, the entire commune still standing rooted to the
spot without caps or hats."[2]

To what extent, one may ask, should the Government be
held responsible for the miserable condition of the peasantry? It is not my purpose to draw up an indictment
against a political body composed of the most heterogeneous elements conceivable, and still less to condemn a minister whom many regard, and not without reason, as a
financial Hercules absurdly employed in spinning wool for
an inappreciative Omphale, a Russian Necker condemned to
play the undignified part of a flippant Calonne, to raise the
wind and allay, for a brief moment, well-founded fears and
just apprehensions. At the same time it is impossible to
blink the fact that Russian credit and Russian solvency
have been made wholly dependent, not only upon the

---

[1] Ploskoff.
[2] *Peasant Proprietorship in the Porkhofski District of the Government of Pskoff.* By G. P. Sazonoff, St. Petersburg, 1890.

intemperance and starvation of the peasantry, which are truly sore evils, but also upon "the prostitution of his mind, the soddening of his conscience, the dwarfing of his manhood, which are worse calamities." More than a third of the ordinary imperial revenue, over 275 millions, is made up of excise duties on alcohol, in the enormous consumption of which the Government cannot and will not allow any falling off.[1] The sober peasant is looked at askance; and an insinuation that he is disloyal or heretical is sometimes enough to ruin him. Now the retailers of liquor, the men whose business is the most lucrative of any other in Russia, are also the money-lending "benefactors" described above. A government truly desirous of filling its coffers could not well quarrel with its chosen instruments, and so the publicans, not being hateful Jews, are tolerated, nay, deliberately encouraged: *vodka* is briskly sold and the needful 253¼ millions flow rapidly in; and thus, if the lambs are not precisely whole and intact, the wolves at least are satiated.

The misery of the peasants, it may be urged, is in great part attributable to their crass ignorance, the vast majority of them being almost as benighted as the six score thousand persons in Nineveh who could not discern between their right hand and their left hand. But this ignorance, it should not be forgotten, is a condition, to the full as indispensable to the success of the financial policy of the Government as the action of the publican and the money-lender; for an educated peasantry, like the Finnish, would very soon adopt temperate habits of life, thus ruining the imperial budget, and would probably grow restive under misrule; so that the economical catastrophe might prove but the prelude to a political cataclysm. Hence the marvellous energy with which education in every shape and form is being suppressed. "In the entire Porkhofski district £30 a year is spent in schools, six cantons contributing small sums to this total, and the remaining twenty-three

---

[1] In 1880 the excise duty on spirits amounted to 223½ millions; in 1889 it reached the figure, 275 millions, that is to say in nine years it increased by 51½ millions, or about 23 per cent., notwithstanding the enormous increase in the excise duty, an increase of more than 32 per cent. These figures, however, are far from showing what the real annual consumption of alcohol in Russia is; for there is a very extensive contraband trade in liquor, besides a great deal of secret distilling going on throughout the country. This is natural enough when we reflect that the excise duty on alcoholic liquors is equivalent to six and even seven times the cost of producing it.

subscribing nothing at all. In several villages of that district (I am speaking of places within two or three hours of the capital) there *is not a man, woman, or child who can read or write*, and every time an official document is received from the Peasant Board (or elsewhere) a special messenger has to be despatched to a neighboring town to seek for some one to decipher it."[1] And yet in that same district there are *seven hundred taverns and public-houses with a yearly turnover of two million roubles*. Many of these taverns were opened against the express will of the peasantry, who unanimously passed emphatic resolutions forbidding them; but the Government not only refused to sanction the will of the village communities, but actually *installed the publicans by force*. One instance, chosen for its typical features, will suffice to give an idea of how the struggle between drunkenness and temperance is carried on.

Eighteen months ago the community of Ploskovo unanimously resolved to allow in their village neither publichouse nor publican. In pursuance of this determination scores of peasants armed with staves and clubs stood on guard at the entrances of the village, relieving each other by day and by night. They refused to entertain any of the alluring promises of the publican, and resolutely drove him away whenever he attempted to enter the village. This state of things continued for several days, until at last the police authorities arrived escorting the publican in solemn procession and installing him by force in the village.[2] The result is not in all respects as satisfactory as even an easy-going Russian Government would desire. "In the village of Goloobtseff," says the *Messenger of Europe*, "fires broke out six different times this year, and each time nearly all the peasants were blind drunk."[3]

The schools, which are at least as effectual preventives of the reign of intemperance as clubs and staves, are being suppressed with equal energy to that manifested in the opening of taverns; for the ignorance and drunkenness of the peasantry are the exact correlative of the temporary solvency of the Government. "It is unjust," we are told by an authority on these questions, "to blame the peasants for the Cimmerian darkness that prevails in the country.

---

[1] Official Report of G. P. Sazonoff.
[2] *Ibid.* Cf. also *Messenger of Europe*, October, 1890, p. 778.
[3] *Messenger of Europe*, September, 1890, p. 360.

The Zemstvos opened and endowed hundreds of schools, making no inconsiderable sacrifices to get the children of the peasants instructed, but the Government of the present Emperor has worked hard to undo all that the Zemstvos had accomplished. Numbers of schools were closed as unnecessary, hundreds were handed over to the clergy, who have not time to attend even to their parochial duties, and consequently maintain the schools on paper only; and the last act of this policy of suppression is enshrined in the ukase published three weeks ago, subjecting all Zemsky schools to the clergy, and forbidding the opening of new ones without the authorization of the clergy, which they have orders not to accord."[1]

In the government of Volhynia, on the borders of Austria, the inhabitants are composed of Russians, Jews, Germans, and Bohemians. Among the three latter nationalities there is practically not one who cannot read and write; while for every one Russian who can do either there are eighty-five who can neither write nor read. The facility with which these unfortunate Russians fall a prey to every scheming swindler that comes along almost transcends limits of credulity. The communes often agree to purchase land, when their own is insufficient for their wants, in the hope that the State Bank, founded with this object, will advance the entire sum, and ignorant of the circumstances that the rules of the Bank, which they possess but are unable to discipher, allow only a certain percentage of the purchase-money to be advanced. This tardy discovery frequently forces them to abandon their intention of purchasing and to forfeit the earnest money paid to the landowner. In the government of Pskoff, for instance, there is a well-known farmer — a nobleman — *who regularly sells his estate every year in this lucrative if unscrupulous way*. More than once he has received £130 earnest-money from the unsuspecting peasants, which they ultimately forfeited from inability to complete the transaction.[2]

But to return to the economic condition of the peasantry, it is highly characteristic of the pressing need of the Government that distraint of property for non-payment of the taxes frequently "takes place long before the arrival of the term fixed by law for that payment. All the auctions, for

---

[1] Cf. *Messenger of Europe*, September, 1890, p. 362, 363.
[2] *St. Petersburgskia Veydomosti*, 1888.

instance, that took place for non-payment of taxes for the first half of 1889 were arranged in the spring of that year, although the term fixed by the law for the payment of the taxes was the 12th of July. These premature and obviously illegal sales of peasants' homesteads are authorized without the slightest difficulty and with unusual promptitude; sometimes permission is granted on the very day it is asked for, although it is a question of a whole series of villages described and valued on forty sheets of foolscap paper. Under this curious system the ruin of a large number of peasants' homesteads and families is effected sufficiently easily and promptly, *even where there are no arrears whatever.*" "Whole farms with complete inventories are knocked down by the auctioneer for £6. From this it is easy to infer the prices realized by the sale of movable property. The last cow, the last horse, is sold literally for a penny."[1] It should not be forgotten that these are the deliberate statements of a responsible official, sent to study the question on the spot, not the rhetorical flourishes of a Russian Liberal newspaper.

But has not every Russian peasant the right of appeal? Have we not been told by an English Radical that the Russian peasant is far better cared for and lives a much happier life than his English brother? To this there are many convincing replies. The following statement gives a sufficiently clear inkling of their drift: — "It occasionally happens that the peasants . . . who feel that this premature distraint is illegal, protest and *earnestly petition* for a few days' grace, but the upshot of it is that they are *prosecuted for resistance* to the authorities."[2] That is what happened to the peasants of the village of Pessok who were ill-advised enough to protest; in the Porkhofski district the peasants who made the same protests were put on trial, found guilty, and condemned.[3]

It would be rash and uncharitable to accuse M. Vyshnegradsky of deliberate complicity in these crimes; for it is difficult to call them by any other names. The fact is that he deals only in general results: it is his underlings who pass beyond, not only the comparatively narrow bounds of decency and humanity, but the broader limits of Russian

---

[1] See Sazonoff's Official Report, &c. Cf. also *Messenger of Europe*, October, 1890, pp. 779, 780.
[2] *Loc. cit.*, p. 780.   [3] *Ibid.*

statute law. *Qui vult finem vult media* is a scholastic saw that continues to hold good even in these days of enlightenment. In Russia, however, the parts are cunningly divided, the Government wishing the end, and its underlings the means, of attaining it. Still it is discouraging to learn that "this premature and energetic collection of the taxes usually calls forth eulogies from the authorities. . . . It does not occur to any one that for the sake of preventing arrears in the present, the very sources of payment in the future are being annihilated."[1] The condition of the peasants is truly harrowing in the extreme. The official report of M. Sazonoff quoted above says of the Porkhofski district (not far from the government of St. Petersburg), "The greater part of the peasants support themselves with the greatest imaginable difficulty, and even then only to the extent of keeping themselves from dying of hunger. To feed their cattle they had recourse to the traditional method — taking down the roofs of their huts and of all the out-houses on the farms, not sparing even such thatched roofs as *were ten years old*. In Zapolya and Krivookha scarcely a roof was left standing. Of course the cattle died in great numbers."[2] Many peasants went about the country begging for alms for Christ's sake.[3]

From peasant proprietorship to professional mendicancy is a terrible fall; but there are far deeper and darker abysses than even that, into which the Russian peasantry are being precipitated by tens of thousands. Numbers of them become serfs, are seized upon by the cruel "soul-dealer" or *dessatnik*, who purchases at nominal prices the future labor of hungry men and women.

"In spring these *dessatniks* drive whole bands of agricultural laborers to forests destined to be turned into pasture lands, to river-banks to tug vessels like horses, and to various factories, having previously resold them to large employers of labor for double or treble the prices they themselves paid. Other dealers scour the villages and hamlets, in search of *children, whom they buy up wholesale*. Many needy parents sell their children for several years to these men for a trifle. Having purchased a score or two of children in this way, the dealer forwards them on in *tumbrils to St. Petersburg, just as cattle-dealers have calves conveyed to town*. In St. Petersburg the children are resold for double and treble the money to manufacturers and shopkeepers. To this same category of trade in human labor belongs the hiring out of peasant

---

[1] *Loc. cit.*, p. 780.
[2] *Messenger of Europe*, October, 1890, p. 770.
[3] *Ibid.*

labor by the Volost Board to the agents of landowners, to timber-merchants, and the owners of works, who journey about the country specially for this purpose, visiting even the remotest districts of Russia. The peasants whose labor is thus summarily disposed of are generally individuals unable to pay the taxes in time, and they are hired out usually without their consent."[1]

The official representative of the Imperial Economical Society states in his report (1890) that he saw a batch of female children, of *from six to seven years old*, walking gloomily towards the fields. "'Where are you going?' he asked them. 'To perform *corvée* (forced service) for the master,' they replied, with a far from childlike calm; indeed their stolid tranquillity might be characterized as imbecile. 'What do you mean? What *corvée* can you have to do?' I involuntarily inquired. 'To the fields to perform *corvée* for the master.' I then put the same question to an adult boy and girl who were at that moment returning from the fields, and I got the same apathetic reply. 'What *corvée* is it?' I asked the Peasants' Assembly. 'Well, that's how we call it, old and young,' was the answer. 'You see it's what used to be before the serfs were freed, only that the service is much harder now that we work for our rich benefactors' (*i.e.*, money-lenders)."[2] "Such phenomena as these have ceased to be exceptional, and threaten to become the universal rule."[3] The sum total of work performed by the peasant borrowers is enormous; "the peasants now work for others *not less than four*

---

[1] Cf. P. A. Sokolovski, Savings Bank Associations, St. Petersburg, 1889, pp. 23, 24. The *Messenger of Europe*, October, 1890, p. 762. No statement is advanced in this paper, or any of the series, without references to some of the British authorities who are responsible for it, and to the official report, whenever it is based upon Governmental sources. This being so, the wild accusations of exaggeration launched by certain English periodicals steadily professing Autonomy and Radicalism, are in reality tantamount to accusations of shameless lying preferred against the very Government they are so anxious to defend. It may interest these gentlemen to learn that a certain foreign Government instructed its ambassador in St. Petersburg to make diligent inquiries into the truth of certain statements that seemed greatly exaggerated in the papers on "Russian Prisons" and on "Russian Jews" that form chapters in this volume. The ambassador, after having thoroughly sifted the evidence brought forward in *The Fortnightly Review*, and a great deal more that was never published, reported to his Government that the alleged facts were perfectly true, and were understated rather than exaggerated. It is earnestly hoped that the statements put forward in this chapter may be subjected to a similar test.

[2] G. P. Sazonoff, *Peasant Proprietorship in the Porkhofski District of the Government of Pskoff*, pp. 189, 190.

[3] *Messenger of Europe*, October, 1890, p. 763.

days a week, that is to say, more than when serfdom existed."[1]

But why do not these little "brown sheep," as an English journalist calls the peasants, appeal to the law or to the Emperor, who surely cannot sanction such inhuman transactions as these which amount to white slavery of the worst possible description, in comparison with which West-End sweating is just and generous? Is he not the loving head-shepherd of Gatchina? The answer is clear, if not precisely consoling. A few years ago a law was framed to meet precisely such cases; and the terms of the law are these. A peasant may enter into a contract to hire out his labor for as many as five years. The conditions to which hunger or drunkenness forced him to give his assent are rigorously maintained by the law, which in all matters touching upon the enforcement of such contracts dispenses with the usual formalities and delays. "The death of the employer," adds the statute significantly, "has not the effect of suspending or abrogating the force of the contract, but merely transfers the rights and obligations of the deceased to his lawful heirs." This law sounds as if it had been framed by a personal enemy of the good shepherd of Gatchina.

The ease with which, in writing of an immense country like Russia, symptoms of merely local distress may be unconsciously magnified into universal misery, makes it incumbent upon those who desire to arrive at right conclusions to scrutinize most carefully the facts, and above all not to confound a district or a government, however large, with the Russian Empire. Nor should there be any hesitation about applying other and more rigorous tests. Thus if want and misery be as widespread in Russia as many publicists of that country would have us believe, the inevitable results should be as evident as the statement is clear: fierce famine would stalk through the empire; blackening masses of miserable wretches would be met with wandering through the weary wastes of that mournful land; fierce fires would fringe with lurid light the long aisles of the forest and the lanes between the well-stocked farmhouses; the people, however patient, would rise up against the authorities, and chaos itself would seem to be quickening in the womb of time. Do we see anything like this in reality?

---

[1] L. Slonimsky, *Messenger of Europe*, October, 1890, p. 765.

To begin with, nothing even remotely approaching prosperity is visible in any corner of the empire. Impoverishment dogs Protection like its shadow. The dimensions of the want and suffering may be accurately gauged without a protracted study of the economical conditions of Russia. The question reduces itself to the compass of a sum of addition and subtraction, the data being furnished by the official organ of the Russian Ministry of Finances. The statistics of the prices of agricultural produce published by that ministry, and divided into four sections headed rye, oats, spring wheat, and winter wheat, constitute the terrible writing on the wall that warns Russia of impending economic ruin. From these tables it appears that wheat is the only crop that yields an income, and as wheat-growing is a branch of agriculture that requires the concurrence of many rare conditions, it is absolutely impossible in immense districts. The other corn crops, rye and oats, which are raised in the larger half of the corn-growing region, show a deficit varying from 1 to 10 roubles a dessateen ($2\frac{1}{4}$ acres) during the most favorable years.[1] On the other hand it is an established fact that rye and oats constitute 40 per cent. of all the corn annually exported from Russia. Half the corn-growers, therefore, work for the foreigner not only gratis, but at a positive loss to themselves. "This explains," says the *Novoye Vremya*, "why it is that in 1887 and 1888, in spite of abundant harvests, the price of land not only did not rise, but continued to fall, still more rapidly than before, while the indebtedness of the farmers went on increasing, as we see, from the reports of the Bank of the Nobility, and likewise from the balance-sheets of private land-banks. What, then, will happen in a bad year?"[2] The present year, 1890–1891, has proved a very bad year, no less by reason of the harvest, for in many districts there was a very great falling off in the crops, than on account of the considerable rise in the price of the rouble, which tells so terribly against the export trade, that we find a minister of M. Vyshnegradsky's intelligence compelled to resort to schoolboy tricks to depreciate in winter his own Russian rouble, which he spends spring, summer, and autumn in raising as near as possible to par.[3]

---

[1] The *Messenger of Finance, Industry, and Trade*, 13th January, 1889.
[2] *Novoye Vremya*, 17th January, 1889.
[3] Cf. *Börsen-Courier* (Berlin), 29th November, 1890; the *Russkia Veydomosti*, November, 1890, etc.

It is needless to descant here on the results of this alarming state of things. They are inevitable. Not a year has passed during the last five years without a famine breaking out in large corn-growing districts, which carries off no man knows how many uncomplaining wretches, its growth every year more and more intense, and spreading over a much wider area. Thus in 1885 there was a severe famine in the government of Kazan, which decimated the population. A public subscription was opened by impecunious Russian students, who themselves cheerfully contributed their mites; but scarcely had the facts begun to be bruited abroad than they were hushed up by the Government. In 1888 the distress became extreme in the governments of Orenburg, the Volga districts, and the Southern governments;[1] and in many places since then the peasants have learned to dispense with ordinary bread, and to live on a substitute made of the husks of rye and the powdered bark of oak.[2]

The harvest of 1890 cannot be regarded as a complete failure, and yet the scarcity of food in most of the governments of European Russia has attained the proportions of a famine. And yet, incredible as it may appear, the first concern of the Russian peasant is not to feed his family or himself, but to pay his taxes and perform his part in mobilizing the finances of the country, even though he should live on refuse and offal.[3] In spite of this, the arrears are accumulating in a geometrical ratio. Distraint, imprisonment, flogging, are equally fruitless. Between 1883 and 1886 the arrears of imperial taxes alone increased by more than 100 per cent.

It would be difficult to determine what part of Russia suffers most from the want of seed corn, of money, of food; from cold, hunger, and disease. Take the Central district, for instance, and what do we find? "One may affirm, with a profound conviction of the truth of the statement, that both landowners and peasants are extremely impoverished, and the signs of impending ruin show themselves with painful distinctness to every impartial observer."[4] In the gov-

---

[1] Cf. *Svett*, 4th April, 1888; *Crimean Gazette*, 15th March, 1888; *Odessa News*, 24th April, 1888.
[2] *Moscow Gazette* (*Moskovskia Veydomosti*), 2nd April, 1888, and April 10, 1888. Cf. also the "Petition of the Imperial Economical Society, St. Petersburg, 1890," p. 120 foll.
[3] *Messenger of Europe*, October, 1890, p. 777.
[4] *Novoye Vremya*, 15th February, 1889.

ernment of Nischny Novgorod the harvest last year was decidedly bad, and the peasants, after having paid their taxes, were left with nothing to sow. "In many parts of the country they had not rye enough for seed for the fields. Half of the district had eaten its corn."[1] In October and November last the peasants were selling their live-stock at ruinous prices; excellent working horses were sold in large numbers *at two roubles per head.* In the government of Tambov the authorities have had to come to the peasants' assistance, and, lest the fields should be waste, advance them a loan of 400,000 roubles to purchase seed.[2] A similar story reaches us from the government of Voronesh: "The farmers have had to sell their live-stock for nominal prices, and whenever they received no offer, to kill them for the meat and the hides. Colts fetched one shilling and even as little as sixpence a head, and during several weeks meat in the markets cost less than one farthing a pound."[3]

In the West the distress is not perhaps quite so widespread, but it is certainly to the full as intense. Thus in the government of Volhynia, "there is," we are assured, "a terrible crisis. Even wheat (the only crop that has been cultivated at a profit for the last few years) is cultivated at a considerable loss. The material condition of landowners is extremely critical."[4] The government of Vitebsk is suffering in a similar way from similar causes by a complete stagnation in the export of timber, which gave subsidiary occupation to thousands of petty farmers. And, as for arrears of taxes, it is wholly out of the question to think of recovering them.[5] Polish landowners do not seem to be a whit better off than their Russian colleagues; owing to last year's failure of the crops they have been compelled to sell their live-stock to purchase food for their families and themselves. Excellent farm horses were sold in large numbers for 2s. 2d. a head. The consequence is that there is no demand for hay and straw, immense quantities of which have been sold for almost nothing and exported to Prussia. Now the peasants themselves have nothing to eat.[6]

---

[1] *Moscow Gazette*, 11th December, 1889; *Novoye Vremya*, 13th December, 1889.
[2] *Novoye Vremya*, 3rd January, 1890.
[3] *Ibid*, 22nd January, 1890.
[4] *West Slavonian News*, 25th November, 1890.
[5] *Ibid.*
[6] *Slavonian Correspondence*, 14th December, 1889.

In the South of Russia, hitherto the granary of the empire, with its rich black loam soil, famous throughout the world, want and misery are as intense as in the North and West. To begin with, last year's harvest was bad in many places, although abundant in other parts of the country, so that when the taxes were paid, the cattle had no fodder and the peasant no food.[1] In large districts of the government of Podolia, where the harvest was likewise a failure, dearth of fodder for the live-stock and of food for the tiller of the soil, has already assumed the dimensions of a famine. "There are no hopes now that the winter crops will prosper," wrote the correspondents sent down by the press; "the position of landowners and land-tillers is critical. Landlords who a short time ago were prosperous are now bankrupt."[2] This was written one year ago. Since then hunger and suffering have been aggravated a hundredfold by the dire results of the bad harvest and the utterly unprepared condition of the population to meet the blow. In the Don territory numerous bands of hungry peasants are to be continually met with, who have come thither from various districts of the South, in the fallacious hope of eking out a few roubles by working. There is no work to be had. "Their feet protected by bast shoes (*lapti*), their bodies covered with tattered, worn-out smocks, miserable wallets thrown over their shoulders, these newcomers have overflowed the land. They wander about from house to house, begging for a crust of bread. But the alms they receive could not possibly still the cravings of hunger."[3] From the government of Kherson the same bitter lamentations are heard. In the district of Odessa, for instance, the peasants were never before in such terrible straits. "You come across whole villages the inhabitants of which utterly lack bread for themselves, food for their live-stock, and seed for the fields. *The imperial and other taxes are being collected with the utmost difficulty.* The communes are begging for a little respite,[4] and the authorities have also been entreated to give or lend the peasants some corn to make bread."[5] The order in which these misfortunes are narrated and the curious climax that results are well worth noting; the fact that fodder and food are as

---

[1] *Novoye Vremya*, 19th October, 1889; *Graschdanin*, 30th September 1889.
[2] *Ibid.* 21st January, 1890.
[3] *Ibid.* 29th June, 1890.
[4] *Ibid.* 10th August, 1890.
[5] *Ibid.* 24th January, 1890.

scarce as snow in midsummer, and the horrors of a famine have begun to be experienced, is rightly looked upon as a grievous calamity. Still it would seem not to be the worst. Far more severe must the distress be if the taxes are being collected with difficulty; for whatever other hardships may be in store for the country, the finances must at all costs be mobilized, and the taxes paid up to the last farthing. And as a matter of fact the peasants have, in many places, given everything they possessed as taxes, afterwards lying down uncomplainingly to die. In the Northern Caucasus the cattle disease has been raging till practically nothing more was left for it to exercise its rage upon; in addition to which the grass and corn crops have proved a miserable failure, so that the people are suffering and dying of hunger and disease.[1] The same story reaches us from Mariapol, where a bad harvest is being followed by a period of terrible want.[2]

The North and Northeast of Russia is, if possible, in a still worse plight. Writing of the large and most fertile district in the government of Saratoff — Balasheff — the *Novosti* assures us that the condition of the peasantry, especially in the northern parts, where the harvest was wretched, is become positively intolerable. Frightful need is everywhere visible. The dearth of corn for subsistence, the lack of work and wages, the scarcity of grass, hay, and straw, and the absolute necessity of paying the taxes, concur to ruin — nay, to exterminate, the peasants. "Numbers have sold their live-stock, and many have gone still further and sold themselves for all next summer and autumn."[3] The local authorities of Saratoff are so deeply moved by the harrowing scenes they daily and hourly witness that they have resolved to ask for a loan of 200,000 roubles merely to keep the peasants from dying of sheer hunger and the fields from lying waste.[4] Many of the peasant proprietors have managed even to part with their land in the hope that in this way they would succeed in shaking off the burden of their debts; but they have had all their trouble in vain, for though they no longer own they still continue to owe as much as before.[5] The govern-

---

[1] *Niedielya*, 14th November, 1890.
[2] *Novoye Vremya*, 31st October, 1890.
[3] *Novosti*, 18th February, 1890.
[4] *Niedielya*, 9th November, 1890.
[5] *Novoye Vremya*, 26th April, 1890.

ment of Samara, that, with due care and reasonable outlay, might be the granary of Eastern Russia, is as badly off as that of Saratoff, especially the Nikolaïevsk district.[1] Vyatka, the government that boasts the most enlightened, capable, and industrious peasantry in all Russia, is struck as low as most of its neighbors. "Poverty, robbery, thieving are therefore increasing there at an alarming rate. Able-bodied healthy men, well able to work, stroll about the country pretending to be deaf and dumb in order to move charitable persons to give them alms. . . . Masses of ragged, half-starved people are wandering throughout the country."[2]

The government of Kazan is an economic ruin. In the year 1885, as we said, there was a regular famine in that vast government, the people lying down and dying of hunger in the streets, on the roadsides, on the steps of houses. At the present moment we have the best possible authority for stating that the population is undergoing equal, if not still greater, hardships than in 1885. It is a question of issuing a loan to save the people from death, and that there is no exaggeration in the accounts published is quite evident from the circumstance that the Minister of the Interior has officially admitted that there are ample grounds for this extraordinary measure.[3] But there is also abundance of other testimony to be had: thus the Governor of Kazan sent in a report at the beginning of the year, in which an appalling state of things is graphically described. In one place, for instance, two hundred families of a thousand souls were, it is stated, discovered without any food fit for human beings; they were subsisting upon a weed known as goosefoot (*Chenopodium*).[4] "Since the autumn of last year," we read in another account, "there has been a famine among the population of the government of Kazan. It is strange that the press should remain so obstinately silent concerning it. The famine of five years ago, which caused such a profound sensation, was not a whit more intense than the present."[5] In the Troitsky district (government of Orenburg) the dearth of corn, hay, grass, etc., is such that the peasants are trying — one may easily divine

---

[1] *Novoye Vremya*, 3rd July, 1890.
[2] *Ibid.* 8th April, 1890.
[3] *Ibid.* 24th January, 1890.
[4] Cf. also *Novoye Vremya*, 10th January, 1890.
[5] *Ibid.* 10th April, 1890.

with what success — to feed the cattle on the foliage of the trees.[1]

A gifted Russian journalist, M. Nemirovitch-Dantshenko, journeyed through the Volga governments investigating the condition of the peasants there, with a lively faith in the inexhaustibility of Russia's resources, and he has now published a book on the subject. His verdict is: "Large numbers of people are dying of hunger. If my wanderings impressed me with a vivid notion of Russia's immensity, they completely shattered my notions of her abundance."[2] The peasants, we read further, are compelled in winter to work in factories in order to earn a miserable subsistence, which neither their own land nor subsidiary agricultural labor affords them.

"And yet, in spite of all that, such is their need, that to purchase food, *they have had to sell their dwelling-houses as fuel for the furnaces of the works*, while they betook themselves to cages. . . . It is scandalous that St. Petersburg should refuse to take these things to heart. Russia might be ruined for all St. Petersburg cares, whose sole concern is that the tax-paying capacities of the masses should suffice for the support of the intelligent and governing classes; but at the price of what bloody sweat these taxes are earned, it recks not one jot.[3] . . . Suffering, tortured, ruined people! Who will stand up for you? It seems as if there were no crawling thing that does not feed upon you! My conception of Russia is that of a huge giant put to sleep by magic spells; every unclean and slimy thing has meanwhile crept upon him, every species of vermin is continuously gnawing him without satisfying its greed. Lichens are on him, and mosses have grown over him. His body is stretched out upon the ground, and a forest has grown up around him; and in the forest God's light is absent; darkness alone prevails."[4]

It is only a couple of weeks ago since the Governor of Ryazan, one of the most flourishing and fertile governments of Central Russia, forwarded a confidential report to the Minister of the Interior, in which he describes the condition of the peasants as almost irremediable. It will take years of very great solicitude and truly paternal government, he says, to better to an appreciable extent the lamentable state of things that now prevails there. The peasants are overwhelmed with arrears of taxes and rates, with loans and debts. Everyone knows what an all-important part is

---

[1] *Niedielya*, 12th October, 1890.
[2] Nemirovitch-Dantshenko, *The Kama and the Ural*, St. Petersburg, 1890, p. 191 (Russian).
[3] *Ibid.*   [4] *Loc. cit.*, p. 318.

played by the farm horse on a peasant's farm, especially in a country like Russia, and the number and condition of the horses is generally a fair index of agricultural prosperity or decay, and he who has but one horse now will, as a rule, have none next year, and be without his land the year after. Now, in the whole government of Ryazan, the governor tells us, or rather tells the minister, 31 per cent. of the peasant proprietors possess but *one* horse; only 18 per cent. possess two horses, and but 12 per cent. have more than two. The proportion of those who have not even one horse is *thirty-nine per cent.*, and there are 26 per cent. who have neither horse nor cow, nor any kind of live-stock whatever.

The only possible issue out of the difficulty would be for the peasant to obtain subsidiary employment, and thus compensate to some extent by winter work for heavy agricultural losses. But, as I have already stated, that is now become a broken reed. Many industrial works have wholly disappeared; others have been closed for a time, and the number of hands employed has everywhere considerably diminished. Thus the rise in the duty on English coal necessitated the closure of the very largest ironworks in South Russia, and of several sugar industries besides. The serious industrial crisis in the extensive manufacturing district of the Petrokovsky government is telling most heavily on the petty farmers who worked there in the winter.[1] The linen industry is positively ruined; this year it received its death-blow; and "not merely in the government of Smolensk, but in all the governments in which linen manufactures exist; one of the consequences is that the peasants engaged in this industry are not receiving even half of their normal wages; and the worst feature in the matter is that the crisis is neither temporary nor accidental."[2] In Krementschoog and the industrial district of which it is the centre, the stagnation in business and industry is extreme, "in consequence of which one hears of nothing but bankruptcies, failures, etc., etc."[3] In Samara similar causes produce similar results, and the depression is intense.[4] Sheep-breeding and the industries dependent upon it are like-

---

[1] Cf. *Novoye Vremya*, 15th March, 1890.
[2] *Ibid.* 29th October, 1890.
[3] *Ibid.* 19th November, 1890.
[4] *Ibid.* 15th January, 1890.

wise rapidly decaying throughout the country, but especially in the governments of Kharkoff, Poltava, Yekaterinoslav.[1] The result is, as usual, a heavy financial crash. Bankruptcies are occurring everywhere, and in far greater numbers than heretofore.[2]

The upshot of all this is easier to imagine than to describe. Mendicity is becoming the profession of hundreds of thousands, possibly of millions. In Nischny Novgorod it is spreading like an epidemic.[3] Immense bands of heavy-hearted lack-alls, with despair in their souls, wander disconsolately through the land eager for work, but finding none to do. In Kharkoff we read of 4,000 peasants gathered together from various parts of the south seeking for employment of some kind, and seeking in vain;[4] much more numerous bands come to Astrakhan in the hope of being put in a way of earning a few roubles for their hunger-stricken families, but the greater number have to return with empty hands, one band of these doomed wretches numbering over one thousand men.[5] In Novotsherkassk the same distressing spectacle is witnessed, and one company of over a thousand peasants returned home travelling hundreds of miles for nothing, as there was nothing for them to mow and nothing to reap. "Many of these men," we are told, "have no scythe, reaping-hook, or wallet, having sold these things and every other article they possessed. Numbers of them affirm that for days together they have not tasted any kind of food; many of them are ill, especially the youths and the women. Every day fresh bands arrive and soon return, having found nothing whatever to do."[6]

No people in the world are so patient and enduring as the Russian peasantry, whose blind obedience, perfect resignation, and absence of care about what the morrow may bring forth would satisfy the aspirations and realize the ideals of St. Francis of Assisi or Sakya Muni. Still it is

---

[1] *Novoye Vremya*, 24th August, 1890.
[2] *Ibid*, 27th February, 1890.
[3] I speak from personal knowledge of this and many other cases mentioned in this paper. But as published and accessible sources of information are always desirable where it is question of such sensational statements, I at all times endeavor to refer the reader to some such. In this case I may quote the *Novoye Vremya*, 2nd January, 1890.
[4] *Ibid*. 20th April, 1890.
[5] *Ibid*.
[6] *Novoye Vremya*, 9th June, 1890.

scarcely to be wondered at if, under such terrible conditions, brought face to face with inexorable, pitiless fate, they turn and toss uneasily from side to side like the groaning Enceladus, unwittingly shaking the empire of which they are the foundation. Moneyless, friendless, helpless, and almost hopeless, the Russian peasantry rise up every year in their tens of thousands and migrate to the south, to the west, anywhere, not knowing whither they are drifting, nor inquiring nor caring what fate awaits them. They move on like swarms of locusts impelled by universal causes of which they have no idea; they are usually buoyed up by a vague half-unconscious feeling that they can create wealth out of nothing, that in their new abodes, with a little fair play, they will be somehow enabled to rise again more marvellously than the phœnix, even after their ashes have been swept away by the four winds of heaven. It is not only from barren soil that these suffering specimens of humanity migrate; fertility of the land linked to hopeless ruin by a well-meaning but demoralized Government, intent merely upon mobilizing its finances, offers no inducement to the hungry peasant to stay and swell the number of victims that perish yearly of famine. In the Balashevsky district of the government of Saratoff, for instance, last autumn, five thousand peasants threw up their land and houses in despair, and set out for the unknown east.[1]

Such is the hopeless misery of these men; we are told that "their condition strikes the beholder with dismay."[2] They set out to seek for fortune, but all of them encounter hardship and misery on the way, many meet with death, and the thousands who return sorrow-laden, and seek for work in their native places, only contribute to lower the existing prices of labor and to ruin others without benefiting themselves. As soon as the navigation was opened last May, a ghastly multitude, numbering fifteen thousand of these silent accusers of a religion and a Government, arrived in Tiumen, in Siberia, the first important halting-place on the weary journey to the Eastern Utopia. There being practically no steamers to take them on, they lived there as best they could in hopes, which (a terrible mortality breaking out among them) death possibly realized for

---

[1] *Graschdanin*, 14th August, 1889. Cf. also *Russian Messenger*, December, 1890, p. 337.
[2] *Northern Messenger*, July, 1890, p. 87.

very many of them, and life bitterly mocked in the case of the rest.[1] Large numbers had to live in the open air, at a time when the frost is still very severe, and the death rate, caused by what a tell-tale euphemism describes as "anti-hygienic conditions," grew so alarming that the Governor of Tobolsk sent a telegram to the Governor of Moscow requesting him to stop the stream of migration as far as depended upon the chief magistrate of the chief rallying-point for them in European Russia.[2] "One has only to glance at these tortured, wind-beaten faces, and at the emaciated bodies covered with ragged smocks," exclaims the *Astrakhan Messenger*, describing a band of them gathered together in that city, "in order to understand what agonies, what exquisite sufferings they must have endured on the way from Nischny Novgorod to Trans-Caucasia. And it is hard to say what awaits them afterwards, for they have no idea what place they are going to. . . . *The only hope for them is contained in the fact that they cannot be much worse off than they are.*"[3] "These living skeletons are to be found in all the towns and cities on the Volga, and their misery-stricken aspect is enough to wring one's heart."[4]

From Tiumen tens of thousands of them move into the interior in steamers, barges, every kind of vessel that floats, "the absence of even elementary accommodation manifesting itself in increased mortality.[5] Like the prisons, the barges always take far more than they can accommodate, so that on the covered deck there is such terrible overcrowding that the passengers all sleep in one indiscriminate heap."[6] The sick and suffering always constitute a numerous body, for in the absence of ventilation disease spreads like wildfire.

"I sometimes went in and cast a glance at the berths of these third-class passengers, but hands, arms, legs, feet, heads, boots, bast shoes, sheepskins, sacks and bags with clothes and dry bread disclosed themselves to my view as one formless mass. I heard the helpless moans of sick children, one of whom was down with small-pox. The atmosphere was fœtid to an intolerable degree: it would positively knock down a person coming straight in from the fresh air. Coffins are left

---

[1] *The Business Correspondent*, No. 90.
[2] *Russian Gazette*, No. 149.
[3] *Astrakhan Messenger*, No. 291.
[4] *Ibid.* No. 299.
[5] *Northern Messenger*, November, 1890, p. 24.
[6] *Ibid.*

behind at every landing-place, containing the remains of peasants who have migrated to the Elysian fields, and scores of children infected with small-pox, with diphtheria, congestion of the lungs, are continually arriving at Tomsk, and augmenting the number of graves."[1]

In damp sheds, thrown up on the banks of the river Toor, thousands of persons are huddled together in Tiumen on dirty straw, without even plank beds to lie on. The children are put to sleep under wagons whenever any can be had. The number of such wanderers passing through Tiumen amounted this year to over 30,000. The rainy weather reduced their scant provisions of fire-dried bread to a pulp, and brought them to death's door. In May, while there were 14,000 persons waiting for the navigation to open, the thermometer registered 23 degrees (Fahrenheit), and more than 13,000 of them had to lie down and camp out in the open air in spite of this cold. A large number of corpses (especially of children) were carted away every day.[2] In Tomsk the wanderers are driven out to camp in a swamp, where there are a few sheds capable of sheltering four hundred persons. The accommodation they enjoy while here may be inferred from the circumstance that they *usually rowed up to the doors of their sheds in boats.*[3]

In all parts of Russia one hears of and sees these woe-begone wretches — pillars of Imperial finance crumbling in dust away. "A new stream of migrants has flowed in here," exclaims the *Tiflis Gazette,* "from the government of Koorsk. The poor wretches sold their horses and wagons before they reached here, hoping to get some work as mowers, but they have been rudely disappointed."[4] "On the 29th May, a party of migrating peasants' families passed through Kieff on their way to Bessarabia. . . . They are suffering extreme misery. Many of them have remained in Kieff subsisting on alms."[5] An army of *over* 20,000 mowers wandered from Taganrog to Yeissk in search of something to do, but found nothing; more than half of them returned the way they came, and endeavored by means of begging for means to move on to other places. *Neither farmers nor others can afford to give them work in*

---

[1] *Northern Messenger,* loc. cit., p. 25.
[2] *Ibid.* p. 27.
[3] *Ibid.*
[4] *Tiflis Gazette,* No. 148.
[5] *Odessa News,* May, 1890, No. 1619.

return for a piece of black bread." [1] What eventually befell this formidable army of starvelings? Its fate has not been disclosed by the press; but possibly the village gravediggers of Russia could account for a very large contingent. It was possibly hunger that ended the sufferings and the wanderings of many members of the hungry band of two thousand mowers from Kieff, Koorsk, and Poltava, who were equally unsuccessful in obtaining temporary employment. A few died before the eyes of the public. "In the broad daylight, in sight of all men, four of them died of sheer hunger. This was confirmed by the *post-mortem* examination." [2]

Men in any other country subjected to such sufferings as these would assuredly not subordinate their anger and their instinctive love of life to any feeling of respect that might still linger in their minds for the property of others; and the forbearance of the Russian peasant in circumstances that seem calculated to stifle the promptings of humanity and throw him back upon first principles, is worthy of profound pity rather than high praise, for it is the forbearance of soulless apathy rather than the discipline of self-control. But at times even the Russian peasant gives signs of life and feeling; proves that his composition is not wholly devoid of what is euphemistically termed human nature. Thus, in Martynovka last summer, there were ten thousand mowers perishing of hunger, but willing and eager to work, even for a mouthful of dry bread. But even on these terms they could get nothing to do. They grew excited, murmurs rustled through the blackening mass of humanity, and noticing some peasants who were carting corn, they seized upon it in a twinkling, and then betook themselves to the stores of a neighboring corn-merchant, where they also took a moderate portion of corn for every man. [3]

In the Balashevsky district the hungry multitude collected outside the house of the representative of the Government and loudly clamored for bread. "For three days we have not broken our fast, for heaven's sake give us bread or corn, or else we'll take it. Our children are moaning at home half dead of hunger; let's have a little corn!" The authorities refused; mumbled something about

---

[1] *Northern Messenger*, July, 1890. Cf. also *The Saratoff Messenger*, No. 121.
[2] *The Crimea*, No. 72, 1890.   [3] *The Don*, speech, No. 66.

sending in written petitions and obtaining the necessary authorization. "We care nothing for petitions, it's corn we want;" and they swayed to and fro for a time, but at last swept on towards the granary. The guard there at first refused to admit them; on reflection, however, he cunningly put the key of the granary on the railing, and dared any man of them to remove it. They knew that that meant Siberia; but necessity sharpened their wits. A long pole was got, and every man touching it with his hand, they all removed the key. This was then attached to a long cord which every man held, moving thus the key to the keyhole. At last the door was opened not by one or two persons, but by the joint efforts of them all, and the corn was taken out.[1] This is narrated by Prince Meshtshersky as a case of desperate insubordination that should be ruthlessly stamped out at once.

These intense sufferings of the Russian peasantry surely constitute one of the strongest arguments that a patriot has ever put forward in favor of the brutal treatment meted out to convicted criminals and honest Jews, and to which very shortly even the harmless Finns are to be subjected. If patriotism is powerless to alleviate the misery of Russian Christians, it should at least prevent its being aggravated by the obtrusive prosperity of odious Jews and Protestant Finns. And if free men and Christians, who are dying like poisoned flies in the desperate attempt to pay taxes that exceed their income, are being flogged and imprisoned in order to give a fillip to zeal, which even the instinct of self-preservation is unable to conjure, why should any tenderness be shown for prisoners who are confessedly guilty of crime?

For poverty, illness, hunger, misfortune are no excuses in the eyes of the Finance Ministry; as borrowing in Russia is a disguised selling, so is tax-gathering a masked expropriation of the capital of the peasants — nay, a masked selling of their bodies into captivity. Since the mobilization of finances began, extraordinary measures have been taken to recover arrears of taxes, and to prevent them from accumulating in future. Thus, for instance, since 1888 the ministry has given orders that all factories, works, shops, etc., are to deduct from the wages of peasant workmen the amount of taxes due at the rate of one-

---

[1] *Graschdanin*, 21st June, 1889.

third of the weekly wages of unmarried persons, and onefourth if the person have a family.¹ Thus the white slave who spends his day of *fifteen hours* in hard work and receives for that his *few pence a week*, must deliver up threepence of it every week as his contribution to the mobilization of his country's finances. The peasant's corn is also taken from him and sealed up till he pay the last farthing, which he can only do by raising money at such rates of interest as were described above. Meanwhile he may literally starve.² Peasants in cities receive no passports, and must return home by *étape*, along with convicts and felons, until they pay every copeck, and their native village, where they are condemned to stay, becomes for them a sort of Ugolino's hunger tower.³ This determination to have the money at all costs is so awkwardly evident that even once, when the authorized representative of the Government received the taxes and spent them on his own pleasures, the peasants were told that the Government could not afford to be at the loss of the money, so they must pay it over again, and when some of them proved that they were absolutely penniless, the police set about distraining their property.⁴

Can the poor peasants be blamed if, under such conditions, they rise up and flee to Siberia, the Caucasus, South America — any whither outside their own native place, become a vast charnel-house? "Where are you bound for?" asked a newspaper correspondent of a batch of intending emigrants to South America. "For Gafrika," one replied. "That's a lie," ⁵ said another; "we're going to Branzolia." ⁶ "We're doing no such thing," broke in a third; "it's Aggripeena⁷ as we're off to." ⁸ Numbers of these wretches were shot down for running off to South America, because, it was contended, they were being deceived by lying agents who discoursed to them of a land overflowing with

---

[1] Cf., for instance, *Day* (*Den*), 6th April, 1888.
[2] *Niedielya*, 17th January, 1890.
[3] Cf. *e.g.*, *Novoye Vremya*, 10th May, 1890.
[4] *Novoye Vremya*, 3rd December, 1888. It should, however, be stated in fairness that, to the best of my belief, the peasants appealed from this decision and obtained judgment in their favor from the competent judicial authorities.
[5] The Russian way of suggesting that the speaker is in error.
[6] Probably Brazil.
[7] Argentina.
[8] Cf. *Novoye Vremya*, 29th October, 1890.

milk and honey. But the truth is, that the misery they were enduring in Russia would impel any man to rush off to any country, were it even to that distant land from whose bourne no traveller returns. Their land was sold long ago to pay taxes, and nothing was left for them but to work to keep their families and themselves in a world in which they seemed superfluous. Many of them could get nothing to do, and those who found employment — the spoiled children of fortune — worked like galley-slaves for fifteen hours a day, receiving *tenpence halfpenny a week, or three farthings per day of fifteen hours*.[1] What diabolical eloquence must have been needed on the part of the foreign agents to persuade these spoiled children of fortune to tear themselves away from their dearly beloved country! And how those who escaped and are now in South America must often sit down by the rivers of Brazil or of Argentina and weep when they remember Russia!

As for those who remain in Russia, until they pay their last debt to nature, they never manage to pay it to insatiable man; they are forced, however pressing their own needs, to contribute to satisfy those of the Treasury. It is not merely that their land and huts are sold by auction, but their labor is sold for the benefit of the Government, and they are systematically flogged lest they should prefer the prior claims of their children and their wives to those of an ingenious finance minister whose reputation is at stake. Yes, systematically flogged and treated as English Jews used to be by greedy Plantagenet kings. Flogging the peasants to compel them to pay taxes is grown very common of late years, so much so, indeed, that a special word has been coined for it — "the threshing out of arrears." "By what advantages," asks the *Law Messenger*,

"is this use of the lash compensated? By none. Flogging does not thresh out the taxes nor the arrears, but brutalizes the man subjected to it. Suppose he have money which he is hiding, he will of course pay up before he submits to this infamous and extremely painful punishment; and if he does not pay under these circumstances, it is obvious that he has not the wherewithal. We could not admit the contrary, unless the ordeal of flogging freed him from all further obligation. This, however, it does not. To whip a man, therefore, who has been unsuccessful in obtaining the necessary sum, notwithstanding the present extreme difficulty of earning anything, and the terribly low rate of

---

[1] *Glos*, 25th November, 1890; *Novoye Vremya*, 30th November, 1890.

wages, is a deed of the most crying barbarity.[1] You sell his property by auction, you break up his farm and home, and compel him by means of physical suffering and infamy to expiate his misfortune, but the upshot of all your measures is that the 'man' perishes and you see in his stead a desperate exasperated individual who works harm to himself and is fraught with danger to others."[2]

"The moral effect of these hard conditions upon the peasants of the young generation is," we are assured, "truly horrible. The notions of law and justice are torn out of their hearts in the most cruel and painful way, and, side by side with utter stupefaction and despondency, one observes the symptoms of unconscious hate, which assumes at times most monstrous forms."[3] "Types have started into being," remarks the representative of the Imperial Economical Society in his official report, "which it is absolutely impossible to match: eternally drunk, with disfigured features, with wandering glance, covered with rags, they look like half-tamed beasts. There lurks an unwonted cruelty and savagery in their entire aspect. They are feared by everyone, by the authorities of the village and district most of all."[4] Sons persecute their fathers, drunken fathers dissipate the property and abandon their families to fate. "This is not a proletariat," exclaims the above-mentioned official; "it is a return to savagery. *No trace of anything human has remained.*"[5] With materials so unpromising as these who but a genuine thaumaturge would attempt to build up even for a brief five years a nation's credit? "It is a matter of surprise," exclaims the most respectable review in all Russia, "how people manage even to exist who are thus ground down on all sides and ruined, who live in a state of perpetual state of hunger, are helpless against any schemer instructed in the arts of reading and writing who comes along, who have spent all their spiritual force in the vain struggle against a combination of injustice, arbitrariness, and violence, and who can nowhere hope to find defence and shelter."[6] And yet a minister has been found capable of solving the apparently insoluble problem of extracting even out of these woebe-

---

[1] "*Dielom samova vopiooshtshova varvarstva.*" — *Law Messenger*, November, 1890, p. 377.
[2] Cf. *Law Messenger*, November, 1890, pp. 377, 378.
[3] Cf. *The Messenger of Europe*, October, 1890, p. 781.
[4] *Ibid.* pp. 781, 782.
[5] *Ibid.*
[6] *Messenger of Europe*, October, 1890, p. 778.

gone subjects the money which they do not themselves possess: he compels them to fulfil his commands more faithfully than even the spell-bound demons executed the strange behests of Michael Scott.

This is not the exaggerated eulogium of an enthusiastic admirer; it would be impossible to be more moderate in praising M. Vyshnegradsky without doing injustice to the facts, of which I shall quote but one example. "In many parts of the government of Ryazan," says the same official Russian organ, "the peasants, for want of rye, *support life on acorn bread.* The official of the district board, sent down to investigate the condition of the peasants on the spot, states that in some families a mixture of the weed called goosefoot (*Chenopodium*), acorns, and rye is eaten; in others bread is made of potatoes, acorns, and rye, and in others, again, of acorns alone. We have often heard," remarks this organ with graceful and well-timed wit, "of acorn coffee, but this is the first time that we have heard of acorn bread."[1] Another official report, frequently quoted in the course of this paper, asserts, in reference to the condition of the peasants of the Porkhovski district — "poverty prevails among them everywhere. In some villages they subsist on —— bread, of which a person unaccustomed to it could not swallow a single morsel." This may seem at first sight an exaggerated description; but it is really a somewhat mild characteristic of bread which, as the official goes on to remark, "*is not so much bread as dry cow-dung.*"[2]

Now it requires a degree of optimism bordering closely upon hallucination to treat men who have to still, without satisfying, the cravings of hunger by swallowing dry cow-dung, as solvent tax-payers; for it is only natural to believe that if these martyrs of financial tactics did occasionally earn or steal a few pence, they would spend it on bread that was genuine rye bread, or at least acorn bread, and not mere dry cowdung, rather than hand it over to the Imperial Treasury. And yet such is not the fact; and it remains one of the most brilliant triumphs of the present minister of finances, who has so often succeeded in gathering grapes from thorns, that he has here also shown his art by extract-

---

[1] *Novoye Vremya*, 12th December, 1890.
[2] G. P. Sazonoff, *Peasant Proprietorship in the Porkhovski District*, St. Petersburg, 1890. Cf. also *Messenger of Europe*, October, 1890, p. 777.

ing gold from dried cowdung. The Russian peasantry, in short, are on the rack of a giant despotism, and, as the years pass, and the tension increases, they are forced to yield not only all that makes life worth living, their flocks and herds, their crops and labor, their homes and home-life, but also at last their very life-blood at the bidding of the Tsar. "'These same peasants,' we are informed, 'are punctual tax-payers, regularly paying the interest on their debts and lodging it in the city bank. These men can scarcely be called human beings; they are more like machines for the payment of taxes, half-unconscious creatures who fancy themselves created solely for the purpose of working on in hopeless toil.'"[1] This is doubtless a very sad consummation, and one that is regretted by no one more profoundly than by the kind-hearted minister himself, who would much sooner alleviate distress than produce it. But why dwell on the inevitable? If, says the Russian proverb, you have called yourself a mushroom, you must jump into the basket. The main point — and one which should not be forgotten by carping critics eager to condemn a minister, whose moral courage equals his ingenuity — is, that he has successfully solved a most difficult problem which a Goschen or even a Gladstone would shrink even from tackling. A stick has been given to him —

> "once fire from end to end,
> Now ashes save the tip that holds a spark " —

and he has cheerfully undertaken the task — which he bids fair to accomplish — to blow that solitary spark with such superhuman force that it will run back and spread itself where the fire lately burned, and impart a bright warm look to what, an instant later, will be recognized by the dullest as cold black ashes.

---

[1] *Messenger of Europe.*

CHAPTER IX.

THE RUSSIAN CENSURE.

THE idea which an Englishman usually attaches to the words, Russian Censure, is that of a strict and irksome control exercised over the periodical press with a view to hinder the propagation of ideas or the publication of facts tending to discredit autocracy in the eyes of Russians; that is to say, an institution unpopular but indispensable as long as the doctrine of divine right is sedulously taught and bolstered up with dishonest interpretations of Bible prophecies, said to contain predictions about the escape of the present Emperor from a violent death at Borki in the Steppes of Southern Russia.[1] Whether the reality is entirely covered by this moderate view, will appear from the following sketch, based upon carefully verified facts which can be supported by most trustworthy evidence.

The definition of the scope of the Censure put forward with all needful clearness in the fourteenth volume of that hell of good intentions called, "The Complete Collection of Russian Laws," is as comprehensive as the most tyrannical autocrat could well desire. "Its function is to scrutinize all productions of literature, science, and art destined to be circulated in the Empire, with the exception of such as are expressly exempted from preventive censure," which, I may explain by the way, are also scrutinized and judged with the same unbending rigor. This paradox is quite on a par with the statement of the Connaught clodhopper, sent to see whether all the pigs were come home, to the effect that he was not quite sure as to their number; he had counted them all except one mottled pig with a curly tail, that kept

---

[1] Serious organs of the Russian press maintained that one of the minor prophets foretold the railway accident at Borki, and the miraculous intervention of Providence in favor of the Imperial family. The most curious part of this theory is the statement that the Emperor's name was mentioned by the inspired writer in full, as was also that of the Empress. The matter was seriously discussed by Russian theologians two years ago. Jeremiah may yet be found to have foreseen, foretold, and lamented the fiasco of the Abyssinian Expedition under Aschinoff, and the bombardment at Sagallo.

running about in such a bewildering way that the wit of man could not count him. Even if jealously confined within these broad limits, the Censure would still deserve to be regarded as an all-important factor in the history of Russian civilization, a sort of serpent-like Nithhöggr, gnawing away at the three-fold root of modern culture — literature, art, and science. In practice, however, it knows no limits; but, striking out successively in every direction, contrives to hedge in thought in all its forms, crushing out every normal manifestation of healthy, moral, and intellectual life, and suppressing with the same ruthlessness a play, a picture, and a private letter. It would be impossible to point to any branch of science, art, or literature on which the Censure has not left deep and abiding traces of its nefarious influence, stunting it in its growth, and warping it from its appointed goal, sometimes into miry paths and marshy byways, whither even the moralist follows it only from afar.

A long, yellow, ugly building in Theatre Street, St. Petersburg, which, appropriately enough, also accommodates the Prisons Board, is the material receptacle of whatever brain-power the Russian Censure may be supposed to possess. It is divided into a home and foreign department, the former of which has its functions as a sort of intellectual excise office, and the latter as a literary custom-house with a prohibitive tariff. It is in one of the stuffy rooms of this dingy building that the official (who probably has never been to a university or even grammar school) told off to censure the Tsar's journalistic literature runs his eye every morning through the damp newspapers, marking with a red pencil the passages which he thinks it prudent and desirable that the Emperor should read, cutting them out with a scissors later on, and pasting them on a few sheets of thick paper. It is in another room of the same edifice that these courtly extracts are conned by a more expeperienced member of the Council — generally the Director-in-chief; after receiving whose *imprimatur* they are carefully copied out in a bold, legible hand, censured by three or four other dignitaries, by each from his own particular point of view, perused by the aide-de-camp in waiting, and served up by him in the digestible form of gossip, spiced with the *chronique scandaleuse* of the day before.

But this spacious building possesses no chamber of horrors, no pandemonium of souls in pain, such as one may see any day in the passport office. The reason is that little of the real labor of sifting the wheat and isolating it from the tares is done in this literary clearing-house, which generally confines its activity to issuing orders, taking official cognizance of their execution, and summarily deciding such cases of doubt as occasionally crop up even here, where a whim is held to be a fair substitute for a reason. Books, manuscripts, engravings, photographs, atlases, music[1] — for the device of the censure is *Humani nihil a me alienum puto* — are being daily received in these quarantine barracks for disinfection or destruction, and from this office they are usually sent to the private lodgings of the Censors, who examine them when they have time, passing a judgment from which there is seldom any appeal. Once a week the Censors come together in solemn conclave, to compare notes and distribute the work on hand.

This wide range of subjects renders it necessary that the Censors should in certain cases modestly content themselves with the functions of a grand jury, and, having found a true bill against the accused, refers to a still less able but also less responsible body the inquiry into details. But no Censor would dispense himself from reading professionally a cookery book on the flimsy pretext that the bearing of the culinary art upon Russian autocracy is so shadowy and remote that an error of judgment in estimating it would prove comparatively harmless. On the contrary, he would first analyze the work from a purely political point of view, and then pass it on to the medical censure, where the hygienic truths it contained would be sifted and winnowed from the heresies, and, the suggested changes having been made by the author, sanctioned for publication. If Lenten fare were descanted upon to any considerable extent, the work would most probably be also submitted to the ecclesiastical censure, whose deliberations are invariably characterized by incredible slowness. A book on logarithms or conic sections, or a treatise on medicine written in Singhalese or Celtic, or any other tongue, of which no subject of the Tsar has an inkling, would, an uninitiated person might suppose, be wholly dispensed from the time-consuming formalities of the Censure Office. This, however, is not the case. The Censure in Russia is as universal as death: no book can escape it; and

---

[1] Cf. § 187, Observ. I. of the Censure Laws.

more than one purely mathematical work has ben suffocated
before it saw the light, owing to the disordered fancy of a
harassed official. Should a special treatise of this kind
contain a sentence in the preface or a foot-note alluding to
the enlightenment of the Emperor or his father or grand-
father, it would, after having been examined in the ordinary
way, be handed over to the Minister of the Court, who
would take counsel as to whether the allusion should stand
or the work be allowed to appear. "How dare you allow
a ribald scribbler to lampoon my imperial ancestors?" said
the Tsar to the Head of the Censure, a few months ago,
alluding to an erudite history of Catherine the Great. A
book that touches even incidentally upon marriage or
burial, a saint or a ceremony, after issuing from the ordeal
of the general censure, must run the gauntlet of the ecclesiastical inquisition; a tragedy or comedy has to be scrutinized by the general censure, the dramatic censure, and
then, according to the range of subjects incidentally
touched upon, by the ecclesiastical, military, or other
appropriate departments; a work on finance — say, Professor Jevons' book on money— would have to pass through
the censure of the Ministry of Finances; and a biography
upon Russian contemporary celebrities would have to be
first sanctioned by all or nearly all of these various censures,
and then by every dignitary and every influential writer
mentioned in the work.[1]

Some works that pass out of three or four such ordeals
unscathed are condemned in the last, and either wholly
annihilated or placed in one of the pigeon-holes of the
archives in Theatre Street — a store-room of unrealized
ideas, wishes, plans, and projects like those with which
Ariosto filled the limbo of the moon. The number of these
records of things that might have been — many of which
disappear every year for want of proper surveillance — is
immense; for the Censure disdains nothing, from formidable folios to tiny leaflets; and only eighteen months have
elapsed since his Majesty's Minister publicly reprimanded
the responsible officials for a culpable lack of zeal in censuring the little gilt paper rings that encircle cheap cigars
and cigarettes, on which one word is printed — the name of

---

[1] *Our Acquaintances* is the title of a humorous work on these lines.
The characteristics of nearly every one of the persons mentioned therein
had to be re-written in very many cases, suppressed in several, modified in
most, and sanctioned in all.

the cigar which implies its strength and quality. The names, it appears, were in many cases printed with Latin instead of Slavonic letters, and were, like the cigars themselves, of Polish, not of Russian origin, and the paper ringlets were, in the interests of good government and public morality, forthwith forbidden.[1] "We have quite a numerous series of censures," wrote one of the few enlightened members of that body; "a General Censure under the Ministry of Public Instruction (now the Ministry of the Interior); a Supreme Board of Censure; an Ecclesiastical Censure; a Military Censure; a Censure in the Service of the Foreign Office; a Dramatic Censure in the Ministry of the Court; a Press Censure; a Censure of the Secret Police; a new Pedagogical Censure; a Censure of Law Books; a Censure of Foreign Works. If we reckon up all the officials occupied in censuring, we find that they are more numerous than the books that are published each year."[2]

The laws laid down for the guidance of the Censors are rigidly absolute in the sense that while the official, prompted by fear of dismissal, desire of promotion, or private animosity, may err with impunity on the side of severity, an attempt to stretch a point in the direction of indulgence would inevitably prove suicidal; a hundred sleuthhounds would scent out the crime, and anonymous denunciations and signed indictments would rain upon the Minister as plentifully as warnings used to pour into the mouth of the lion of St. Mark's in troublous times of sedition and discontent, leaving the Minister no choice but to punish the culprit. The Censor, told to bear in mind that excess of zeal may possibly be rewarded but will never be punished, whereas indulgence is almost certain to be followed by dismissal, frequently succumbs to the temptation to commit most arbitrary acts, against which the public, which is quite accustomed to be treated with cynical contempt, has no remedy. I was once on terms of intimate acquaintance with the Censor of the Foreign Department, enjoying a favorable opportunity of observing the manner in which he — an unusually indulgent official — acquitted himself of his official duties. He explained to me the working of the Postal Censure, which receives daily all the foreign reviews, newspapers, books, music, and printed matter of every

---

[1] *Grashchdanin*, 27th October, 1889.
[2] Cf. *Russian Antiquity*, March, 1891, p. 632.

description which pass through the post to persons living in Russia. The examination is sometimes tedious, and the result frequently unfavorable; but if the book or journal be registered, it may be expected in the long run to be either delivered to the addressee or returned whence it came; otherwise the chances are considerable that, whether approved or condemned, neither the sender nor the addressee will ever set eyes upon it again. My own experience amply confirms this statement. Hundreds of copies of English, French, and German newspapers, reviews, and books sent to me and to my personal friends have been intercepted in this way.[1]

This friend of mine in the Censure Office was in the habit of receiving bundles of publications twice or thrice a week addressed to people living in Russia; and I think I can honestly say that he never once made a present of any of them to his friends, or gave them a place in his own library. The language they were written in was not Russian, and the number of persons who speak or read it in the Russian Empire is extremely limited, so that he enjoyed a liberty to do almost anything he liked without fear of control; moreover, as he occupied a dozen other lucrative posts in the city, his leisure was too limited to allow him to be pedantic or minutious. He seldom mutilated, and still more rarely prohibited a book or review. "Works in the ———— language," he used to say, "are as likely to be read by Russians as the inscriptions of Rameses the Great; and it does not signify one jot what they contain." He was wont to read, for his own pleasure, two periodicals addressed through the post to persons who lived several hundreds of miles from St. Petersburg, often keeping them back a month or two for the purpose.. I once paid a tribute of praise to the patience of the two distant subscribers, to whom it seemed to make no difference that they received in February a periodical published abroad in December of the year preceding. "Well, worse evils might befall them than waiting," he once exclaimed. "I have never yet cut off any one's supplies of periodical literature, though I

---

[1] It is only a few weeks since several copies of the English translation of Count Tolstoï's tale, *Work while ye have the Light*, forwarded by English booksellers to Englishmen living in St. Petersburg, were returned by the authorities. One of the gentlemen whom it was feared the perusal of this work might demoralize is the lector of English at the University of St. Petersburg — an Oxford scholar.

might do so at any time. They feel that this power is a Damocles' sword ever suspended above their heads."

Circumstances that occurred much later made me better acquainted with the extent of the discretionary power thus vested in men whose intellectual development is generally much inferior to that of those to whom they stand in the capacity of mentors. A weekly periodical which I was in the habit of receiving possessed an irresistible attraction for the Censor appointed to read it, whose education had been rather neglected in his youth. Being compelled somewhat late in life to give lessons in English grammar and literature, he was laudably desirous of acquiring, for his own satisfaction, a knowledge of the language which he was being paid to teach. He selected my periodical for his experiment, and began to read it over slowly and with difficulty, working most zealously with the dictionary for ten days at a time, while I, ignorant of his efforts, was engaged in an angry correspondence with my bookseller on the subject of the delay. Several numbers never reached me at all.

Once when more than usually desirous to see the periodical, in order to read an interesting paper that had appeared therein, I applied to a Russian acquaintance who, I was aware, occasionally received a copy. On inquiry, however, he proved to be merely a borrower, not a subscriber; but he kindly promised to endeavor to procure me the number I was seeking for. He kept his word and sent me the journal, which I found, to my extreme surprise, to be my own copy, paid for by me, but read and owned by the Censor, who had lent it to the friend from whom my Russian acquaintance had borrowed it. It was only lent to me for that one day, and I never set my eyes upon it afterwards. An official whom I consulted as to the advisability of lodging a complaint against the Censor strongly dissuaded me on the ground that I should do more harm to myself thereby than to this indomitable student of the English tongue.

The circumstance that many of the Censure laws run counter to common sense is never treated as a reason for not enforcing them, and even the most meaningless and absurd of them all is executed with the same puerile pedantry in virtue of which the sentry, told off to stand guard over the rose to which the Empress Catherine once took a fancy, was maintained there for half a century after the rose had withered and the Empress mouldered away in dust.

Thus the law ordains that all books and papers in the possession of strangers or natives crossing the Russian frontier be taken from them and forwarded to the Censure Committee of the nearest city, which may be hundreds of miles distant from the traveller's destination; and the circumstance that these are well-known Russian works, published in the Empire and bearing the *imprimatur* of the Censure on the flyleaf, is not enough to ensure their exemption from this costly and irritating formality.[1] It is only fair to say that even to this rule there are some exceptions: "A foreigner has the right to take with him one note-book, one almanac, one small dictionary, one album, and one keepsake" (*sic*), if, in addition to other negative characteristics, to be verified at the custom-house, they are found to contain nothing subversive of morality and are not of a religious or political character. Rubinstein's musical manuscripts were taken from him in this way, as they aroused the suspicions of the officials, and the Censure in the fulness of time either confiscated or lost them. The maestro never saw them any more. A traveller who should take his *Encyclopædia Britannica* with him would probably be annoyed to see himself deprived of it on the frontier, and exasperated to find, on receiving it back, that hundreds of paragraphs had been blackened with printer's ink, and scores of pages cut out in a most slovenly manner. It must not be forgotten, however, that, like the blast tempered to the shorn lamb, this seemingly harsh treatment is deprived of a little of its sting by the provision made in section 195 of the Censure Laws, which thoughtfully enacts that the Censors are to fold up carefully the pages thus cut out and, at the desire and expense of the owner, forward them across the frontier by post to any address he gives.

It would be difficult to imagine a code of regulations more childishly pedantic, more wantonly irksome than the 306 paragraphs of which the Censure Laws are composed, which, comprehensive though they are, constitute but the warp of the web, the woof being made up of secret instructions and galling prohibitions which would seem positively ludicrous to a Chinaman and oppressive to a Turk.[2] Editors

---

[1] Cf. § 196, Obs. I. of the Censure Laws.
[2] Neither this nor any other statement of mine is intended to be taken for a figure of rhetoric: it is the expression of a fact. In Russia it is still the custom to laugh at the Chinese system of government, and the word, *Kitayshtshina* (*Gallicè, chinoiserie*), is a synonym for utter chaos. And

are frequently summoned by letter, as Members of Parliament are by a three-line whip, and enter the Council Chamber in Theatre Street in fear and trembling, uncertain whether they have not committed an expiable crime, the wages of which is literary death. There they listen in silence to the High Priest of public morality, who reads out a list of topics to which they must under no circumstances allude: — the emigration to Brazil, perhaps, the migrations of peasants in Russia, the famine in various districts of the interior, the frequent cases of armed resistance to the authorities, the drunken brawl between Prince X. and Count Y. at Cubat's on the Grand Morskaïa, the flight of T.'s wife, the movements of the Tsar, Tolstoï's *Kreutzer Sonata*, and a dozen others.

No book or writing can be exempted from the Censure on the ground of its universally acknowledged moral tendency, nor even for the more intelligible reason that it has already been approved by the Censure, and published scores of times — nay, that it has been specially recommended by the Ministry of Public Instruction; and the imprudent printer or publisher who should issue a new edition or a new translation of the *Imitation of Christ* or a Homily of John Chrysostom without first obtaining the written sanction of the authorities, would have to atone for his crime by a maximum fine of £40, and a term of imprisonment not exceeding three months,[1] besides putting himself under a cloud of suspicion that would damp his energies and clog his efforts for years to come. The excusable desire to weave into the wording of that portion of the Censure Laws which is accessible to the public, the proof that these restrictions are not the result of obscurantism, but emanate from enlightened solicitude for the welfare of the people, gives rise to passages of unrivalled *naïveté*. Thus the Censors are informed that they need not necessarily prohibit a work, say a history of Germany

---

yet Russians should know better. Privy Councillor Vassilieff, Professor of Chinese at the University of St. Petersburg, informs his countrymen, with more enthusiasm than befits a loyal Privy Councillor, that " in China there is no such thing as censure. Periodicals, pamphlets, and books are published without any examination "; and he further communicates the interesting fact that when, on a certain occasion, "a work was published against the reigning Manchov dynasty in China, the Emperor contented himself with answering the book by a book." — (Vassilieff, *Chinese Progress*, St. Petersburg, 1883, p. 14.)

[1] Cf. Russian Criminal Code, Section viii., § 1024.

or a treatise of metaphysics, on the sole ground that reprehensible opinions are quoted therein, "provided always that a reasonable amount of indignation be expressed by the author of the work, or a sincere attempt made to refute them;" though, even then, the question of sanctioning or condemning the work is deemed too momentous to be decided by any one official; it must be referred to the Central Censure Committee for final solution, the members of which are as eager to compete with each other in patriotic zeal as were the French regicides after the king's death, and far more deeply impressed by the truth embodied in the Russian proverb, which says that "a man's shirt is nearest his own skin."

The Censure Laws depend largely for their efficacy upon the complete control exercised by the Government over printing offices, type foundries, booksellers' shops, circulating libraries, and all cognate trades and callings in the Empire; and the most analytical of German professors would gape in admiration at the wonderful minuteness and thoroughness of this control. None of the above-mentioned establishments can be opened without a very special authorization which it is a Herculean labor to obtain. A most searching inquiry is invariably made into the antecedents of the applicant, the sins and backslidings of fathers being visited upon sons and daughters, and the imprudence of the children recoiling upon their parents. When the permission is finally obtained, the heavy responsibility that goes with it, the galling restrictions that fetter the successful applicant, and his helpless dependence in business matters upon a number of venal officials devoid of scruples of any kind, is sufficient to crush out whatever enterprise he may have been originally endowed with. Every new printing machine, every set of type bought, sold or repaired,[1] every book or pamphlet destined to be printed, must be first announced to the authorities, verified by them, next entered in detail in a number of books, and then sent to the Censure for examination. If a printer gets one of his presses altered and neglects to notify the

---

[1] My object being to give a faithful picture of things as they are rather than an unfavorable comparison with other countries, I think it right to point out that in England, down to 1869, no one might make or sell type without a special license, and that every person so licensed was obliged to keep an account, in writing, of all persons to whom types or presses are sold; "and to produce such accounts to any Justice of the Peace requiring the same, under a penalty of twenty pounds."

fact to the authorities, he is fined five hundred roubles, besides being visited with other and more serious pains and penalties.[1] If a journal, having been read by the Censure, is sanctioned for publication, but the written authorization should happen to be delayed, the printer who dared to set it up in type and publish it, would be fined three hundred roubles and imprisoned for three months.[2] A person who sells type, printing presses, hectographs, etc., is in duty bound to look upon the intending purchasers as conspirators against the State, and must, in his own interests, turn them away, unless he knows them personally, and is in possession of their real names and address. Nor is this acquaintance considered sufficient to allow of business relations: he can deal only with authorized printers, and he is exposing himself to a heavy punishment if he part with a set of type without having first seen, with his own eyes, the authorization to the buyers to purchase and keep a printing press.

Permission to open a bookshop, a circulating library or a reading-room is more difficult to obtain than a railway concession, and the melancholy list of pains and penalties for infraction of any one of a long category of rules and regulations makes the man's life an intolerable burden. The petition or petitions — for there is a whole series of them — in which he humbly prays for the boon, and in the framing of which as many elaborate formalities have to be observed as in the preparation of certain of the specifics of Paracelsus, is certain to be rejected, if the applicant's name is found inscribed in the black books of the Secret Police — a sort of recording angel's register in which are carefully entered, to use the Hibernicism of a late Member of Parliament, the record of all the political crimes prevented by the vigilance of the police as well as the intentions and velleities of persons suspected of disaffection by the experienced thought-readers of this redoubtable Third Section. It occasionally happens, for obvious reasons, that the applicant is but a figure-head, who possesses neither the capital nor the experience needed to carry on the business, but once he receives the authorization, the real proprietor, who has no power to remove him without the consent of the authorities, is merely a puppet in his

---

[1] Criminal Code, § 1010.
[2] Criminal Code, § 1024.

hands. It is scarcely necessary to point out the abuses to which these regulations give rise, especially should the unfaithful steward be wise enough in his generation to make friends to himself of the complaisant Censors.

But on no profession in Russia does the nightmare of the Censure weigh so heavily as upon journalism; an editor's life in one of the mushroom cities of the Far West, who is one day short of the letters l and v, another day short of money, and a few days later on is hurled into eternity by a pistol-shot, is tame in comparison with the checkered life of some Russian journalists.

To foreigners it is a mystery how a capitalist can risk his money in such a precarious investment as a newspaper; Russian journals, however, require but a small capital to start them, and even that seldom belongs to the editor, who generally begins his journalistic career with credit, continues it in debt, and frequently ends it in bankruptcy and ruin.

Newspapers may be broadly divided into two classes: those which cannot be even printed until they have been approved by the authorities, and those which may be printed but cannot be published without the authorization of the Censure; the latter category consisting of a very few newspapers published exclusively in St. Petersburg and Moscow. The division really rests on a distinction with a scarcely perceptible difference. So trained are the editors of the latter class of periodicals that they cut and mutilate the contributions destined for their journals with the same unerring judgment, the same unbending vigor as the paid official. Like Violenta in the fairy tale, some of them can almost smell the voice of a man that has the faintest tones of disloyalty in its composition. A curious instance came under my own observation some time ago. An acquaintance of mine, whose name is well and favorably known in Russia, offered a story for publication to the editor of the *Messenger of Europe*. M. Stassiulevitch agreed to insert it on condition that a certain number of pages (eleven or twelve, I think) were cut out, as he feared the Censure might take exception to them. The authoress, deeming M. Stassiulevitch *plus royaliste que le roi*, refused to allow her story to be lopped and pruned by a timorous journalist, and laid the manuscript before the editor of *Russian Thought* in Moscow. M. Goltseff, ignorant of the circumstance that it had been offered to another editor, read it and accepted it on condition that certain passages (exactly the same as those marked by M. Stassiulevitch) should be erased. The authoress again refused and sent the manuscript to the editor of a journal which is censured before being printed, and the Censor authorized its publication, after having struck out the identical passage objected to by the first editor.

Editors' intuitions, correct though they are, are not the only guarantees against a disagreeable surprise; the proof-sheets of every newspaper, review, and book, which is theoretically exempt from preventive Censure, must remain a certain time (calculated in hours for daily newspapers and in days for reviews and books), before publication; and even on the expiration of this term a special authorization in writing must be placed in the hands of the printer before he can allow the copies to be removed from his office. A line, a word, nay, the absence of a word, is quite enough to cause the permission to be refused, and the edition must then be printed anew in a modified form at the expense of the editor. The *Messenger of Europe* for April, 1890, while lying on the table of the Censure Committee, awaiting the written permission to appear, was read by some zealous person who objected to certain passages in a paper by M. Issaieff, on the migration of the peasants in Russia. The editor was called upon to make the necessary alterations at once, and to reprint the whole edition.[1] This would have taken him several days, as it was Saturday morning when the order arrived, and the date on which the review should appear had already come. The thing was found impracticable, and the Censure *tore out twenty pages* of the paper by M. Issaieff. In this condition the review was delivered to subscribers.[2] Another still more curious case occurred on Saturday, the 28th of September, 1889. The *Universal Illustration*, a weekly illustrated paper, was already printed. Tens of thousands of copies were lying addressed to the subscribers, ready to be delivered to the post office for distribution. The proof-sheets had been read by the Censor, and approved, but at the last moment the watchful eye of a zealous literary policeman spied the disloyal words: "The journey of their Majesties," etc. The adjective "Imperial" had been unwittingly omitted before the word

---

[1] A number of the *Messenger of Europe* contains about 450 pages.
[2] Pp. 828-849.

"Majesties." The Council was hastily summoned together, as the proprietor of the journal declared that the loss of money and time would be enormous if he were compelled to destroy the entire edition and print a new one, on account of the accidental omission of a word, the absence of which would pass unnoticed. The Council discussed the question in considerable detail, and took the opinion of the Director of the Censure, after which they decided that the edition must be annihilated, and a corrected edition printed, with the missing adjective "Imperial" added. And yet no people in the world laugh more immoderately at the absurdities of the Turkish Censure than Russian journalists.

So shadowy, even in theory, is the difference between the unprivileged periodicals that § 140 of the Censure Laws[1] forbids editors to touch upon any topic withdrawn from discussion by secret circulars or verbal prohibitions, which are as numerous as the sands of the sea, and likewise compels them by inference to insert without change or commentary, and as coming from the editor himself, any statement or opinion which it may be found desirable to have propagated. It is the old story — if the masters say the crow is white, the servants must not assert it as black. The *Novoye Vremya* and the *Graschdanin* are continually publishing such paragraphs, which are occasionally copied by the Russophile press in England as evidences of the state of public opinion in Russia.

This being the fate of the dry wood, one can readily imagine what happens to the green wood. The sorrows of the editors of unprivileged journals are more poignant than those of Werther, and the knowledge that they are inevitable scares away those rare writers whose literary talents, careful habits of thought, and unbending honesty, would prove an inestimable boon to the Russian press were it only as a leaven. But the vacant places are taken by rusticated students, returned convicts,[2] liars who boast of their mendaciousness,[3] thieves who have "done their sentences,"[4] and

---

[1] *Laws concerning the Censure and the Press*, printed at the Imperial printing office in St. Petersburg, 1886, pp. 20, 21.
[2] I take it that the total number of convicts and *ci-devant* political suspects engaged in journalism amounts to about fifty-five per cent.
[3] Cf. Chapter I.
[4] Cf. Chapter IV., where a short sketch is given of Mr. Goldberg, the respected journalist, who was convicted of stealing, sentenced to a year's imprisonment, and having "done" his sentence, resumed his journalistic

drunken bullies who, when a leading article is required, have to be sought for in the taverns and disorderly houses of the city.[1] None of the vigorous philippics and biting satires of Russian liberals are calculated to give such a fair idea of the difficulties against which an editor has to contend as the matter-of-fact description of the steps he must take in order to obtain permission to found a journal, and the perspective that stretches out before him when he has at last reached the pinnacle of his ambition. I will endeavor to make that description as brief as may be.

The unhappy mortal whom hope or despair drives into journalism and who seeks to found an organ of his own, must first of all draw up a petition to the Minister of the Interior, giving his name, address, profession, the type of journal he proposes to found, its size, detailed programme, a list of the topics it will touch upon, its name, price, the number of times it will appear every week, an autobiography of himself, and a biography of the responsible editor, together with the baptismal certificates and all other official documents relating to their life and activity.[2] The omission of any of these details would cause the petition to be sent back. Such is the present posture of affairs in Russia that out of every ten such petitions, the writers of which were found to be without reproach (no one in Russia can be truly said to be without fear except certain religious fanatics), nine would be returned at once with an emphatic negative. But suppose the circumstances to be unusually favorable and the petition allowed to take its course; a private inquiry would be next set on foot by the police of the city into the antecedents of the applicant, and in this investigation the Governor-General of the province would be asked to take part; the books of the secret police would be overhauled, and the correspondence on the subject would swell to an unwieldy size, while the petitioner would be obtaining an insight into the meaning of hope deferred.

But let us suppose all these formalities paid for and past, and the applicant's perseverance rewarded by the desired permission to found a journal in Kieff or Kazan. His

---

duties. I am personally acquainted with two other very well known Russian journalists of still worse antecedents, whose history I learned long after I had met them in respectable society.

[1] One of the most forcible leader-writers on the staff of the *Moscow Gazette*, under Katkoff's editorship, answers to this description. Another is M. Sytschevsky, one of the best literary critics of the provincial press.

[2] Cf. Censure Laws, § 119.

troubles begin forthwith. His staff falls very short of his own modest ideal, and is as casual as the guests at the wedding party described in the Gospel, being composed of stragglers and vagabonds taken from the highways and byways; reporters who know neither shorthand [1] nor grammatical longhand; writers of weekly letters who are in the pay of his rival; correspondents who take bribes when they can get them; leader-writers who have as much claim to be termed journalists as Carlyle's distressed needlewoman, with an occasional professor eager to change his fancied talents into the small coin of the empire; in a word, men in whose tragic career journalism is but a fleeting episode — a halfway house on the *facilis descensus Averni*.

It is no easy matter to make a web of bottled hay, but Russians are justly famous for their optimistic ingenuity, and so trifling are the drafts they present on Fortune's bank, that the editor I have just described would deem himself lucky indeed were he free to put the services of even his motley crew to the best account. But he might as well sigh for the moon. Suppose him fortunate enough to make the important discovery that for years past, in some town or district, the Government had been systematically defrauded to a fabulous extent, or that the judges in one of the law courts had made a practice of selling the justice or injustice which they had paid for the privilege of administering — he is forbidden to hint even remotely at the mere possibility of such enormities, *if the price of his journal for a year be less than seven roubles*. If it exceeded this sum, and the circulation was therefore presumably smaller, he would enjoy the right to hem and haw and beat vaguely about the bush, suppressing names, and not mentioning places;[2] but even this is no more than a theoretical right which no Censor in the enjoyment of his normal faculties would allow him to exercise. If the editor learns from the most trustworthy source that the Government intends to introduce some new project of law, paragraph § 100 strictly forbids him to make his information public; and were the law less emphatic the Censors would not fail to make good the omission.

But if the publication of news received at first hand is forbidden fruit to a Russian journalist, it seems natural to

---

[1] I have heard of only three Russian reporters who can read or write shorthand.
[2] Cf. Censure Laws, §§ 98, 99.

suppose that they have full liberty to use their scissors and paste upon all books and journals expressly authorized by the Censure to appear and circulate through the Empire. As a matter of fact, however, paragraph 63 of the Censure Laws absolutely forbids them to reproduce or even summarize any article or item of news published in authorized books, journals, and reviews, without first asking an express authorization in each particular case, which the Censors are extremely chary of according. Thus in Kieff and Odessa, during the disturbances at the Universities, the press was strictly forbidden to allude even remotely to the subject; and when the University of the former city was closed, six journals of Odessa were forbidden to communicate the intelligence to their readers or even to copy the details which the seventh, an anti-Jewish organ, was permitted to publish. The real cause of the loss of the steamer *Vesta*, three years ago, was carefully hidden from the Odessa public, no newspapers of that city being allowed to discuss the subject, while the press of Sebastopol analyzed it in detail. And yet in both these cases all the newspapers were equally subject to preventive Censure.

Driven off the debatable ground of politics the hopeful editor takes refuge in the vast domain of social topics, art, and literature, endeavoring to give a faithful picture of the events of the day, "to shoot folly as it flies." An interesting law suit, a local *cause célèbre*, may possibly be going on in one of the law courts, and as the most lengthy account of the proceedings in the organ of his most serious competitors is fully two days behind, he resolves to steal a march on his rival and take the lead. Engaging at considerable expense a reporter who can write a little shorthand, he prints on Tuesday night, for Wednesday's issue, a verbatim report of Monday's proceedings, intending to astonish the town by his unparalleled expeditiousness. But the wary Censor coldly reminds him that § 77 of the Censure Laws absolutely forbids him to publish any such report of law cases now or at any other time, as this is a very special privilege not lightly accorded to provincial journals. Among the eight newspapers that actually appear in Odessa only one enjoys this rare privilege, and that one is the rabid anti-Jewish organ alluded to above.

Again discomfited, the editor, if not wholly disheartened, starts in search of other items of intelligence, and discovers, perhaps, that the Mir or Peasants' Commune has passed certain resolutions, or that the Assembly of Nobles has adopted strong measures against some long-standing evil. He writes one or two paragraphs, and possibly a leading article, on the subject, hoping that the Censor will allow them to pass unchallenged. But the vigilant official returns the proofs marked with a red pencil, and the words, "See § 82 of the Censure Laws," which strictly forbids the publication of items of news on either of the topics just named without a special authorization from the governor in each particular case; and the governor may be two hundred miles distant at the time.

Thus a Russian journalist, like his Spanish colleague described by Beaumarchais, if he only eschews politics, religious and social topics, steers clear of political economy, finance, philosophy, and certain epochs of history, is careful not to offend persons who, whatever their official position, can resent fancied insults, sedulously avoids such burning questions as the taxes, the laws, the economic condition of the peasantry, the press, medicine, education, and the partial famines in the empire, enjoys considerable liberty in the choice of topics for his paragraphs and themes for his leading articles, subject, of course, to the caprice of a timorous Censor, who is painfully aware that his career may be irreparably destroyed by a single mistake on the side of indulgence.

These and numerous other topics being removed from the purview of journalism, a newspaper is generally very uninteresting reading indeed. But there are occasions when a dictionary or an old almanac are read with avidity; "a crab," says the Russian proverb, "is a fish when you can get nothing more like one." But let us suppose the newspaper at last made up, the latest telegrams received, and the reporters gone home for the night. The editor's next step is to obtain the Censor's imprimatur. At about eleven o'clock, P.M., a messenger is despatched with the proofs, which the wearied official, who has been working, or purporting to work, all day, takes and reads at his leisure, keeping the office-boy waiting generally for two hours on ordinary occasions, and three or four on public or private holidays, when he goes to the play, or spends his evening in jovial company. It is comparatively easy to imagine the feelings of an energetic editor who, after having impatiently waited for several hours for the authorization to print, keeping his workmen idle, ready to begin work at a moment's notice, at last receives back the proofs at two or three o'clock A.M. with the leading article, which formed the *pièce de résistance*, rejected *in toto*, the cleverly-written feuilleton kept back for further consideration, and the only two interesting items of news struck out.[1] This means that about one whole page is left a perfect blank which it is his duty straightway to fill up; for were he to allow his paper to appear with a blank space, or even with too suggestive asterisks, his journal would cease to appear, and his own place would know him no more. As he has now no time to write leading articles, and what is still more important, no right to trouble the Censor's well-earned sleep, he is forced to fall back upon stale news, oft-repeated anecdotes of famous men, recipes from authorized cookery books and other ordinary makeweights, none of which he can use unless they have been previously approved by the identical official, who now censures his journal. This vamping up of events long past as news of the day is now so common in Russia that it excites no manner of dissatisfaction among readers. In the *St. Petersburg Svett* of the 30th October, 1887, we find the important intelligence that—"In 1882 the population of Moscow amounted to 753,469 souls, and that of St. Petersburg to 861,303." This reminds one of Elia's unimaginative friend who, when at a loss for a smart paragraph, was wont to communicate the interesting information that—"It is not generally known that the three balls outside a pawnbroker's establishment are the ancient arms of Lombardy."

I have myself observed several cases of newspapers being fettered and expurgated till they ceased to exist, and I have had my own leading articles cut and mutilated, and wholly forbidden. But as in these cases it is always desirable to have published testimony rather than the unsupported assertions of individuals, it may be interesting to give the experience of a provincial journal as described in the review, *Memoirs of the Fatherland*, at a time when the Censure was much less severe than at present. "The prohibitions were numerous, or rather innumerable, and the upshot of them all was simply this, that no matter what topic the editorial staff found it needful to discuss, it was

---

[1] This is no imaginary case. I was once present on the return of the office-boy bringing the proofs, with the most important portions of the newspaper struck out, and heard the editor apostrophize the absent Censor in language that was quite equal to the occasion.

always 'a very delicate question.' . . . They were forbidden to allude to the fact that letters were being constantly lost in the Post Office or delivered to the addresses with broken seals and opened,[1] because the Post Office was under the Governor-General, and an article or even an allusion to the matter would tend to cast a shadow on the good government of the province; neither was it lawful to point out the unsatisfactory condition of the Moscow Tract, and for the same reason; it was strictly forbidden to discuss the terrible fire that had devastated the city, to complain of the exorbitant prices of provisions, of the lack of corn for the people, etc., and the Censure drew a red pencil across a passage in which a comparison was instituted between the prices of provisions in Irkutsh and those that obtained in St. Petersburg. . . . It was forbidden to allude to the Benevolent Society because the Governor-General was its President. The distribution of relief to the sufferers from the fire, which was arranged in such a way that the owners of large storehouses received thousands of roubles while the real sufferers were left to vegetate in holes amid the ruins of their houses, was also placed upon the index of forbidden subjects. . . . It was not lawful to write a word about statistics, because the Censor was the Secretary of the Statistical Committee, nor about the peculation connected with the hiring of the theatre, etc., etc. . . . And as if all this were not enough, it was deemed almost a crime that the editor and the staff had never once praised a general in this paper."[2]

It is, perhaps, superfluous to remark that the principles by which Censors are guided in forbidding or permitting leading articles, stories, etc., are as difficult to discover as those which determined Buridan's ass to choose one haystack in preference to the other. What was permissible yesterday is illegal to-day, and the article that may appear without prejudice in the newspaper printed on one side of the sheet, would amount to constructive high treason if it appeared in the journal published on the other. One of the most recent instances occurred last February, when the *Graphic* crossed the Russian frontier with an illustration presenting the Tsarewitch with a tiger killed at his feet.

---

[1] This practice is more widespread than ever it was before, and is likely to continue so until vigorous representations on the subject are made by foreign Governments to the Russian Foreign Office.
[2] *Memoirs of the Fatherland*, March, 1881, p. 37.

It would be as difficult to discover anything hostile to Russia in this picture as to find the philosopher's stone in a wagon of Newcastle coals. But the Censor, with sight sharpened by prospective hunger, descried disrespect to Imperial Majesty therein, and blackened out the offending cut. A fortnight afterwards the *Graphic* reprinted the illustration, and with it a fac-simile of the blackened page as it was delivered to Russian readers, with the evident object of casting ridicule upon the Censors. Yet this was allowed into the country without let or hindrance.[1]

An enterprising editor with a fair capital at his back would naturally spare no pains or money to procure special telegrams from the chief cities of Europe, until he made the painful discovery that it would profit himself and his readers just as much if he distributed his money in bribes to the official meteorologist in the hope of obtaining better weather than his fellows. All such telegrams, whether the journal in which they are destined to appear be privileged or the reverse, must first go to the Ministry of the Interior; and, should the nature of the topics seem to render it advisable, to the other ministries concerned. This procedure, which may sometimes be perfectly justifiable, can always be used by the Censure to delay the appearance of important telegrams and to thwart the intentions of the editor. No newspaper in Russia enjoys such privileges as the *Graschdanin*, which is subsidized by the Emperor. And this is an instance of how the *Graschdanin* testifies to the efficiency of the telegraph Censure: — "We were unable to insert the telegrams of our special correspondents this morning, owing to the circumstance that the Censor appointed to examine all telegrams was not at home all night — at least he had not come home up to two o'clock in the morning."[2]

The advertisements, which afford no scope for the display of an editor's energy and enterprise, would seem to be the only portion not dished up by government officials. And yet even they do not constitute an exception to the rule: all advertisements, whatever their character, must be carefully censured, in the first instance by the police, and then by those other departments of the State which are

---

[1] Not being in Russia or England, I did not see either of the copies of the *Graphic*, and my description of the illustration is founded merely on hearsay.
[2] *Graschdanin*, 27th October, 1889.

authorized to take cognizance of the things advertised. Thus an advertisement recommending or offering for sale tickets for a foreign State lottery would have to be expressly approved by the Minister of Finances, a patent medicine puff by the Medical Council, etc. This law is very rigorously enforced, and the editor who should presume to publish an advertisement, even for a cook or a coachman, without the written authorization of the police officer, who possibly may be absent from home or with faculties too clouded to allow him to sign his name, would be put on his trial and infallibly punished. I have sometimes seen three editors on their trial together for this crime, and I remember M. Liberman, of the *Tiflis Listok*, who was tried more than once for this offence, and always found guilty and punished.[1]

It would seem that when all these minute regulations have been literally complied with, the paper brought out, and the editor's troubles over for the moment, there is no reason why his recollections of them should be embittered by a feeling of constant apprehension for the results. And yet, strange as it may appear, he is never wholly free from this feverish uneasiness. For if the Censor have failed to weed out every trace of Liberalism, if he have neglected to inquire into the hidden meaning of some equivocal word or allusion, he may, and very probably will, be condignly punished, but all the real thunderbolts are sure to fall upon the devoted head of the editor, whose journal may be suspended for six months or forbidden ever again to appear, in virtue of Section 154. For, as I remarked above, printed words are looked upon in Russia as caterpillars, and their creators are held responsible not only for their existence but likewise for the acts of the future butterflies. The manifest injustice of this law cannot fail to strike the unbiassed reader. A journalist hands in the proof sheets of his newspaper and virtually says to the Censor: "I will print only as much of this as you may declare desirable; any passage across which you draw your pencil will disappear, any interpolations you suggest will at once be inserted; I am wholly in your hands." Numerous erasures and additions are then made by the Censor, who at last says: "By the authority vested in me by the Government, I approve this day's issue and sanction its publica-

---

[1] Cf., for instance, the *Law Journal* of the 21st December, 1887.

tion." And yet if the authorities be dissatisfied with this authorized version, the unfortunate editor will suffer quite as much as if he had surreptitiously printed the offending passages. Thus out of nine journals suspended during the short space of nine months, five were newspapers that passed through the hands of the preventive Censor, whose every suggestion had been scrupulously carried out; among them were the *Saratoff Leaf*, which was suspended for one month, the *Odessa Messenger* for three, the *Siberian Messenger* for four, and the *Siberian Gazette* for eight months.[1]

One of the usual measures adopted by the Government against journals to the existence of which it is desirable to put a speedy end consists in the refusal to appoint a Censor in the city in which they appear. In all Russia there are but eight Censure committees, besides those of the capital; and four of the eight are crowded together in the Baltic Provinces. The Government, by the exercise of paternal indulgence, may allow an official employed in the service of the Crown to censure a journal founded in a provincial town, without regarding him as an official Censor; but this is a privilege and may at any time be withdrawn. Thus one occasionally reads announcements like the following: "The censuring of the *Dniepr* (an excellent daily paper) is transferred from Yekaterinoslav to Moscow," *i.e.*, to the distance of over a thousand versts, so that if the proofs of Thursday's issue were posted to the Censor on Wednesday evening at six o'clock, they might in the most favorable case be delivered into his hands on the following Saturday evening at seven or eight o'clock, and reach the editor on the following Wednesday, exactly a week after they had been posted; in winter they would take occasionally as long as a fortnight to go and return. Of course the journal immediately ceased to appear. In 1881 the editor of the *Tver Messenger* was ordered to send in future the proof sheets of his journal to Moscow to be censured, in consequence of which it ceased to exist.[2]

If the editor finds that the sale of his journal is unfavorably affected by its high price, he is powerless to lower it, and if he agrees to take the yearly subscription in easy instalments, he has committed a crime, not provided for by any published or secret law, but for which he will have

---

[1] Cf. *Russian Courier*, 17th January, 1889; *Novosti*, 19th January, 1889.
[2] *Russian Antiquity*, August, 1888.

to pay dearly;[1] if it appear only six times a week, and he wishes to issue it on every day of the seven, like the papers of his rivals, he might as well propose to lay claim to the Imperial throne as to give effect to his wish; if he is anxious to enlarge the dimensions of the journal by a few square inches, he would infallibly ruin himself and it, were he to do it without a special authorization, which it is most difficult to obtain and even dangerous to ask for.

In Russian society, bereft, as it is, of public opinion, and of public conscience, which lies at the root of all healthy public opinion, Censors are, to some extent, pariahs, or, at least, men of an inferior caste. This is keenly felt by the few Censors who were originally destined for something better — by the two Censor poets, Maikoff and Polonsky, for instance, who black out pages of Huxley and Buckle, Swinburne and Byron, in the morning, write "inspired" pæans to liberty and the Muses in the evening, and at all times when poetry or the Censure is mentioned, guiltily "hang their heads, and a' that." One may reasonably find fault with a man for bartering away his birthright for a handful of silver and a ribbon to stick in his coat, but, the purchase once concluded, one can scarcely blame him for guarding his acquisition with the aggressive jealousy of a miser. The fact that most Censors do this is the true explanation of the ridiculous scrupulosity with which they object to the most harmless article, scent treason in a note of interrogation, and heresy in the form of a letter of the alphabet,[2] thus rendering their own lives supremely miserable, and driving editors to the verge of madness.

This painful anxiety is natural enough on the part of men who, to employ the technical terms of the law, "can be dismissed from the service for misdemeanors which it

---

[1] Last January M. Pobedonostseff wrote a secret complaint to the Minister of the Interior, to the effect that several quasi-Liberal periodicals, among which he mentioned the *Novosti*, the *Observer*, *Nablindatel*, the *Northern Messenger*, the *Week*, and the *Messenger of Europe*, were demoralizing the youth of the Empire by allowing them to pay the yearly subscription in instalments. He requested the Minister to forbid this practice in future, and to deal more severely in general with these pernicious publications.

[2] That such trivial matters as these do not always depend upon the caprice of the individual Censors is evident from the law cited *in extenso* in a former number of this journal, according to which all books and articles in the Russian language in which the letter i is formed as in English, instead of like an N upside down, are forbidden.

is impossible to prove that they committed. And it is hereby decreed that no petition or explanation offered by any individual so dismissed shall be entertained or received."[1] One day the Minister of Justice, displeased at some article, insisted that the Censor who sanctioned its publication should be punished. "Certainly," was the conciliatory reply, "but would it not be as well if we first called him up and heard what he has to say to the charge?" "No, it would not," angrily replied the Minister (Count Panin); "I insist on his being punished first. Afterwards, if you wish, you may ask him for explanations."[2]

Treatment of this kind drives the Censors to extremities which would raise a smile on the lips of a Russian *tschinovnik*, if related of the Turks. An authentic list of incidents of this kind as a volume of humorous anecdotes would be certain of success. I shall mention two as illustrations. When the so-called Mazeppa dance was invented in Paris, a humorous article on the subject appeared in the organ of the Imperial Academy of Sciences in St. Petersburg, in the course of which the writer hazarded the conjecture that in a short time the new dance would spread over all Europe. This observation seemed wantonly seditious to the Minister, who, discovering therein a covert sneer at Russia, called up Dtschkin, the editor, reprimanded him very severely, and threatened him with the utmost rigor of the law.[3]

Private letters are censured on much the same lines as books and newspapers, although it is in the nature of things that very many of them should escape. There are Censors of private correspondence as there are Censors of science, art, and literature, and the results of their labors are registered in the books of the Recording Angels of the Third Section,[4] where human misery is being eternally brewed as in a witch's cauldron, where the thread of life of many a young and harmless man and woman has been ruthlessly cut. The broad principle observed in the Censure of Private Correspondence is that a certain fixed percentage of letters taken at random, is opened and read, besides all letters to and from persons whom there is any real or fan-

---

[1] Cf. *Russian Antiquity*, March, 1890, p. 635.
[2] *Russian Antiquity*, September, 1890, p. 618.
[3] *Novoye Vremya*, 2nd March, 1890; *Novosti*, 2nd March, 1890; *Russian Antiquity*, March, 1890.
[4] The name of the Russian secret police.

cied grounds for suspecting of hostility to the Government. My own experience of the practice was varied, curious, and unpleasant. One evening an acquaintance of mine rushed breathless into my room, exclaiming: "What do you mean by enclosing a photograph of your soul in every letter you send to your friends, just as if there were no one to read them but yourself and they?" "Are my letters then really tampered with?" I asked. "Well, yes, I should think they were. Just listen to this music and tell me who composed it. 'My dear X.,'" and he proceeded to quote several consecutive sentences from a letter of mine to a friend abroad, which I thought were as secret as if I had merely whispered them to the rustling foliage of a solitary oak. The letter was registered; moreover, I had handed it in and had received the receipt for it myself. "How did you learn the contents of my letter?" I asked, after I had recovered somewhat from my astonishment. "From the Censor — a silly young man," he replied. "You should make his acquaintance and enlarge your gallery of types."

I did make the acquaintance of the young fellow, who lived in somewhat straightened circumstances, and was struggling hard to keep his head above water; and I found him extremely communicative over the walnuts and the wine — a diversion of the day which he had not previously been in the habit of making. With the utmost simplicity and blandness he told me extraordinary stories of intrigues and counter-intrigues, of damnable lies told and mortal blows struck by unseen assassins whose consciences left them untroubled because they never themselves actually shed innocent blood but only sold it[1] to others. These disclosures startled me, and for days I kept recalling the expressions and allusions contained in my previous letters, calculating the interpretations to which they were open. That such innocent allusions may be, and frequently are, quite as dangerous as real crimes, I have had ample and terrible proof. Three years ago a number of grammar-school boys were arrested and put in prison without knowing or even conjecturing what they were accused of. The secret

---

[1] I confess to having occasionally written letters to friends, knowing that they would be opened and read by the authorities, and desiring it, in order to save innocent men from ruin. Cases have also come to my knowledge — infamous cases — of men having written apparently confidential letters to others for the purpose of compassing their ruin.

investigation was tedious, but when it was completed the juvenile prisoners were set at liberty. Some time later, the cause of their arrest leaked out. It appears that one of the boys had written to another, during the Easter holidays, enclosing his subscription for the "good cause." The letter was intercepted, read, and interpreted as a missive from one dangerous conspirator to another, and the boys were imprisoned in consequence. The official investigation established the fact that it was only a question of the regular annual subscription organized by the scholars for the purpose of bribing the man who had charge of the written examination papers to disclose them a day or two before the written examination.

The Censure of spoken words and phrases and private conversations, the systematic abuse of the conventional forms, of social life, of hospitality and friendship for the purpose of tempting men and women to think aloud in the presence of living phonographs who, not content with simply repeating, often exaggerate, aggravate, and even invent, the consequent air of profound mystery, the look of mistrust, the attitude of fear with which people converse together in the streets and public places — these things constitute a special branch of the subject, which deserves a paper to itself. The degree of terror that lies at the root of all this can readily be imagined; it has been sketched scores of times; among others by an intelligent Censor who enjoyed the confidence of two Emperors, and who in spite of his official position could not refrain from exclaiming: "In sober truth it is a very painful position for men to be in who, though conscious that they never harbored any criminal designs, and have always led irreproachable lives . . . feel themselves daily, nay, hourly, in danger of being irretrievably ruined, merely in consequence of a secret denunciation, of calumny, of misunderstanding, of the bad humor of others, or of a false construction put on their words or deeds. Harassed and hounded down as they are, it is infinitely better for such men to renounce once for all their right of living and working — to waive that right in the name of —— in whose name, O God?"[1]

It is a matter for wonder that under the Upas-like shadow of the Censure any embodiment of thought has been permitted to spring into existence, to which by even

---

[1] A. V. Nikitenko, *Russian Antiquity*, March, 1890, p. 648.

the widest stretch of courtesy the names of literature and science could be applied. There can be no doubt that the representatives of the Government have been, and still are, desirous of arresting, if possible, the very process of independent thinking, and at the worst of confining it within the narrowest conceivable limits. They rightly feel that any presentation, literary or plastic, of the aspects of Russian life must, by the very nature of the subject, excite disgust at the reality; and it is only natural that the conclusions of science should appear quite as redoubtable in this respect as the types and forms of art and literature; for if the staff be crooked, its shadow cannot well be straight, whether the intercepted rays be those of the midday sun or the flickering light of a tallow candle. "It is my desire," exclaimed the Minister who at the time was Chief of the Censure, "that Russian literature should wholly cease to exist. Then at least we shall have obtained a definite result, and I, at any rate, shall be permitted to enjoy unbroken slumber."[1]

Bearing this avowed aim of the Government in mind, one cannot affect surprise on learnng that innumerable works of literature and science have been either wholly forbidden or mutilated till they were fit only for the trunkmaker's and the pastry-cook's. There was nothing abnormal — judged by this standard — in the refusal of the Censure to sanction Count Uvaroff's work on Grecian Antiquities in Southern Russia, because the word *demos* was rendered by "the people." "If you wish your work to appear, you must change the word *people* into 'citizens,'" exclaimed the Censor, proud of his ingenuity and confident of his power.[2] Not less logical was the rigorous exclusion of the word *progress* from all literary and scientific works, native and foreign, destined to circulate in Russia, owing to the demoralizing train of ideas which it is naturally calculated to suggest;[3] and it would be cruel to reproach the Censure for considering a series of full-stops following in close succession as a satisfactory proof of

---

[1] Cf. *Novoye Vremya*, 14th December, 1890, quoting extract from the review *Russian Antiquity*, December, 1889.

[2] Cf. Nikitenko, *Russian Antiquity*, March, 1890, p. 637. Deliberating on the advisability of employing the word *citizens* in a book or article, Saltykoff condemns it: "It seems to me that the word 'citizen' should be struck out. Just fancy what it smacks of." Cf. *In the Midst of Moderation and Correctness*, p. 170.

[3] Cf. *Russian Antiquity*, September, 1890, p. 599.

hostility to the Government, and an unanswerable reason
for suppressing books and articles that would otherwise
have proved not merely harmless, but eminently beneficial.
In England one is tempted to scoff at these things; in
Russia they are stern realities that draw forth tears of blood
from the very strongest men, none of whom felt disposed
to laugh when Censor Akhimoff, mindful of his duty,
refused to sanction the publication of an arithmetic, in
which the rows of figures of two problems were separated
from each other by a series of two suggestive dots, behind
which the wit of man could not divine what diabolical
ideas might be lurking. One can scarcely refrain from
speculating what, under such conditions, would have
become of the irreverent Aristophanes, with his seventy-
eight syllabled words, of Rabelais, with his *Antipericata-
metanaparbeugedamphicribrationes Toordicantium*, or of
Dante, with his cabalistic *Rafel mai amech Zubi almi?*
Surely their productions would have been promptly chopped
up into little shreds on Holiday Island, near St. Petersburg, and they themselves — if they had the misfortune to
be subjects of the Tsar — placed under police supervision.
That is what happened to Shevtschenko, the national poet
of Little Russia, who was forbidden to put pen to paper,
and who scribbled down some of his most charming poems
with a pencil on scraps of greasy brown paper, which he
hid away in his boots, for which, when discovered, he was
cruelly flogged. It is only a very few years since M. Shel-
goonoff was banished from St. Petersburg and threatened
with a similar or even worse fate; and at this moment his
works in two volumes are being mutilated in such a manner
by the Censure that he himself finds it difficult to recognize
them as his own. Most of Count Tolstoï's later writings
are on the index of prohibited books, and nothing that
comes from his pen can be sanctioned by any one Censor,
no matter how harmless it seems. Every line of his must
first be laid before the Censure Committee in St. Petersburg, to be read later on by M. Pobedonostseff, and practically nothing that he writes ever reaches the Russian
printer. Even the series of moral pamphlets which he
wrote for the peasantry, and being highly approved by the
authorities, went through numerous editions, are now being
withdrawn from circulation by the Censure, owing to a
letter on the subject written to the Minister of the Interior
by the restless M. Pobedonostseff, who is shocked at their

immorality, while the unredeemed filth of the novels of Alboff and of Zola is propagated like some new and saving gospel.

In the history of no ancient or modern literature is the chapter of might-have-beens so long or so full of tragic interest as in Russia. Scarcely more than half the manuscript works of the gifted Saltykoff have seen the light. Leskoff, one of the foremost literary men of the present day, is practically reduced to silence because he offended the Director of the Censure, by drawing a too faithful portrait of him twenty years ago. It is almost as difficult for literary men to live on the produce of their labors in Russia as it is for astrologers to "hitch their wagons to a star" in England. Lately one very respectable member of the fraternity died of hunger, and some of those who are yet alive are in fear of meeting a similar fate, while the only fear that possesses others is that they may not die quick enough. "Russian literature, indeed!" exclaims Saltykoff; "why you may die of hunger if you rely upon literary work for a livelihood. I am a living example myself of the fate that overtakes literary men. I do not earn enough to keep my old hack from dying of starvation. No one but an egregious fool would commit such an inexcusable blunder as to devote himself to literary work in Russia."[1]

One of the most celebrated men of letters in contemporary Russia, whose name is favorably known in France, Germany, and England, is at this moment condemned to silence and poverty by the Censure. And he has absolutely no redress, and not the shadow of a hope of better things. Can he not appeal to the Tsar, English Radicals will ask; the just Tsar whose private virtues are belauded even by his enemies? He did so appeal, I reply, in a letter of deeply respectful loyalty and attachment which touched his Majesty's heart. This occurred some three months ago. The Emperor called for the Minister of the Interior, showed him the letter, and inquired: "Is this true? You are persecuting X.?" "Certainly not, your Majesty; we have employed no exceptional measures against him. But I will make strict inquiries on the subject." The Minister then summoned M. Fesktistoff, the Head of the Censure.

---

[1] *Hist. Messenger*, October, 1889. Cf. *Novoye Vremya*, 12th November, 1889.

"What's this X. has been writing to the Emperor?" he asked. "I hope you have issued no exceptional orders against X. in writing?" "Certainly not, your Excellency; I should never think of doing such a foolish thing.". "No, I thought not. All right. Order the police to inform X. that his letter was read by his Majesty, and the allegations it contains found to be untrue. Good morning." And the police duly informed X., whose confidence in the sterling virtues of the Tsar was far more lively than that of the most rampant Radical Russophile, that his letter to the Emperor was —— a lie. If Mr. Pitt, having received a complaint against Warren Hastings from the eunuchs who had been tortured at Lucknow, were to refer the matter to the accused for investigation, and having received from him an emphatic denial, were to inform the complainants through the police that they lied, we should have a parallel to the case of the unfortunate X.

The Director of the Censure spoke the truth when he said that it would have been foolish to issue written orders against any one writer, singling him out for exceptionally harsh treatment. For there is a comprehensive law which delivers up every writer to the mercy of the Censors, so that even the just themselves may be condemned. According to this law, a pamphlet or book being printed, the form must be *instantaneously* decomposed, and the type distributed, otherwise the inspector of printing offices is empowered to take cognizance of the fact, and the book is then *ipso facto* and absolutely forbidden. That is to say, the author and the publisher are liable to be severely punished because the printer is not endowed with the gift of working miracles. It would be charitable to suppose this law obsolete, if we had suppositions instead of facts to deal with; but truth compels me to affirm that it is in full force at this very moment. The last case that came under my notice was that of a book compiled by M. Shidkoff and printed by M. Pavlenkoff, of Moscow, some three years ago. The inspector was purposely sent round the moment the printing was done, and he merely took cognizance of the state of the form, with the result that the large edition of this useful book is now mouldering away, and will never see the light.[1]

---

[1] The book was a Russian reading book for schools. The real motive for arresting it was private animosity.

Few branches of science are so cramped and crippled as history, possibly because his Majesty himself plays at historian to the extent of taking the chair and ringing a bell at the meetings of an historical society in the palace, the secretary of which is M. Bytchkoff, brother of the infamous criminal who was deported to Siberia several years ago. In M. Smaragdoff's work on history, the President of the Censure Committee noticed that a considerable number of pages were devoted to the life and doings of a certain "fanatical vagabond named Mohammed," and he indignantly protested and insisted that they should be erased or the book prohibited, basing his demand on the historico-ethical ground that Mohammed was "a scoundrel and the founder of a false religion to boot."[1] One of the most gifted and conscientious historians of contemporary Russia is Professor Bilbassoff, who has spent the best part of a laborious life in the patient study of the published and unpublished documents relating to the life and times of the Empress Catherine II. After years of research in dark libraries and dusty archives he completed the first volume of his *History of Catherine II*. Being a large work it was printed without censure, but being a book it could not be published with the usual sanction. The term fixed in such cases for the deliberations of the Censure is only seven days, but this work remained there two months, and with the utmost difficulty was at last authorized. The Emperor having since read a portion of it, has severely reprimanded the Minister for allowing "my imperial ancestors to be lampooned." The second volume of this history appeared a few months ago, and was kept eleven weeks in the Censure. A couple of weeks since the secret fiat at last went forth, the dream of a scholar's life was dispelled by the word of a Vandal, and a work that would have built up the reputation of the author on a solid foundation has been chopped up into little bits on an island outside St. Petersburg, where a book on Russian finances had met the same fate a few months before. In a biographical dictionary of Russian men of letters, now being brought out by M. Vengheroff, we find under the name "Bakoonin," which, if treated on the scale employed throughout the work, should give occasion for dozens of pages of critical and biographical remarks, the following:—"A family which

---

[1] Cf. *Russian Antiquity*, May, 1890.

supplied the ranks of Russian culture with many noteworthy workers. *Certain reasons compel us* to defer writing anything more about them until we reach the end of this volume."

In all this written law plays no important part. Even secret circulars are superfluous. A verbal command is more than sufficient. *Verbum sat sapienti.* A Russian writer, whose name I purposely withhold, lest he should be spirited away like Madam Tsebrikoff, lately wrote a most interesting paper on a series of abuses that positively cried to heaven for vengeance. A faithful description of them might well be taken for an unpublished page of Dante's "Inferno." The Russian writer narrated the facts in a dry statistical style, the simplicity of which brought them out in stronger relief. As the Government had not the remotest intention of laying the axe to the root of the evil, the article was forbidden. The author was poor and hungry; he had written the paper in the hope of gaining a crust of bread, and the Censure, like an unclean harpy, had snatched it from his hand as he was about to convey it to his mouth. He perseveringly begged for indulgence, but indulgence was denied him. At last an influential official, touched with pity and intent upon extracting good from evil, told him that permission to publish it would be accorded, if only he would consent to strike out a number of the salient facts, tone down all the rest, and pen a few lines stating that all these horrible evils had been completely remedied by the present humane and provident Government, and that his remarks had but a historical interest. His own urgent needs and despair of effecting any good for the cause he had at heart compelled him to act upon this advice, and his article at last saw the light. "But a more damnable lie I never uttered in my whole life!" he exclaimed, and tears trickled down his hunger-pinched cheeks, tears of compassion for the forlorn wretches whose sufferings he had thus contributed to perpetuate, as he stood trembling, talking to me in the cold, piercing wind that found easy ingress through the threadbare garments he wore; and coughing the cough of the consumptive, he turned sadly away, saying: "A heavy sin lies on my soul. May God pardon me!"

And yet his Majesty the Emperor is an honorable man, and the Censors are all honorable men.

TYPOGRAPHY BY J. S. CUSHING & CO., BOSTON.

www.ingramcontent.com/pod-product-compliance
Lightning Source LLC
Chambersburg PA
CBHW032057220426
43664CB00008B/1043